THE COMPLETE BOOK OF Steam Cookery

D1449654

Also by Coralie Castle:

The Art of Cooking for Two
Country Cooking of Many Lands
Country Inns Cookery
Edible Ornamental Garden
Hors D'Oeuvre Etc.
Leftovers
Real Bread
Soup
The Whole World Cookbook (co-editor)

THE COMPLETE BOOK OF Steam Cookery

Tasty and Healthful Dishes from
Around the World

With Instructions on
Equipment and Technique

Coralie Castle

JEREMY P. TARCHER, INC.
Los Angeles
Distributed by St. Martin's Press
New York

Library of Congress Cataloging in Publication Data

Castle, Coralie.
  The complete book of steam cookery.

  Includes index.
    1. Steaming (Cookery)   2. Cookery, International.
I. Title.
TX691.C37   1985   641.5'87   85-16851
ISBN 0-874-77365-2
ISBN 0-874-77366-0 (pbk.)

Jeremy P. Tarcher, Inc.
9110 Sunset Blvd.
Los Angeles, CA 90069

Design by Tanya Maiboroda/Robert S. Tinnon
Illustration by Jeanette Lendino Gurney

Manufactured in the United States of America
10 9 8 7 6 5 4 3 2 1

First Edition

Contents

Introduction

Can you imagine what it's like to be surrounded in a mist of steam eight hours a day, seven days a week, for months on end? Your hair gets either kinky or, in my case, straight and unmanageable. The kitchen wallpaper flakes off and painted surfaces gradually develop mottled grease clots as the steam works on the film accumulated through years of frying foods. The exhaust fan wears out and must be replaced. The windows take on what seems to be a permanent haze.

At the same time, your complexion is smooth and glowing. The plants in your kitchen are thriving beyond your wildest dreams. The oven never needs cleaning, and the utility bill has dropped perceptibly because you've been economizing on fuel by steaming everything in one large pot. Pounds have fallen away from your figure owing to the reduction of fats in your diet, and you feel great because you know you've been eating in the most healthful way possible.

As the mist clears, I can reflect on my experience in the steam world with some perspective. Writing this book has been a real challenge. There has been a proliferation of cookware geared to steaming, but the recipe booklets that accompany the appliances are limited to those particular products and are often poorly put together. General cookbooks usually contain only a handful of recipes for steamed dishes and there are surprisingly few works on the market that address themselves specifically to steam cookery. What books I have found either lack sufficient directions for the reader or define steaming in a far broader sense than I do.

This book does not include information on braising and roasting above water in the oven, grilling in foil packets on the barbecue, microwaving, or pressure cooking (which deserves a book of its own). It is a book about steaming on top of the stove: the foods are either placed in a dish set over

1

or in boiling water, or they are placed directly on a rack over boiling water. The circulating steam is what cooks the food. This may sound restrictive, but my experience proves otherwise—as you will discover in the following pages.

The Complete Book of Steam Cookery will open up a new and exciting world of cooking to you, one that is healthful and flavorful. There are few kitchens today without a collapsible-basket rack for steaming vegetables, thanks to nutritionists who have been touting the advantages of steamed vegetables for years. There may be no published statistics showing that more minerals, water-soluble vitamins, and fiber are retained with steaming than with boiling, but it is logical to believe that nutrient retention is greater because steamed vegetables are not immersed in water that leaches out their nutritional value and because they have such a fresh, vital taste. The days of overcooked, heavily sauced boiled vegetables are long gone.

As you'll quickly discover here, steaming means more than just vegetables. This book will rid you, as it did me, of preconceived ideas about what can and cannot be steamed. I had always steamed a number of fish and chicken dishes, but until recently I didn't realize how tender and moist steamed red meats could be. I had assumed that these meats would "shrivel up," that they would take a long time to cook, and that the seasonings would go up in mist. How wrong I was! Steamed red meats remain moist and succulent, and in some cases they cook even more quickly than by other methods. Seasonings permeate better and the final result is one of full-bodied flavor and delicate texture.

There are a host of additional advantages to steaming almost any food. You can avoid cooking with butter and oils, and much of the fat in meats is drawn out in the steaming process. A complete meal can be prepared in the steamer with little advance preparation and only minor attention once the cooking has started. Fuel is saved and cleanup time is shortened.

Given all of these facts, I can only wonder why the fine cookbooks of the American Heart Association and the American Diabetes Association include almost no recipes for steamed foods other than those for vegetables. While magazines and newspapers warn of the dangers of high cholesterol and salt consumption, they almost never mention that steaming is a good way to minimize the need for salt because foods retain their natural flavors, or that little or no cooking fat is needed.

In a cursory examination of this book, you will find butter, salt, cream, egg yolks, and other ingredients that are avoided by those on medically restricted diets or those who are closely watching their weight. This is not meant to be strictly a health/diet book, but rather one that gives the reader options. Some recipes contain none of these ingredients; others are modified to reduce the fats. To adapt the recipes to your needs, substitute polyunsaturated margarine for butter, no-salt herb seasoning for salt, and low-fat dairy products for the cream and sour cream (see Terms and Ingredients). The sauces and sugary desserts can be completely ignored. There will still be many wonderful, exciting, and exotic recipes to delight you and your guests.

For centuries, Asians have understood the advantages of steaming, but other cultures have relied far less on this cooking method. There are, of course, exceptions, such as the couscous of North Africa, tamales in Mexico, and Boston brown bread. My greatest challenge has been to adapt, without contrivance, dishes that are commonly roasted, stewed, braised, or fried.

Some of the adaptations did not work; the success of certain culinary preparations requires the use of their classic cooking techniques. Other dishes, I discovered, fare even better when steamed than when prepared by their customary method. A corned beef brisket, for instance, has a finer texture and more robust flavor when steamed than when boiled.

My successful adaptations appear in this book. They are meant to be tried and enjoyed, and at the same time to act as guidelines for cooks who wish to create their own repertoire of steamed dishes.

I have included an excellent representation of classic dishes, too. Traditional Asian recipes could easily have dominated, but I have kept a good balance of continents and exotic ingredients in order to please a wide range of readers. One of the current trends in cooking is to combine the ingredients, herbs, and spices common to a variety of ethnic groups in one dish, and to serve the dishes of different nations at the same meal. I have done some of this mixing and matching and encourage the reader to elaborate on this idea.

This book is easy to use. Information on steaming equipment and techniques follows this introduction. Read these sections carefully; they contain everything you'll need to know to become an enthusiastic and successful "steam chef."

The Terms and Ingredients section describes some of the less familiar terms and ingredients, as well as such points as what size eggs to use or how to substitute dried herbs for fresh.

Next come the recipes, which for the most part are grouped in chapters as they would be in a conventional cookbook. Only the Vegetables chapter is organized somewhat differently than usual. It is a detailed how-to section, with suggestions for purees, marinated vegetables, and stuffed vegetables.

Finally, there is a listing of some cookware companies and the steaming equipment they manufacture.

Equipment

Today, kitchen shops and the cookware sections of department stores offer a wide range of steamers and steaming equipment in a variety of styles and materials. The bounty of choices is dizzying at first, but armed with some knowledge about what basic designs are available and how they are used, you can thread your way through this equipment labyrinth.

The world of steaming paraphernalia is divided into two broad categories, which I refer to as complete-system steamers and steaming equipment. In the first are those steamers that need nothing more than an energy source to make them function: the all-purpose steamers, which can be used to prepare almost anything that will fit into them; specific-use steamers, such as those designed for cooking asparagus or clams; and electric steamers, which include both multi-use types and those commonly called rice cookers.

The second category, steaming equipment, includes a variety of items, from collapsible-basket racks and shallow ceramic dishes to bamboo steamers and Yunnan pots, each of which must be combined with a piece of standard kitchen equipment—a large pot, a roasting pan, and so on—to create a steaming unit. Here, too, I include improvised steamers, those units ingeniously devised from common kitchen objects designed for other uses: wire cooling racks, a French fryer basket, or an empty tuna fish can.

Steaming is a simple cooking technique, and equipment considerations are equally straightforward. Basically, you need a pot or other vessel in which water can be boiled. Whether it is made of a material that conducts heat especially well or is thick- or thin-gauge is not critical. There is no difference in taste and texture between something steamed in a hundred-dollar molded aluminum steamer and a fifteen-dollar lightweight stamped aluminum one from the Far East.

5

There are, however, a few things to keep in mind when selecting equipment. First, the pot must be wide and deep so that the steam circulates freely around the food. The pot must also be large enough to hold racks, dishes, and bowls of various sizes and shapes. Then, too, the lids of all steamers or standard pots that hold steaming equipment must be tight-fitting.

The best choice of steaming equipment is the one that appeals to your aesthetics and pocketbook. I have included what I consider a good basic selection in Recommended Basic Steaming Equipment, which follows this section.

Complete-System Steamers

This group is marked by its seemingly endless choice of materials. These steamers range from very expensive all-copper ones to low-price, light-weight aluminum three-piece units. In between you find high-quality molded aluminum (Magnalite); high-quality stamped aluminum (Leyse); stainless steel; stainless steel with copper bottom (Revere Ware), carbon-steel core; aluminum core (Cuisinart); porcelain-on-steel ware (Granite-ware); copper-coated exterior with a stainless-steel interior; enameled aluminum; and enamelware. (For information on specific manufacturers' products that include some of these materials, see Equipment Sources.)

ALL-PURPOSE STEAMERS

The most common member of this group and probably of the entire line of equipment is what is called the three-piece steamer. It consists of a solid lower pan, which is the water reservoir; a perforated-bottom upper pan, used for holding the food to be steamed; and a tight-fitting lid. The four-piece steamer is the same basic design as the three-piece, with an additional perforated pan that permits steaming on two levels. In cookware literature this is often called a three-tier steamer, which is a misnomer because it actually has only two tiers.

The handsome, expensive Magnalite cookware line manufactures a four-piece steamer and an optional insert that can be used as a third tier. The more tiers, of course, the more items that can be steamed at the same time, making it easier to prepare a fully steamed meal over one burner.

Graniteware, the popular blue-speckled porcelainware company, manufactures a "5-Piece Everything Pot." This reasonably priced set includes a seven-quart cooking pot, a spaghetti cooker/blancher (a deep perforated basket), a colander/steamer, a perforated trivet, and a lid. The "jumbo" version has an 11-quart pot that is 10½ inches in diameter, 3 inches larger

Yunnan Pot on Saucepan

Aluminum Three-Piece Steamer

Couscousière

Roasting Pan

Two-Tiered Steamer

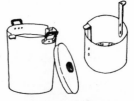

Asparagus Steamer (and detail of insert)

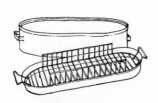

Fish Poacher

Gadget for Trivet Removal

Pan-shaped Steamer Insert

Clam Steamer

Electric Rice Cooker

Yunnan Pots

Tiered Steamer Set

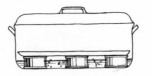

Improvised Steamer with Cans

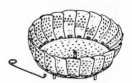

**Collapsible-Basket Rack
with Lifter**

**Bamboo Steamer
(with top view)**

Metal Steaming Trivet

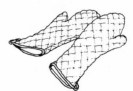

Long Oven Mitts

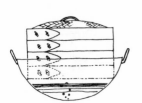

Bamboo Steamer in Wok

Steamer Tray in Wok

**The Towel-Sling
Removal Method**

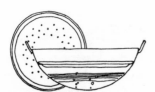

Perforated Tray and Its Position in Wok

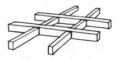

Interlocking Grid Trivet

Basket Rice Steamer

than the smaller set. Only if you already have the more versatile four-piece (two-tier) steamer should you consider adding this set to your kitchen equipment.

There are two additional all-purpose complete-system units, each designed to fulfill two important kitchen-equipment needs. The roaster/broiler pan with rack and lid is sold as both a traditional roasting pan and an ideal steaming arrangement because of its rack for holding foods above the cooking liquid and its tight-fitting lid. It would be suitable for whole fish, corn, or the simultaneous steaming of a number of small, shallow dishes.

The steamer/double boiler combination has a lower saucepan and two upper pans, used separately. One has a perforated bottom for steaming and one has a solid bottom for the double-boiler function. This piece of equipment is practical only if you need a double boiler, as the steaming possibilities are limited to a single small shallow dish or vegetables.

SPECIFIC-USE STEAMERS

The term "specific use" is somewhat misleading. Though these steamers are marketed as being specially designed for cooking a certain food, they are considerably more versatile than that. In fact, construction on some of them is so similar as to make distinctions superfluous.

The asparagus steamer is a tall pot, usually about nine inches high and seven inches in diameter (smaller ones are available), with a deep hanging-basket insert that can be lifted out for easy removal of the vegetables. There is little space between the base of the basket and the pan bottom, so in addition to asparagus this steamer can only be used for quick-cooking vegetables like corn or broccoli. It is also good for steaming long-cooking foods in tall basins that are partially immersed in the steaming water, such as Boston brown bread steamed in a coffee can.

Though larger than an asparagus steamer, a clam or lobster pot is designed in essentially the same way, and thus could be used to cook good-sized portions of corn or asparagus in addition to shellfish.

A pasta steamer has the same basket-insert arrangement as the above steamers, but the pasta is immersed in boiling water, not cooked over it. The basket simply eliminates the need for draining the pasta in a colander. This doesn't mean that you shouldn't add this piece of equipment to your cupboard, but rather that it has the same practicality as a clam pot.

There is also a pot more squat than those described above, with a shallow basket insert and a tight-fitting lid. The insert reaches only halfway down into the pot rather than nearly to the bottom, as with the above steamers. These shorter steamers are designed for cooking vegetables. They are good for long-steaming ones such as potatoes and beets because the bottom pot will hold plenty of water. Two things limit their usage: they are generally rather small in diameter, and, unlike multi-tiered steamers, there is only one level for holding food.

Leyse manufactures a stovetop rice steamer/cereal cooker that can be used to cook up to four cups of raw rice. It has a deep solid-bottom upper pan that fits into a lower pan. The rice or cereal and a specified amount of liquid are placed in the upper pan and the pan is covered. Water is brought to a boil in the bottom pan, the top pan is placed into the bottom pan, and the grain is steamed. Tiny perforations in the upper pan just below where the two pans meet allow the steam from the boiling water in the bottom to circulate around the grain.

This Leyse steamer illustrates one of the exceptions to the common definition of steaming. In this case, rice and cereals are combined with liquid *and* cooked over boiling water, rather than only cooked over water. The Rival and Waring electric steamers described below work on this same principle. In either case, I find this to be a round-about way to cook rice. It is far easier to prepare rice in a saucepan on the stove (see Steaming Rice and Grains) or in an electric rice cooker (see below).

The *couscousière* is a specialized double steamer for cooking couscous, a popular North African dish (see Couscous). The classic couscousière of North Africa is made of unglazed earthenware, while those available in the United States are generally lightweight aluminum. This steamer is a three-piece design, with a solid bottom pan in which liquid boils and a shallower top pan with a perforated bottom where the couscous grains cook in the rising steam. Though a lid comes with the steamer, it is unnecessary, as the grains are traditionally steamed without a top.

An egg "poacher" is actually a steamer, since the egg sits above rather than in the water. The poacher has three parts: a tray with three round indentations to hold the eggs, a pan to hold the water, and a lid. The tray, which rests on the rim of the water reservoir, has a few tiny holes for the steam to rise through and cook the eggs.

ELECTRIC STEAMERS

Rival, Waring, and Hitachi are the principal manufacturers of all-purpose electric steamers. The Rival and Waring models have a reservoir with a heating element in the bottom. The reservoir is filled with water and the element heats the water to produce steam. The Hitachi does not have a water reservoir. It works on the principle described below for rice cookers and therefore is included in their description. Its use, however, is not limited to cooking rice and rice dishes.

Rival's "The Steamer" has a steamer basket for cooking vegetables, puddings, and breads, and a bowl for cooking rice with liquid as well as foods with sauce. Its oval shape is practical for holding "long" items such as corn on the cob or fish fillets, and the high-domed lid permits stacking of foods. Included with the Rival are complete directions for its use and a comprehensive recipe book.

The Rival's major drawback is that there is no on/off switch. The appliance is turned on by plugging it in. When the food is ready, the timer light goes out but the steamer does not turn itself off; the cook must promptly remove the plug. Thus, too much of a busy cook's time is taken up with attending to what is designed to be a convenience appliance.

Waring's Food Steamer/Rice Cooker works in the same way as the Rival, and has both a basket and a bowl. It also lacks an on/off switch. The major difference between these two appliances is that a built-in thermostat shuts off the heating element in the Waring if the liquid in the reservoir evaporates.

The rice-cooker market is dominated by Japanese manufacturers and, of these, the National brand is a particularly reliable one. The rice and water are combined in a solid pan that fits inside a shell with a heating element in its base. The pan is covered, the cooker is switched on, and when the element detects the complete absorption of the water, the machine shuts off automatically; the rice continues to steam until the grains are tender. This cooker works on much the same principle as the boil-and-steam method for steaming rice on top of the stove (see Rice and Grains). Information on the amount of rice and water to use and how long to let the rice sit once the light has gone out is provided by the manufacturer. Some models also have a "warm" setting that holds the cooked rice at the proper temperature without drying it out.

A few rice cookers, including the National, come with a flat metal plate with tiny perforations that fits flush against the bottom of the pan. This must be used when cooking plain rice or rice to which small bits of food and seasonings have been added. Its value may be that it permits the tiniest bit of steam to circulate beneath the rice.

Some rice-cooker manufacturers also provide a steaming rack for cooking vegetables or small dishes of food above water. Hitachi, however, is the only company that supplies an adequate booklet with directions and recipes for general steaming of a wide variety of different foods, including vegetables, fish, chicken, shrimp, foil-wrapped sandwiches, fondue, tamales, and hard-cooked eggs. Their Chime-O-Matic Food Steamer/Rice Cooker has transformed the common rice cooker into a practical unit I highly recommend. No longer does the valuable, specialized rice cooker need to be restricted to cooking just rice.

A much-appreciated advantage of the Hitachi is the chime that rings to let you know the rice has absorbed the water and is now steaming, so you can plan your meal accordingly. Hitachi's newer models have a much-appreciated nonstick inner pan. The Hitachi Chime-O-Matic is available in three sizes: 10-cup, 8.3-cup, and 5.6-cup. For a family of four, the medium or large model would be best.

The electric egg cooker has a bottom pan that is the water reservoir, a rack, an insert, and a lid. The rack, which sits directly on the pan bottom, is a disk with a series of up to seven round holes along the outer edge. In the center is a tiny indentation with an upright pin. To soft- or hard-cook eggs, you first pierce the round end of each egg by gently pushing it down on the pin and then place the egg, round end up, in one of the holes along the edge of the rack. Add the specified amount of water, cover, and switch on the cooker. (The amount of water determines how long the eggs cook.) When the switch goes off the eggs are ready.

The egg cooker insert sits directly on top of the rack (which of course must be empty) with airspace around it. It consists of up to four triangular-shaped cups. To prepare "poached" eggs, add the specified amount of water to the pan, break an egg into each cup, cover, and switch on the cooker. It goes off when the eggs are done.

An electric egg cooker is by no means a kitchen necessity, but it is a very nice appliance to have. My Sunbeam cooker has been servicing me well for twenty years.

Steaming Equipment

The items that follow must be used with another piece of equipment to form a complete steaming unit. All of them are used for holding foods in an all-purpose steamer, such as a two- or three-tier unit or a roaster/broiler pan, or in a conventional saucepan with a lid. Unless otherwise mentioned, these items can be found in most department-store housewares sections or in kitchenware shops.

COLLAPSIBLE-BASKET RACK

This inexpensive, versatile steaming utensil should be a kitchen standard. The basket of interleaved perforated panels is expandable from about five to ten inches in diameter, making it possible to transform a wide range of standard pots into steamers. It stands on three legs that lift the food above the water. Select a basket of heavy-gauge stainless steel, with legs as tall as possible and side handles or a removable central post. Some models have a post with grooves to which a separate handle is fitted for lifting the basket from the pot. Having one with a permanent post is fine if you only want to use the basket for vegetables, which can be arranged around it; but a permanent post makes it impossible to have the basket double as a rack for holding a dish of food, or for steaming a whole cauliflower.

STEAM PLATE

Made of aluminum or light-gauge stainless steel, this perforated plate, with very shallow sides, is usually about eight to ten inches in diameter and is ideal for placing in a wok or flare-sided saucepan where it rests halfway down in the vessel. The plate can hold a shallow dish or bowl, or the foods may be placed directly on it. If it fits only on the bottom of a saucepan, however, there is not enough space below it for sufficient water, so it can only be used to hold basins that may be partially immersed in water.

PAN-SHAPED STEAMER INSERT

Available in two types, this perforated insert rests inside a standard kitchen pot, which acts as the water reservoir. The sides of one type are concentrically ridged, permitting it to be used with lower pans of differing diameters. The second type is without ridges and fits only one pot size. A domed lid is often sold with the ridged ones. When purchasing either of these, coordinate their sizes with your present kitchen equipment. Pan-shaped steamer inserts are good for steaming vegetables or anything in a shallow dish such as fish fillets, chicken parts, or meatballs.

BAMBOO STEAMER

Round, woven Chinese bamboo steamers are attractive enough to go to the table. They come in several sizes, from small ones at about four to five inches in diameter on up to ones a foot or more across. They are sold with slightly domed lids. When stacked (you can only stack those of the same diameter) they economize on fuel, since three or four tiers cook above a single heat source. The food can be placed on a plate in the steamer, or the basket can be lined with lightly dampened cheesecloth and the food placed on the cloth.

A wok is the ideal water reservoir to use with a bamboo steamer, though you may find you prefer to have a special wok for this purpose, as boiling water in a well-seasoned one wears away the hard-won finish. (Alternatively, the steamer can be set over the top of a pot with a lipped rim, but the fit must be tight so that no steam escapes at the edges.) Add water to the wok. The water level should be one inch below the base of the bamboo steamer.

Use one bamboo steamer basket, or stack up to four of them in the wok and top the last one with the bamboo lid. If using more than two baskets to cook the same dish, switch top to bottom halfway through steaming so that all the food finishes cooking at the same time. If cooking different foods in the layers, put the shorter-cooking ones in the top layers.

Before using bamboo steamers for the first time, immerse them in water and then place them empty over boiling water. Leave for an hour or so, pouring hot water over them occasionally. This will reduce the strong bamboo smell to a mild, pleasant one. Subsequently, never wash these steamers with anything other than plain hot water; if you use soap, the foods will absorb its taste. Dry well before storing to prevent mildewing.

Though bamboo steamers are available in department stores and cookware shops, they are generally much less expensive in shops in Asian neighborhoods.

SHALLOW DISH

Along with vegetables placed directly on a collapsible basket, steamer tier, or insert (generically referred to as a rack in the recipes) above boiling water, food arranged in a shallow dish above water is the most common steaming arrangement. A "shallow dish" is as it sounds: any low, flare-sided, heatproof ceramic or glass bowl or platter of a suitable size to hold whatever food—anything from chicken pieces and whole fish to stuffed bell peppers—you wish to steam.

The dish, which should be attractive enough to go from the steamer to the table, must not fit too snugly in the steamer or it will be difficult to lift out when the food is cooked and the dish is still hot. Ideally, there will be just enough room on the rack to lift the dish out with hands protected by pot holders. There are also inexpensive metal utensils with two arms, similar in principle to a canning-jar lifter, that grasp the rim of the dish so that it can be carefully lifted out.

Remember, too, juices collect as foods cook, so select a dish that is large enough to contain the additional liquid. If the liquid threatens to overflow the dish, ladle it out into a jar and save to heat and serve on the food being steamed or for stocks, soups, or sauces.

BASIN

A basin for steaming foods is defined as any pudding mold; soufflé dish; casserole; timbale mold; loaf, cake, or bundt pan; muffin tin; or any ceramic, glass, or metal bowl that is high-sided. In most cases, the covered basin is placed in a pot atop a rack, folded towel, or other platform, and water is added to reach two-thirds up its sides. The platform is necessary to prevent possible cracking of the basin and to keep it from "dancing" around in the boiling water. Basins are sometimes placed on a rack over water, such as when steaming breads, some egg dishes, or cakes.

Glazed Chinese basins with lids, in attractive designs and a wide range of sizes, can be found in Oriental markets and in import and cookware stores. Traditionally, these basins are used for steaming meats and making clear soups, but they can be used for any food you would normally steam in a conventional basin.

YUNNAN POT

Named for the southwest province of China where it originated, the Yunnan pot is an unglazed clay or glazed ceramic bowl with a lid. It sometimes has small side handles, which make it easier to transport. Most Yunnan pots available in the United States range in capacity from about one quart to three quarts.

The Yunnan pot has a central chimney that forms an interior trough where the food, with or without liquid, is arranged. The pot is covered with its own lid and set over a saucepan (it must fit snugly into the rim; it acts as the saucepan's "lid") of boiling water, or on a rack over boiling water in a large covered vessel. The steam rises up through the chimney, condenses on the ceramic lid, and falls over the food in a light mist. Some food writers direct the cook to place the Yunnan pot on a rack and add water to reach halfway up the pot sides. With this method, though, water is drawn up through the chimney and bubbles out over the steaming food, thus diluting it. I do not recommend immersing the pot.

In Yunnan, this pot is used for cooking the province's best-known dish, delicate chicken pieces in broth lightly seasoned with ginger, green onions, and rice wine. You can, however, easily go beyond this traditional preparation and use this unique basin for cooking fish steaks, lamb or veal shanks with or without vegetables, or any stewlike dish. Once you have cooked with a Yunnan pot, it will become a kitchen favorite. It is attractive, easy to use, beautifully self-contained, and performs as the serving dish as well as the cooking basin.

Yunnan pots imported from China can be found in Chinese shops. Kira Designs, Inc. of Boston has recently begun manufacturing Yunnan-style pots in New England. They are made of high-fired porcelain and go by the name The Steampot. Attractive handcrafted Yunnan pots can also be purchased directly from the potters who make them (see Equipment Sources).

SOUTHEAST ASIAN BASKET RICE STEAMER

Glutinous rice, also known as sweet rice, is commonly eaten with daily meals in some areas of Southeast Asia, especially northeastern Thailand and Laos. There it is traditionally steamed in tightly woven broad baskets with flared sides. The rice is put into the basket and the basket is set over boiling water in a saucepan. The rice is covered with a saucepan lid and steamed. (See Glutinous Rice.) Look for these baskets in shops catering to a Southeast Asian clientele.

IMPROVISED STEAMERS AND STEAMING EQUIPMENT

If the equipment you already have is not quite adequate for the dish you want to prepare, or you're not sure you want to invest in special steaming equipment, there are numerous ways to improvise. These adaptations can range from placing two parallel chopsticks, broad ends opposite and about an inch apart, across the top of a shallow dish to permit the stacking of a second dish, to using an electric frypan as a steaming vessel. There are improvised steaming equipment possibilities in every kitchen; don't be limited to the ideas suggested here. The most important thing to remember is that a steaming unit must have a tightly fitting lid.

Steaming Vessel: The water reservoir may be of any shape or size, and of any common cookware material, including flameproof earthenware. As previously noted, a wok is a particularly good steaming pot, as most racks or chopstick-fabricated platforms will work in it and the domed lid will accommodate large items (see Bamboo Steamers).

Platforms: There are a number of common kitchen items that can be used to hold steaming foods above water, or in water in the case of some basin-steamed dishes: wire cooling racks, trivets, canning-jar rings (but not ordinary jar lids, as they will slide on the pot bottom), an empty tuna fish can with both ends removed, a folded kitchen towel or dishcloth (especially good for steamed puddings), or a small shallow bowl such as a custard cup. (If using the latter, fill it with water so that it won't float, set it on a towel, and top it with a rack or a pair of chopsticks on which to rest the dish of food.) Whichever platform you choose, it must be sturdy and reliable or the food may tumble into the water.

Electric Frypan: To transform an electric frypan into a steaming vessel, put a platform, such as a canning-jar ring or trivet, on the bottom. Add water, cover, and bring to a boil. Place a plate of raw food on the platform, cover the frypan, and open the air vent slightly so that water does not drip on the food from the underside of the lid. (It would not be possible to wrap the lid in a towel to prevent this condensation.) Steam as you would normally. The frypan is ideal because of its large size, its spacious domed lid, and its independence of the stovetop.

Roasting Pan: Use any roasting pan with a rack or trivet and a tight-fitting lid for steaming good-sized pieces of meat and other large items, or a series of small dishes.

Fish Poacher: A fish poacher need not be restricted to cooking fish. It makes a versatile steamer, especially if the rack can be raised slightly so that more water can be added to the pan. Use canning-jar rings to prop up the rack. In addition to whole fish, you can steam custard cups; bamboo leaf, parchment, or foil packets; or vegetables.

Colander: Place an ordinary kitchen colander, French fryer basket, or any metal strainer with short legs in a large pot and use for holding foods above water as they steam. Use in place of a collapsible basket.

Improvised Lids: To improvise a lid for a basin, take a piece of aluminum foil slightly larger than the diameter of the dish to be covered, lay it flat, and make a one-inch pleat in the center. Centering the foil on the dish, crimp the edges against the rim, and, if possible, secure the cover with a rubber band. If pressure builds in the dish during steaming, the pleat will expand to accommodate it.

Recommended Basic Steaming Equipment

In the preceding equipment descriptions I have outlined to the best of my knowledge what steaming equipment is available. Here are my recommendations for outfitting your kitchen with the basics. Of course, selections depend on your personal taste, your existing cookware, and your pocketbook, so what appears can only be suggestions. With just these few utensils, however, you will be able to explore the whole world of steam cookery.

The single most important item is the collapsible-basket rack for combining with saucepans and skillets of various sizes. An eleven- to twelve-inch four-piece (two-tier) steamer in lightweight aluminum is a good complete-system, all-purpose unit. I have specified aluminum because its weight makes it easy to maneuver (for information on aluminum, see Steaming Techniques). The saucepans and skillets and the steamer must have sturdy handles and tightly fitting lids.

If you don't have the storage room for a tiered steamer, look for a concentrically ridged pan-shaped steamer insert with a domed lid to transform your saucepans into a single-tier unit.

Shallow dishes in two sizes, 6½ and 8½ inches in diameter, are the most useful for the majority of households. You may want a platter for whole fish, and basins ranging up to an eight-cup capacity for some of the puddings.

A must if you are going to have fun with steaming and entertain in a dramatic, unusual way is the Yunnan pot. Get one before your friends do. It will be the source of many great meals and the focus of conversation at the dinner table. If you order your Yunnan pot from a potter, request colors that complement your dinnerware.

Other equipment is really frosting on the cake. My only additional recommendation is that rice lovers buy an electric rice cooker. The Hitachi Chime-O-Matic is the best choice, because it is also a practical all-purpose steamer.

Steaming Techniques

Steaming is an easy cooking method. The principles are simple and most of the specialized equipment is uncomplicated and widely available. Overcooking is the only real concern, and this possible problem is restricted to egg preparations, such as custards and mousses, breads and cakes, and fish dishes. Should you overcook a vegetable, it can be turned into a puree or soup. Most meat and poultry dishes are forgiving, because they do not dry out as they do when cooked by other methods.

Most foods are steamed in essentially the same manner: held above bubbling liquid. The depth of the liquid is determined by the height of the rack that holds the food and how long the food steams. A long-steaming dish will require more steaming liquid than a short-steaming one. The important thing is that the liquid not touch the food or the rack, dish, or basin that is holding it. Exceptions to or elaborations of these basic rules are noted in appropriate equipment descriptions, in recipes that go beyond this simple steaming procedure, and in sections devoted to directions on preparing a particular type of dish, such as puddings or steamed rice.

Each recipe specifies whether the food is placed in a dish or set directly on a rack. Though many books recommend steaming meats and seafood on a rack, I usually prefer to put them in a dish so that the juices will collect and the flavorings will not be lost. The juices can then be served in place of a high-calorie sauce. There is a negligible difference in texture between the foods steamed in a dish or on a rack, but the flavor is more pronounced in the former.

The majority of recipes direct you to steam food over boiling water. This means that the water should be bubbling but not at a hard boil. If a recipe specifies gently boiling water, the water should be just above a simmer so that the bubbles break softly on the surface.

Whether you have a gas or an electric stove, take into consideration the size of the pot, the size of the burner, the amount of steaming water, and how hard the water should boil, then adjust the burner accordingly. A gas stove reacts instantly to adjustments of the burner knobs and maintains a steady heat level, so it is easy for the cook to control the degree of heat. An electric stove is slower to react, so it may take a little longer to master your range.

Start timing the cooking when the liquid in the bottom of the steamer starts to boil and steam is just visible. (Unless otherwise specified, water does not necessarily have to be boiling when the food is set on the rack.) Steaming time will vary according to whether items are set directly on the rack of the steamer or in a dish on the rack of a steamer. The latter will take a little longer. If foods are packed tightly, they too will take longer because the steam cannot circulate freely. Times given in recipes may need to be increased or decreased according to these factors. If ingredients come straight from the refrigerator, times may need to be increased.

There are several terms that repeatedly appear in the recipe methods. *Rack* refers to a collapsible basket, the tier of a steamer, a steamer insert, or a metal steam plate or cooling rack. A *platform* is any low rack, canning-jar ring, or folded towel or dishcloth (see Platforms). *Reservoir* or *vessel* is the pot that holds the steaming water. For other unfamiliar, less frequently encountered terms, see the preceding section on equipment.

The Aluminum Controversy

There has been talk in some medical circles about the possible dangers of using aluminum cooking vessels. It is believed that these utensils might give off injurious trace elements that can be absorbed by the human body. Therefore, I have reservations about saving the vegetable steaming water from an aluminum pot for adding to soups and stocks and about cooking in foil. I have suggested forming an aluminum "boat" for steaming a whole salmon, but have lined it with plastic wrap to be on the safe side. My improvised foil lids (see Improvised Steamers and Steaming Equipment) do not touch the food they are covering.

Though the virtues of cooking in foil have been described in glowing terms in many magazine articles, I find that the foods steamed in a shallow dish or a Yunnan pot turn out better. Foil doesn't breathe and thereby gives the dish a stewlike texture, while foods steamed in ceramic or glass containers retain their identities. In the case of those recipes using bamboo or other leaves, the flavor and consistency of the finished dish is not the same if done in foil. Packets made of parchment paper may be substituted. If you must use aluminum foil for packets, line it with plastic wrap.

Steaming Facts and Hints

This is a catchall section, but an important one. Many of the hints deal with those situations you face every time you steam, such as how to lift the steamer lid or what to do with the steaming liquid. A number of directions I have included elsewhere are repeated here to give them emphasis. Finally, there are some general cooking tips.

Each type of pot takes different heat and thus slightly different timing. Learn your equipment and your stove.

Start timing when the steam is first visible.

The closer the rack is to the water, the faster the food will cook.

Foods continue to cook in a covered pot once the heat is turned off. Take this into consideration, especially when steaming vegetables or fish, since they can easily overcook.

If you open a pot to check a dish you are steaming, turn up the heat slightly when you re-cover it to return the water to a boil, then readjust.

If cooking a long-steaming dish, check the water level from time to time and add boiling water as needed to maintain original level.

If a pot lid "sputters" during steaming, wrap it in a lightweight towel. Be careful the towel does not hang down and catch fire.

Always wrap the lid of the steamer when steaming uncovered cakes, breads, and egg dishes to prevent condensation from dripping on them.

When steaming foods such as puddings and mousses in a covered basin, do not uncover the basin until after the time designated in the recipe directions has elapsed. If you uncover these foods, they will not set up properly.

For easy removal of basins: Make a twine sling and rig it onto the filled basin before lowering the basin into the steamer. Coil the end of the sling on top of the basin so that it can be easily grasped. Or open a tea towel on a flat surface, place the filled basin in the center of the towel, bring up opposite corners, and tie securely. Repeat with remaining corners and then lower into the steamer. To remove from the steamer, push the handle of a long wooden spoon under the knots and carefully lift out.

Your steaming vessels may develop a thin white film on the interior due to minerals in the water. Wash them occasionally with distilled white vinegar. A pinch of cream of tartar added to the steaming water will help minimize the buildup.

To insure even cooking, place the steamer squarely on the burner, and place the platform with the basin on top directly on the center of the pot bottom.

Unless using an aluminum pot, save the steaming water from vegetables for use in sauces, soups, and gravies. If you are steaming a vegetable that cooks for a short amount of time, such as snow peas, use only a little water so that it will have more concentrated flavor.

To check a pot during or just after steaming, lift the cover *away* from you, letting any water drip down into the reservoir, not into the dish.

If you should be burned by steam, immediately put the burned area under cold running water and leave it there until the pain ceases.

Set Yunnan pot evenly on saucepan. Otherwise it will tip easily.

Open the lid of a Yunnan pot away from you and don't put your arm over the chimney. The steam can seriously burn you.

Add seasonings, such as garlic, onion, and herbs, to the steaming liquid for long-cooking dishes, though seasoning the foods themselves is the best way to impart flavor.

To reheat leftovers, place in a shallow dish or wrap in plastic wrap and then aluminum foil and reheat while steaming another dish. Or place food in a colander, cover with a dampened cloth, cover pot, and steam ten minutes or until heated through.

Use Lecithin Butter or Lecithin Oil (see Terms and Ingredients) to grease a basin and the foods will never stick.

Special terms or unusual ingredients appear in the Terms and Ingredients section.

For best results, egg whites should be at room temperature before beating and heavy cream should be chilled before whipping.

Follow directions for readying the steamer before starting to prepare any recipe that calls for baking soda or beaten egg whites. These dishes won't rise properly if the mixture sits.

If you have assembled a dish ahead of time, allow it to come to room temperature before steaming.

Use scissors or kitchen shears to cut dried fruits rather than trying to chop them. It's much easier and they don't stick to the scissors as they would to a knife.

For easy peeling of garlic cloves and to release their essence, smash lightly with the flat side of a broad knife blade.

A general substitution rule for herbs is that one part dried equals three parts fresh (see Terms and Ingredients).

Eggs, unless otherwise specified, are always Grade A Large.

Polyunsaturated margarine may be substituted for butter in most recipes, though the taste will not be as satisfying.

Dairy substitutes (see Terms and Ingredients) may be used in all recipes except puddings, mousses, and timbales. The consistency, however, as well as the taste, will not match the original.

Salt is always optional. Herb seasonings with no salt, or just a small amount of salt, may be purchased in natural and health-food stores and some supermarkets.

Unless tomatoes have very thick skin, there is no need to peel them.

Terms and Ingredients

Acidulated water: To each 2 cups water add 2 tablespoons white or cider vinegar or fresh lemon or lime juice. Use to prevent the discoloration of vegetables and fruits.

Bean Curd: See **Tofu.**

Bean Thread Noodles: Also called glass, cellophane, and silver noodles, Chinese vermicelli, transparent noodles, and long rice. Very thin, whitish noodle made from mung bean starch. Packaged by weight in cellophane and sold in Oriental markets and some supermarkets. Store indefinitely in airtight container in cool, dry area.

Black Bean Sauce: A sauce of black beans with various spices such as ginger and garlic (see also **Fermented Black Beans**). Available in jars in Oriental stores and many supermarkets.

Black Beans, Fermented. See **Fermented Black Beans.**

Brown Bean Sauce: Sometimes called yellow or ground bean sauce. A brownish, thick, salty sauce of ground or partially mashed small brown beans. Available in cans and jars at Oriental stores and many supermarkets. After opening, transfer canned sauce to a jar with a tight-fitting lid and refrigerate up to 9 months.

Butter: When a recipe lists "butter" as an ingredient, it means standard salted butter. Unsalted butter or margarine (preferably without preservatives) may be substituted.

Chile Oil: Called *aji* oil by the Japanese. An oil flavored with hot chile peppers. It is reddish in color and can be purchased in Oriental markets

24

and some supermarkets. To make your own, crush 1 to 2 dried hot red chile peppers and add to ½ cup each Oriental sesame oil and peanut oil. Place mixture in a jar, cover, and let stand 2 days, or until oil has absorbed chile flavor to taste. Strain into a squeeze bottle or cruet and store at room temperature for up to 6 months.

Chinese Plum Sauce: See **Plum Sauce.**

Chinese Rice Wine: A cooking and drinking wine of China made from rice that is dark yellow in color and somewhat sweet in taste. Available in Oriental markets. Substitute high-quality dry sherry.

Coriander, fresh: Called *cilantro* in Latin American countries and in some parts of the United States, and Chinese parsley in Asian communities. A pungent herb that looks somewhat like Italian parsley. It can be grown in the home garden and is available in Oriental markets and most supermarkets.

Daikon: A large, long, white radish with a slightly peppery flavor. Popular in Japanese and Korean cooking. Available in many supermarkets.

Dairy Substitutes: For approximately 1¼ cups substitute cream, whirl in blender or processor ½ cup each low-fat cottage cheese and nonfat milk. Add 1 tablespoon noninstant, nonfat dry milk and whirl briefly. Refrigerate in covered jar as dictated by the pull dates of the cottage cheese and the milk.

For approximately 1½ cups substitute sour cream, whirl in blender or food processor 1 cup low-fat ricotta cheese, ¼ cup plain yoghurt, 1 tablespoon noninstant nonfat dry milk, and 2 teaspoons fresh lemon juice, or to taste. Refrigerate in covered jar as dictated by the pull dates of the ricotta and yoghurt. Prepared horseradish may also be added to taste.

Dashi: Basic Japanese broth made from *kombu* (seaweed) and *katsuobushi* (dried fish flakes). Available in instant form in Japanese markets and some supermarkets.

Dried Shrimp: Tiny dried shrimp with a salty, concentrated taste. Available in cellophane bags in Oriental markets. Must be soaked to soften before using. After opening, may be stored almost indefinitely in an airtight container in a cool, dry place.

Dried Tangerine Peel: The sun-dried peel of tangerines. Available in small cardboard boxes and cellophane packages in Chinese markets.

Eggs: Eggs called for in recipes, unless otherwise specified, are Grade A Large eggs.

Fermented Black Beans: Also called salted black beans, Chinese black beans. A Chinese seasoning of brined and fermented black soybeans with ginger or orange peel and sometimes five-spice powder (not recommended). Packaged in heavy plastic bags and sold in Oriental markets and some supermarkets. After opening, store indefinitely in airtight container in cool, dry area.

Fish Sauce: Also called *nam bla* or *nam pla* (Thai) and *nuoc mam* (Vietnam). A brown sauce, thin and salty, made of salted fish. Available in Oriental markets and some specialty markets.

Five-Spice Powder: A dry spice combining star anise, fennel, cinnamon, cloves, and Szechwan peppercorns. The fragrant, reddish brown spice of finer grind is preferred to the coarser grind. Store in an airtight container in a cool, dark area. Available in Oriental markets and many supermarkets.

Garlic Chives: Also called Chinese chives. A hardy chive with a flat blade and a light garlic flavor. Easily grown in the home garden. Available in Oriental markets and some supermarkets.

Garlic Olive Oil: Fill a small jar or a cruet with a top with olive oil. Add 2 to 3 garlic cloves, lightly mashed. Let stand to steep for at least 2 days to let flavor of garlic permeate the oil. Store at room temperature for up to 3 to 4 weeks. Use when a light garlic flavor is desired.

Golden Syrup: Imported from England in 11-ounce jars, a cane sugar syrup rather like a cross between maple syrup and honey. Available in specialty food shops and many supermarkets.

Green Peppercorns: Green (not dried) peppercorns, usually from Madagascar. Available in small jars or cans in specialty shops and many supermarkets.

Herb Seasoning: Any of a wide variety of herb mixtures, many of which contain no salt. Available in health- and natural-food stores. Choose the one you prefer.

Herbs: Some recipes call for dried herbs, others for fresh. To substitute, use 1 to 1½ teaspoons crumbled dried herbs, or ½ teaspoon powdered, for 2 to 3 teaspoons minced fresh herbs. Sprigs of fresh herbs are sold in many supermarkets; if not available, start an herb garden.

Hoisin Sauce: A thick, dark reddish brown sauce of soybeans, garlic, sugar, chile, and spices. Available in jars or cans in Oriental markets and some supermarkets. Once opened, canned sauce must be transferred to a jar with a tight-fitting lid. Store in the refrigerator indefinitely.

Lecithin Butter: Liquid lecithin is a primary ingredient in nonstick spray coatings for pots and pans. It keeps foods from sticking far better than oil or butter, and can be found in health- and natural-foods stores. By preparing your own nonstick coating mixture, you save money and avoid using a spray can. To make lecithin butter, blend 2 teaspoons liquid lecithin thoroughly into 4 tablespoons softened butter. Cover and refrigerate for as long as 1 month or freeze up to 2 months. Bring to room temperature and let soften before using. No more sticky pans! **Lecithin Oil** may be substituted.

Lecithin Oil: Mixture of oil and liquid lecithin (see preceding entry). In a squeeze bottle, measure 3 parts safflower or corn oil and 1 part liquid lecithin. Shake well before using. Store at room temperature for as long as 4 months. **Lecithin Butter** may be substituted.

Lemon Grass: Also known as citronella, or *da kry* in Thailand, *sereh* in Indonesia. A tall grass with a lemony flavor. One teaspoon sereh powder may be substituted for 1 stalk lemon grass. If the stalk and powder are unavailable, substitute 1 teaspoon grated lemon peel, but the flavor will not be as good.

Lop Chiang (Chinese sausage): Sweet and spicy pork sausage sold packaged or loose in Chinese markets and some supermarkets.

Oriental Sesame Oil: Golden brown in color, an oil made from toasted sesame seeds. Strong and distinctive flavor, more like an extract than an oil. Do not confuse with sesame cooking oil sold in health-food stores and supermarkets. Once opened, refrigerate for as long as 6 months.

Oyster Sauce: Thick, dark brown sauce made of oysters, soy sauce, and brine. Has a slight oyster flavor. Available in jars and cans in Oriental markets and most supermarkets. If using canned, once opened transfer to a jar with a tight-fitting lid and refrigerate almost indefinitely.

Roasted Pepper: Roasted sweet peppers purchased packed in jars in specialty shops and many supermarkets. To make your own, wash red (or green) bell peppers, dry with paper toweling, and place on a baking sheet. Broil, turning so all sides are exposed to the heat, until skin is blackened. (If you have a gas range, blacken the peppers directly over the flame.) Transfer the peppers to a paper bag, close bag, and let the peppers steam for 10 to 15 minutes.

Remove peppers from bag and peel off the blackened skin. Remove and discard seeds and veins, cut peppers into eighths, and pack into sterile jars. Pour safflower or olive oil into jar to cover peppers completely. Cover tightly and refrigerate for as long as 1 month.

Plum Sauce: Chinese condiment of plums, chiles, and spices. Available in cans or jars in Oriental markets and some supermarkets. If canned, once opened transfer to a jar with a tight-fitting lid and refrigerate up to 1 month.

Rice Vinegar: A vinegar made from rice. Always use white rice vinegar for the recipes in this book; the red and black versions are too strongly flavored. Available in Oriental markets and some supermarkets. Do not purchase seasoned rice vinegar, as it contains sugar, salt, and MSG, which would conflict with the seasonings in the recipes.

Sake: Japanese rice cooking or drinking wine. Sold in Oriental markets and some supermarkets.

Shichimi: Also known as seven-spice seasoning. A seasoning of chile powder, sesame seeds, and spices. Available in Japanese markets and some supermarkets.

Shiitake Mushrooms: Also called Chinese dried black mushrooms or black forest mushrooms. Packaged by weight and size (1 inch to about 2¼ inches in diameter), with or without stems. Available in Oriental markets and many supermarkets.

Shrimp: See Dried Shrimp.

Tangerine Peel: See Dried Tangerine Peel.

Tofu: Pressed bean curd cakes made of pureed soybeans, called *dow fu* in Chinese, popularly called by the Japanese name *tofu*. Often sold in 14-ounce or 1-pound packages. The cakes of firm bean curd (Chinese bean curd) are approximately 2 inches square and ½ inch thick (4 per package), or 3 × 4 × 1 inch (2 per package). The cake of soft bean curd (*kinugoshi*) is approximately 5 × 4 × 1½ inches. Three ounces firm or soft bean curd will yield approximately ⅓ cup mashed; 1 ounce firm bean curd will yield approximately ¼ cup when cut into small dice.

White Rice Vinegar: See **Rice Vinegar.**

APPETIZERS AND FIRST COURSES

Dim Sum

Baos

Spareribs in Black Bean
   Sauce

Rice-studded Meatballs

Chicken Liver Pâté

Cold Whole Salmon with
   Avocado Sauce

Stuffed Mushrooms

Dolmades

Lingcod with Garlic
   Mayonnaise

Eggplant Caviar

Swiss Chard Soup

Curried Broccoli Soup

Carrot Soup

Green Bean Soup

Pumpkin Soup

Appetizers and First Courses

A steamed appetizer or first course can be the perfect introduction to a fully steamed meal or the light prelude to a richer repast. Here you will find flavorful stuffed mushrooms, Greek *dolmades*, elegant fish fillets with garlicky mayonnaise, and a vinegary eggplant caviar.

Dim sum, the foods featured in Chinese tea houses, are not classically served as appetizers. I have included them because they are good light, informal fare. They are brought to the dining or buffet table in their attractive bamboo steamers, making the presentation easy on the cook.

Pureed steamed vegetables can be transformed into delicate soups suitable for a sit-down or walk-around first course. Recipes for five distinctive soups appear—Swiss chard, broccoli, carrot, green bean, and pumpkin. With these as guides, you will be able to create your own versions with vegetables you have on hand.

The majority of preparations conventionally served as appetizers and first courses, such as savory pastries, canapés, cheeses, and so on, do not lend themselves to steaming. Pâtés and terrine-type molds, which are usually baked in a water bath (*bain marie*), can be steamed; though the texture will be slightly different, the flavors will be similar. My fine-textured, delicate liver pâté illustrates this move from the oven to the steamer.

For a very simple first course, marinate any lightly steamed vegetable in a vinaigrette dressing and serve plain or on a bed of crisp lettuce leaves. See Marinated Vegetables for vegetable, dressing, and garnish suggestions. The South Asian or Garlicky Mussels or Clams would make a spicy first course that could be followed by a hearty entrée salad, while the Cold Salmon with Avocado Sauce would glorify any buffet table.

Dim Sum

Dim sum, a Cantonese specialty literally translated as "little heart," describes a way of eating as much as it does a specific list of foods. At midday, the Chinese crowd into tea houses to eat, drink great quantities of tea, and converse with their friends. From this centuries-old social custom, a vast array of delicious preparations has evolved.

Many different kinds of savory and sweet foods appear at tea houses. There are deep-fried egg rolls, wontons, and paper-wrapped chicken; cold and hot fried noodle dishes; spicy shrimp fritters; and braised stuffed tofu, to name just a few of the items. Here the focus is on the steamed delicacies: dumplings, meat or seafood mixtures encased in thin dough skins; *baos*, yeast buns filled with meat or vegetables; pungent black bean spareribs; and rice-studded meatballs.

Prepare a selection of the *dim sum* foods that follow and serve them as a Chinese buffet. Alternatively, prepare only one or two of the dumplings to precede Chinese Whole Fish with Brown Bean Sauce and a stir-fried green, or any other Chinese fare.

Offer small bottles of soy sauce, chile oil, white vinegar, and Oriental sesame oil and small bowls of finely minced garlic and ginger root and Chinese hot mustard for guests to mix their own dipping sauces. Provide diners with chopsticks, small plates, and sauce dishes.

TO FORM AND STEAM DIM SUM DUMPLINGS

The wonton skins used for dumplings come in rounds and squares, usually about 60 to a package, and can be found in Oriental markets and some supermarkets. If you are unable to find round ones, which are needed to prepare dumplings, make an impression on a small stack of square wrappers with a 3-inch round cookie cutter or a glass, then cut out rounds with kitchen scissors. I have decided against including a recipe for making your own wonton skins, as it is a tricky and very time-consuming process.

Well-wrapped wonton skins may be frozen up to 2 or 3 weeks; defrost them in the refrigerator. For best results, use the skins as soon as possible after purchase, as they dry out and crack if stored too long.

When forming the dumplings, work with only 4 to 6 wrappers at a time. Keep the remainder well wrapped and covered with a lightly dampened tea towel. Very lightly dab water around the outer rim of the wrapper; this will help to hold the dumpling in its formed shape. Loosely cup the wrapper in the palm of your hand and place 1 tablespoon of filling in center. Bring sides up to cover the filling, making pleats around the top to resemble an opened tulip. The wrapper should tightly hug the filling, and the top of the filling should be exposed. If desired, place a tiny coriander or parsley leaf on the filling. Gently flatten the bottom of the dumpling by pressing with your fingertips.

As the dumplings are made, place them upright, not touching, on a board or platter and cover with a tea towel. Once all of the dumplings are ready, they may be steamed immediately or well covered with plastic wrap and refrigerated up to 6 hours. Alternatively, arrange dumplings on a baking sheet and freeze; when frozen, wrap well and store in the freezer for 2 or 3 days. Defrost in the refrigerator before steaming.

Use Chinese bamboo baskets for steaming the dumplings. Place each dumpling on a 2-inch square of aluminum foil and set them directly on the basket rungs. The foil may overlap, but the dumplings should be at least 1 inch apart. Stack the baskets in a wok or other vessel over water (the water should be no closer to the base of the bottom steamer than 1 inch), cover the top basket with its lid, and steam 20 minutes. (For more information on using bamboo steamers, see Equipment.)

If you do not have bamboo steamers, place the dumplings on a wire rack in a large pot or on the perforated tiers of a two- or three-tier steamer. Wrap the pot or steamer lid in a light kitchen towel to prevent condensation from dripping onto the dumplings.

Four dumpling fillings follow. Despite a similarity in ingredients, each has its own special taste and texture.

Har Shui Mai (Shrimp Dumplings)

MAKES 40 DUMPLINGS

1 pound uncooked shrimp, shelled, deveined, and minced

5 water chestnuts, finely minced

4 dried shiitake mushrooms, soaked in warm water 30 minutes to soften, drained, stemmed, and finely minced

2 teaspoons finely minced green onion

½ teaspoon very finely minced ginger root

1 tablespoon minced fresh coriander

2 tablespoons light soy sauce

1 egg white

2 teaspoons cornstarch

2 teaspoons water	40 round wonton skins
1 teaspoon Oriental sesame oil	Tiny fresh coriander or parsley leaves
¼ teaspoon ground white pepper	

Combine all ingredients except wonton skins and coriander leaves. Place a teaspoon-size portion of shrimp mixture in a small shallow dish, set on a rack over boiling water, cover pot, and steam 5 minutes. Taste and adjust seasonings. Form and steam dumplings as directed.

Siew Shui Mai (Pork Dumplings)

MAKES 40 DUMPLINGS

4 or 5 Napa cabbage or romaine lettuce leaves	stemmed, and finely minced
¾ pound lean ground pork	3 tablespoons minced bamboo shoots
2 tablespoons minced green onion with tops	1 egg, lightly beaten
1 large garlic clove, finely minced	1 tablespoon Chinese rice wine or dry sherry
1 teaspoon finely minced ginger root	1½ tablespoons soy sauce
4 dried shiitake mushrooms, soaked in warm water 30 minutes to soften, drained,	2 tablespoons cornstarch
	40 round wonton skins Tiny fresh coriander or parsley leaves

Place cabbage leaves on rack of steamer. Set rack over boiling water, cover pot, and steam 1 to 2 minutes, or until leaves are limp. Remove from rack, pat dry with paper toweling, and finely chop to measure approximately 1 cup. Combine with all remaining ingredients except wonton skins and coriander leaves. Place a teaspoon-size portion of pork mixture in a small shallow dish, set on rack over boiling water, cover pot, and steam 5 minutes. Taste and adjust seasonings. Form and steam dumplings as directed.

Ngaw Shui Mai (Beef Dumplings)

MAKES 40 DUMPLINGS

- 1 pound lean ground beef
- 3 tablespoons minced green onion tops
- 2 teaspoons minced garlic
- 1 teaspoon minced ginger root
- 2 tablespoons oyster sauce, or 1 tablespoon each oyster sauce and soy sauce
- 1 egg, lightly beaten
- 1 tablespoon Chinese rice wine or dry sherry
- 1 tablespoon cornstarch
- 40 round wonton skins Tiny fresh coriander or parsley leaves

Combine all ingredients except wonton skins and coriander leaves. Place a teaspoon-size portion of beef mixture in a small shallow dish, set on rack over boiling water, cover pot, and steam 5 minutes. Taste and adjust seasonings. Form and steam dumplings as directed.

Gai Shui Mai (Chicken Dumplings)

MAKES 40 DUMPLINGS

1½ cups minced raw chicken
⅓ cup finely minced lop chiang or Smithfield or similar ham
3 dried shiitake mushrooms, soaked in warm water 30 minutes to soften, drained, stemmed, and finely minced
1 tablespoon minced chives or green onion tops
1 egg white

1 tablespoon cornstarch
2 teaspoons Chinese rice wine or dry sherry
2 teaspoons hoisin sauce
1½ teaspoons peanut oil
½ teaspoon Oriental sesame oil
1 teaspoon soy sauce
40 round wonton skins
   Tiny fresh coriander or parsley leaves

Combine all ingredients except wonton skins and coriander leaves. Place a teaspoon-size portion of chicken mixture in a small shallow dish, set on rack over boiling water, cover pot, and steam 5 minutes. Taste and adjust seasonings. Form and steam dumplings as directed.

Baos (Chinese Buns)

Baos are those snowy-white puffs one always sees on the carts at *dim sum* restaurants. Most often they have a savory barbecued pork filling. I have included that favorite, plus five-spice chicken and mixed-vegetable versions. In the Dessert chapter, you will find a sweet red bean one, as well. *Baos* may also be steamed unfilled to serve as an accompaniment to a Chinese meal.

These buns, unlike most yeast breads, steam perfectly. Also, because they are traditionally steamed, we do not miss the golden color associated with baked breads. You may substitute whole-wheat pastry flour for half of the unbleached flour, but the buns will not rise as high or be as fluffy.

MAKES 16 BUNS

1½ teaspoons active dry yeast	¼ teaspoon salt (optional)
1 cup lukewarm water (110° F)	2½ cups unbleached flour, or as needed
1 tablespoon granulated sugar	

In a large mixing bowl, sprinkle yeast over water, stir in sugar, and let stand 10 minutes until foamy. Add salt and gradually stir in flour, beating well. Turn out onto lightly floured board and knead, adding more flour only as needed to prevent sticking, until smooth and elastic, about 10 minutes. Form into a smooth ball, place in oiled bowl, turn to coat all sides with oil, cover bowl with a lightly dampened tea towel, and let rise in warm place 1½ hours or until doubled in bulk.

While dough is rising, make one of the fillings that follow. Alternatively, halve two of the recipes and fill half of the buns with each.

Punch dough down, knead briefly, and divide into 2 equal portions. Roll each portion into a log approximately 16 inches long. Cut each log into 8 equal pieces, cover pieces with tea towel, and let rest 10 minutes. With hands, form each piece into a round ball. With a rolling pin on a very lightly floured board, roll each ball into a 3-inch round. While rolling, keep remaining dough covered with tea towel.

Place 2 to 3 teaspoons filling in center of round and bring sides of dough up around to encase filling, pleating and pinching as you go. Twist top to seal completely and place each filled bun, pleat side down, on a 3-inch square of waxed paper. Arrange 2 inches apart on baking sheet, cover with tea towel, and let rise in warm place 45 minutes or until almost doubled in size.

Carefully remove paper-lined buns to bamboo steamer tiers, placing them at least an inch apart. Following directions in How to Fill and Steam Dim Sum Dumplings, set steamer tiers over boiling water, cover, and steam 20 minutes.

Cha Siew Bao (Pork Buns)

MAKES 16 BUNS

¾ pound barbecued pork (cha siew), shredded (see Note)	¼ cup pork stock
1 tablespoon finely minced green onion tops or chives	1 tablespoon brown bean sauce

Combine all ingredients, place in a shallow bowl, set on rack over boiling water, cover pot, and steam 5 minutes. Let cool. When filling buns, transfer the filling to dough rounds with a slotted spoon to drain off juices.

Note: Barbecued pork may be purchased at a Chinese delicatessen. If unavailable, substitute cooked pork roast or chops; add 2 teaspoons hoisin sauce to mixture.

Gai Bao (Chicken Buns)

MAKES 16 BUNS

1   *whole chicken breast, skinned, boned, and finely chopped*

½   *to 1 teaspoon 5-spice powder or curry powder*

2   *green onions with tops, minced*

2   *teaspoons Chinese rice wine or dry sherry*

1   *teaspoon light soy sauce*

1   *large garlic clove, finely minced*

2   *dried shiitake mushrooms, soaked in warm water 30 minutes to soften, drained, stemmed, and finely minced*

Combine all ingredients, place in a shallow dish, set on a rack over boiling water, cover pot, and steam 5 minutes. Let cool. When filling buns, transfer the filling to the dough round with a slotted spoon to drain off juices.

Choy Bao (Mixed-Vegetable Buns)

MAKES 16 BUNS

2   *tablespoons chopped bamboo shoots*

2   *tablespoons chopped water chestnuts*

¾   *cup chopped steamed bok choy (Chinese cabbage) or other green, well drained*

2   *dried shiitake mushrooms, soaked in warm water 30*

minutes to soften, drained, stemmed, and finely minced

1   *teaspoon soy sauce*

1   *teaspoon Chinese rice wine or dry sherry*

¼   *teaspoon ground white pepper*

Pinch of granulated sugar

Combine all ingredients, place in a shallow bowl, set on rack over boiling water, cover pot, and steam 8 minutes. Let cool. When filling buns, transfer the filling to dough rounds with a slotted spoon to drain off juices.

Dow See Pai Gwat
(Spareribs in Black Bean Sauce)

Follow these tiny, flavorful ribs with a platter of steamed shrimp surrounded with a variety of Chinese dipping sauces.

MAKES APPROXIMATELY 40 INDIVIDUAL SERVINGS

2 pounds pork spareribs, cut into 1½-inch lengths	3 tablespoons fermented black beans, rinsed and drained
1 to 2 large garlic cloves, bruised and peeled	1 tablespoon soy sauce
¾ to 1 teaspoon grated ginger root	1 tablespoon Chinese rice wine or dry sherry
	Coriander sprigs

Place spareribs on rack of large steamer. Set rack over boiling water, cover steamer, and steam 10 minutes. Meanwhile, mash garlic in a mortar and pestle. Add ginger root and black beans and mix together well, crushing the beans as you mix. Transfer to a large bowl and stir in soy sauce and rice wine. Add spareribs and toss to coat well with sauce.

Transfer ribs to a shallow bowl, set on rack over boiling water, cover, and steam 30 to 35 minutes, or until tender. To assure even cooking of spareribs, move and turn them with chopsticks or forks several times during cooking. Garnish spareribs with coriander sprigs and serve from the dish.

Rice-studded Meatballs

A bright change from the standard chafing-dish meatballs seen at too many predinner functions. Accompany these "porcupines" with the condiments listed in the *dim sum* introduction.

MAKES 4 DOZEN

1 1/3 cups long- or short-grain white rice
1 pound lean ground beef
1 egg
5 water chestnuts, minced
2 tablespoons minced fresh chives
1 teaspoon finely minced ginger root
1 tablespoon cornstarch
1 1/2 tablespoons soy sauce
2 teaspoons Chinese rice wine or dry sherry
1 1-inch piece dried tangerine peel, soaked in warm water 15 minutes to soften, drained, and finely minced

Wash rice until water runs clear, cover with water, and soak 1 hour. Drain and spread out on board or baking sheet to dry slightly while you prepare the meat mixture.

Combine all remaining ingredients. Place a teaspoon-size portion of meat mixture in a small shallow bowl, set on rack over boiling water, cover pot, and steam 5 minutes. Taste and adjust seasonings. Chill until mixture holds together well, about 30 minutes.

Shape meat mixture into 48 smooth balls, each about 1 1/4 inches in diameter. With the palm of your hand, gently roll each ball in the rice until outside is completely coated with kernels. With fingertips, lightly press rice into meatballs, being careful not to misshape them. If using bamboo steamers, line baskets with lightly dampened cheesecloth and arrange balls about 1 inch apart directly on cloth. If using metal steamer racks or tiers, lightly coat with lecithin oil and then arrange meatballs directly on them. Place baskets or racks over boiling water, cover, and steam 20 minutes.

Chicken Liver Pâté

This olive-flecked pâté stands out on a buffet table or can be the opening course for a large dinner party. The rich flavor and smooth texture of this elegant dish will prompt compliments from your guests, and the olives may even be mistaken for truffles.

Sieve one or two hard-cooked eggs separately and decorate the pâté once it is unmolded onto the serving plate. Lightly sprinkle with paprika and tuck watercress sprigs around the pâté. Arrange Melba toast, rye, or pumpernickel rounds, baguette slices, and/or plain wheat crackers on an attractive plate nearby.

MAKES APPROXIMATELY 30 BUFFET SERVINGS

*½ pound chicken livers,
trimmed of fat and cut up
Brandy or dry sherry to
cover*
1 egg
½ cup diced onion
1 large garlic clove, minced
*2 tablespoons butter, cut up,
at room temperature*
*2 tablespoons unbleached
flour*

½ cup heavy cream
¾ teaspoon salt
*¼ teaspoon freshly ground
white pepper*
¼ teaspoon ground allspice
*⅛ teaspoon freshly grated
nutmeg*
¼ cup chopped ripe olives
1 bay leaf

Place livers in a nonmetallic dish and pour brandy over. Refrigerate, covered, overnight. Butter a 3-cup basin, soufflé dish, or mold with lecithin butter; set aside.

Drain livers and place them in a blender or food processor fitted with metal blade. Add egg, onion, garlic, butter, flour, cream, and seasonings. Puree until smooth. Add olives and blend *just* until mixed.

Spoon liver mixture into prepared basin and place bay leaf flat across center. Cover tightly (see Improvised Lids), set on rack over boiling water, cover pot, and steam 45 minutes. Remove to cooling rack and let stand 15 minutes.

Uncover, cool completely, re-cover, and refrigerate overnight. With a thin-bladed knife, loosen pâté from pan sides. Place a serving platter on top of pâté and invert pan. Present as described above.

Cold Whole Salmon with Avocado Sauce

This elegant salmon will be the highlight of your next buffet table. An artistic garnish for the avocado-masked fish would be lemon slices, ripe olive strips, capers, and watercress or parsley sprigs.

Arrange small, thin slices of black, pumpernickel, and/or rye bread near the platter and set out short, broad-bladed silver knives, bowls of capers, and remaining Avocado Sauce. Guests help themselves to the salmon, placing it on the bread to make small open-face sandwiches.

MAKES APPROXIMATELY 40 BUFFET SERVINGS

1   *whole salmon (5 to 7*
    pounds)
    Fish stock, or equal parts
    water and dry white wine
3   *tablespoons fresh lemon or*
    lime juice
1   *small onion or 2 leeks,*
    sliced
½   *cup celery leaves*
2   *bay leaves, broken*

½   *teaspoon ground mace*
4   *whole cloves*
6   *white peppercorns, lightly*
    crushed
2   *thyme or tarragon sprigs*
    (optional)

    Avocado Sauce (recipe
    follows)

Follow Basic Instructions for Readying Whole Fish in the fish chapter, but do not score. You will need a fish poacher or a roasting pan for a fish this large. (See Equipment for hints on adapting fish poachers and roasting pans to steaming.) With aluminum foil, form a boat- or cradle-shaped container to hold the fish lying flat; the sides should rise about 2 inches above the height of the fish. Line the "boat" with plastic wrap. Place the fish in the foil container and set aside.

Place rack in fish poacher or roasting pan and add fish stock to come within 1 inch of the bottom of the rack. Set fish in its foil container on the rack. Pour lemon juice evenly over fish, then strew with onion, celery leaves, bay leaves, mace, cloves, and peppercorns. If desired, top with thyme sprigs.

Cover steaming vessel and bring steaming liquid to a boil. Steam 25 to 35 minutes, or until fish tests done. Remove fish to cooling rack (or set poacher rack on a cooling rack) and let stand until cool enough to handle. Discard vegetables and herbs. While fish is still warm, carefully peel away skin, using your fingertips and a small knife. Gently flip the fish onto a serving platter and remove the skin on the second side. Let fish cool completely, cover with plastic wrap, and refrigerate up to 24 hours.

When ready to serve, cover fish with a thin coating of Avocado Sauce and garnish fish and platter as suggested above. Spoon remaining sauce into a bowl to place on the buffet table.

Avocado Sauce

MAKES APPROXIMATELY 2 CUPS

3   *large ripe avocados*
3   *tablespoons fresh lemon or*
    lime juice
½   *to ¾ cup plain yoghurt*

1½   *teaspoons dried dillweed*
¾   *teaspoon salt*
½   *teaspoon freshly ground*
    white pepper

With a fork, mash avocado and lemon juice until smooth (or whirl briefly in a blender or food processor if a very smooth mixture is preferred). Stir in all remaining ingredients, taste, and adjust seasonings.

If not using sauce immediately, cover and refrigerate until just before masking the salmon. Sauce should be made no more than 4 hours ahead of time, or the proper flavor and consistency will be lost.

Stuffed Mushrooms

When stuffed mushrooms are steamed rather than broiled or baked, they retain more of their natural flavor and moisture. I have included three scrumptious fillings—garlicky pesto, nutty ham, and creamy blue cheese. Each recipe will fill 12 large mushrooms. Select the filling that complements the other dishes you are serving.

Garnish serving platter or individual serving plates with parsley or watercress sprigs. Bring mushrooms to the table while they are still very hot.

SERVES 4 TO 6

12   *large fresh mushrooms*
     (approximately 2½ inches
     in diameter)

Fresh lemon juice
Approximately ¾ cup
filling (recipes follow)

Gently clean mushrooms with a soft brush. Cut off any discolored part of stems and snap stems off, being careful not to break the caps. Rub caps with lemon juice and set aside. Mince the stems and steam until tender (see Vegetable Steaming Methods).

Combine stems with filling and mound into caps. Place caps close together (barely touching) either in a shallow dish or directly on rack over boiling water. Cover pot and steam 7 minutes, or until just tender; watch carefully to avoid overcooking. Transfer to serving platter or individual plates, garnish as desired, and serve with picks or forks.

Fillings for Stuffed Mushrooms

Pesto Filling: Combine ½ cup Pesto or Watercress Pesto (see Basic Savory Sauces), ¼ cup fine dry breadcrumbs, and reserved steamed stems. Sprinkle filled caps with freshly grated Parmesan cheese and paprika. Steam as directed.

Ham Filling: Lightly beat 1 egg and mix in ½ cup finely ground cooked ham, 2 tablespoons chopped ripe olives, 3 tablespoons finely chopped walnuts, ⅓ cup freshly grated Gruyère cheese, 3 tablespoons fine dry breadcrumbs, and 1 teaspoon dry mustard, or to taste. Combine ham mixture with reserved steamed stems. Fill and steam as directed.

Blue Cheese Filling: With fork, combine ½ cup crumbled blue cheese, ⅓ cup Crème Fraîche (see Basic Savory Sauces), 1 tablespoon *each* minced green onion tops and minced fresh parsley, and 1 teaspoon minced fresh garlic chives. Combine cheese mixture with reserved steamed stems. Fill and steam as directed.

Dolmades

Traditionally, the classic Greek *dolmades*—stuffed preserved grape leaves—are simmered in water that has been flavored with fresh lemon juice, olive oil, and garlic. *Dolmades* can, however, be steamed rather than simmered. Serve these tiny rolls hot or at room temperature—plain, with Greek Lemon Sauce, or with plain yoghurt seasoned to taste with finely minced garlic and fresh lemon juice.

There are approximately 50 grape leaves in a pound. They come packed in jars in a brine solution, which can be found in gourmet shops and most supermarkets. Remove the leaves from the jar, rinse well with cold water, place in a bowl, and pour boiling water over. Drain and carefully separate, then cut away stems and any tough stem portions that remain on the leaves. Spread leaves on paper toweling shiny sides down. If not stuffing all of the leaves, layer the extra ones on the steamer rack to serve as a decorative bed for the rolls, or use as a garnish for the serving platter.

Large nasturtium, beet, or spinach leaves, or average-size Swiss chard, lettuce, cabbage, or fresh grape leaves can be used in place of the preserved grape leaves. All of these leaves are prepared for stuffing in the same way: Wash well and cut off stems. (In the case of Swiss chard, save the stems for steaming as vegetables.) Place the leaves flat on a board and cut away any tough stem portions left on them. If the leaves are very large and the ribs are thick, cut the leaves in half lengthwise and cut away the ribs. Each leaf will then make two wrappers. Steam the leaves in a single layer on a rack above boiling water until limp, about 1 to 2 minutes. Remove the leaves and spread on paper toweling rib sides up. (The "rib side" is the one on which the rib is more pronounced.)

To stuff grape or other leaves, place a tablespoon of filling on stem end of each leaf. Roll one turn, fold in sides, and roll like a jelly roll. Place close together (barely touching) seam side down directly on rack and drizzle with garlic olive oil and fresh lemon juice. Place over boiling water, cover, and steam 15 to 20 minutes for grape leaves and 12 to 15 minutes for other leaves.

Transfer rolls to serving platter and drizzle with additional olive oil. Garnish with tiny grape clusters and lemon slices. If not including the *dolmades* in a buffet, serve them as a supper dish with a salad of tomatoes, feta cheese, and Greek olives.

Rice Dolmades

MAKES 48

1 cup minced onion	2 to 3 tablespoons pine nuts, coarsely chopped
2 tablespoons olive oil	
1 to 2 large garlic cloves, finely minced	3 tablespoons dried currants
	2 teaspoons chopped fresh oregano
1 cup long-grain white rice, washed and drained	1/2 teaspoon ground allspice
1 1/2 cups water	1/2 teaspoon herb seasoning or salt
2 tablespoons fresh lemon juice	1/2 teaspoon freshly ground black pepper
1/2 cup chopped fresh parsley	48 grape leaves

Sauté onion in olive oil, stirring often, until onion begins to turn golden. Stir in garlic, cover, and cook 1 minute. Add rice, water, and lemon juice. Cover, bring to boil, lower heat, and simmer 15 minutes. Remove lid and let any moisture boil away.

In a mixing bowl, combine all remaining ingredients except grape leaves. Toss in precooked rice and adjust seasonings. Fill grape leaves and steam as directed.

Lamb Dolmades

MAKES 48

1 pound lean ground lamb	1/2 teaspoon freshly grated lemon peel
1/4 cup minced green onion with tops	
1/4 cup minced fresh parsley	1/2 teaspoon herb seasoning or salt
2 large garlic cloves, finely minced	1/2 teaspoon ground cumin
	2 tablespoons fresh lemon juice
2 tablespoons minced fresh dill or mint	48 grape leaves

In a mixing bowl, combine all ingredients except grape leaves. Place a teaspoon-size portion in a small shallow bowl, set on rack over boiling water, cover pot, and steam 5 minutes. Taste and adjust seasonings. Fill grape leaves and steam as directed.

Lingcod with Garlic Mayonnaise

For an elegant first course, steam small fresh fish steaks and serve with homemade garlic-flavored mayonnaise. If you cannot find lingcod in the market, use monkfish, sea bass, albacore, swordfish, salmon, or halibut. Halve steaks that are too large for first-course portions.

SERVES 6

6 small lingcod steaks (approximately 3 ounces each)	*Minced fresh or crumbled dried basil*
¼ cup fresh lemon juice Freshly ground white pepper Salt	*Garlic Mayonnaise (see Basic Savory Sauces) Small fresh basil leaves or watercress sprigs*

Arrange fish steaks in a shallow dish. Sprinkle with lemon juice and let stand 10 minutes. Season with pepper and salt to taste and strew minced basil over. Place dish on rack over boiling water, cover pot, and steam 8 to 10 minutes, or until fish flakes easily; be careful not to overcook.

With slotted utensil, transfer fish steaks to heated individual serving dishes. Top each with 2 to 3 teaspoons mayonnaise. Garnish with basil leaves.

Eggplant Caviar

This piquant spread is bound to be a hit. Prepare it a day ahead, cover, and refrigerate to let the flavors meld.

Serve the "caviar" garnished with halved cherry tomatoes and a generous sprinkling of minced fresh parsley. Accompany with a basket of pita bread triangles and/or baguette slices. This spread also makes a delicious relish for broiled meats.

MAKES APPROXIMATELY 2 CUPS

1 *large eggplant*
   (approximately 1½ pounds)
1 *medium onion, finely*
   chopped
2 *large garlic cloves, minced*
2 *tablespoons olive oil*
1 *large ripe tomato, coarsely*
   chopped
   Pinch granulated sugar

½ *teaspoon salt, or to taste*
¼ *teaspoon freshly ground*
   black pepper, or to taste
   Cayenne pepper to taste
1 *tablespoon fresh lemon*
   juice, or to taste
¼ *to ½ cup drained roasted*
   pepper, cut into thin slivers

Trim and halve the unpeeled eggplant. Place halves, cut side down, directly on rack over boiling water. Steam 12 minutes, or until tender. Remove eggplant to a work surface and let stand until cool enough to handle, then peel and chop coarsely. Set aside.

In a large covered nonstick skillet or saucepan, cook onion and garlic in oil 5 minutes. Add chopped eggplant, tomato, sugar, seasonings, and lemon juice. Cook, stirring occasionally, 15 minutes, or until excess moisture has cooked away. Taste and adjust seasonings.

Remove skillet from heat and gently stir roasted pepper into eggplant mixture. Transfer to a bowl, cool, cover, and refrigerate.

Soups from Steamed Vegetables

Soups do not fit easily into this book. Clear soups prepared in covered ceramic basins or Yunnan pots would be appropriate first courses, but it is quicker and easier, and thus more practical, to cook them directly over the heat. I have included the following soups because they are made with steamed vegetables, and because of my particular affinity for soup making.

Through the years of cooking for family and friends, the most frequent praises have come when I serve soup, whether as a main meal, a first course, or as part of a buffet. However, the query "What is this delicious soup?" can never be accurately answered. Each time the pureed vegetable or vegetables have been combined with different stocks and seasoned with whatever my mood has dictated.

One time it might be cooked lentils mixed with the asparagus steaming water I have stored in the freezer and the green beans I have pureed from last night's dinner. On another occasion, the combination could be steamed cauliflower pureed with the sorrel sauce I was testing the day before, and then thinned with chicken stock and seasoned with fresh herbs.

My hope is that these five recipes will guide you in the creation of soups from vegetables you have deliberately oversteamed, or from those that went unfinished at a recent meal. It is not necessary to puree the vegetables immediately upon cooking. Chop and store them, covered, in the refrigerator for up to 2 days, then puree them with the other ingredients for the soup. One cup of chopped steamed vegetables will yield about ¾ cup of puree. You may also use a vegetable puree that was originally intended as a side dish; in this case, consider the original seasonings when preparing the soup.

To prepare a simple soup with a steamed vegetable, boil down the vegetable steaming water to reduce and concentrate the flavor, then puree the vegetable with this liquid. Transfer the mixture to a saucepan and heat with seasonings and enough stock to form the consistency you desire. If you prefer a richer soup, add half-and-half cream, milk, or one of the dairy substitutes.

Combine two or more vegetable purees for a more elaborate preparation. Use the combination guidelines for Vegetable Purees in the Vegetables and Grains chapter, or develop your own, keeping color and complementary flavors in mind. The addition of lightly sautéed onions, garlic, shallots, and/or mushrooms adds extra flavor. Mashed or riced potatoes (or cubed cooked potatoes) can be pureed with the vegetables, eliminating the need to thicken the finished soup with flour. An egg-yolk binder is also a good thickener, but adds unnecessary fat.

Any soup may be made without thickeners and without cream or milk. If the stock, whether vegetable, meat, or poultry, is richly flavored with herbs, the puree will stand on its own. A special taste dimension, however, is added by dairy products, especially when the soups are being served cold. In the latter case, heavy cream is a must. Omit half-and-half and chill the soup well. Add heavy cream to taste, re-chill, and adjust seasonings. Serve in chilled bowls with colorful garnishes.

Serve any of the soups as a first course, or as a luncheon main dish with the addition of cooked grains or small pastas. Garnish attractively, again keeping color in mind.

Swiss Chard Soup

Spinach or tender beet greens can be substituted for the chard. Use any rich stock you have on hand.

SERVES 4

- ¼ cup minced onion
- 1 garlic clove, minced
- 1 tablespoon butter and/or
   rendered chicken fat

1   tablespoon unbleached
     flour
1½   cups rich chicken, turkey,
     or vegetable stock
1½   cups chopped cooked Swiss
     chard
1½   cups half-and-half cream
     or milk

⅛   to ¼ teaspoon freshly
     grated nutmeg
     Fresh lemon juice, freshly
     ground white pepper, and
     herb seasoning to taste
1   hard-cooked egg, yolk and
     white sieved separately, or
     grated Gruyère cheese
     Paprika

In a covered nonstick skillet cook onion and garlic in butter until softened. Sprinkle flour over and cook, stirring occasionally, 2 minutes. Remove from heat and gradually blend in stock. Return to heat; cook and stir until smooth and slightly thickened. Stir in chard and puree the mixture in a blender or food processor. Transfer to saucepan and add half-and-half and nutmeg. Reheat gently (do not boil) and season with lemon juice, pepper, and herb seasoning. Ladle into heated soup cups and top each serving with sieved egg or grated cheese and a sprinkling of paprika.

Curried Broccoli Soup

Cauliflower, or a combination of cauliflower and broccoli, may be prepared in this fashion. Add minced fresh parsley or chives to the sun-dried tomato garnish.

SERVES 4

3   tablespoons minced onion
2   tablespoons minced celery
1   large garlic clove, minced
1   tablespoon butter and/or
     rendered chicken fat
½   to 1 teaspoon curry powder,
     or to taste
1   tablespoon unbleached
     flour

1½   cups rich lamb or other
     stock
1½   cups chopped steamed
     broccoli
1½   cups half-and-half cream
     or milk
     Fresh lemon juice, freshly
     ground black pepper, and
     herb seasoning to taste
     Minced sun-dried tomatoes

In a covered nonstick skillet cook onion, celery, and garlic in butter until softened. Sprinkle with curry powder and flour; cook, stirring occasionally, 2 minutes. Remove saucepan from heat and gradually blend in stock. Return to heat; cook and stir until smooth and slightly thickened.

Stir in broccoli and puree mixture in a blender or food processor. Transfer to saucepan and add half-and-half. Reheat gently (do not boil) and season with lemon juice, pepper, and herb seasoning. Ladle into heated soup cups and top each serving with 4 or 5 tiny pieces of sun-dried tomato.

Carrot Soup

SERVES 4

$1/4$ cup chopped green onion with tops	$1\frac{1}{2}$ cups rich chicken or turkey stock
2 tablespoons chopped fresh parsley	2 cups chopped steamed carrot
1 tablespoon butter and/or rendered chicken fat	$1/2$ cup half-and-half cream or milk
$1/8$ teaspoon ground ginger	Herb seasoning and freshly ground white pepper to taste
1 tablespoon unbleached flour	Minced fresh chives

In a covered nonstick skillet cook onion and parsley in butter until onion is softened. Sprinkle with ginger and flour and cook, stirring occasionally, 2 minutes. Remove saucepan from heat and gradually blend in stock. Return to heat; cook and stir until smooth and slightly thickened. Stir in carrot and puree mixture in blender or food processor. Transfer to saucepan and add half-and-half. Reheat gently (do not boil) and season with herb seasoning and pepper. Ladle into heated soup cups and sprinkle with chives.

Green Bean Soup

Vary this soup by adding $1/2$ cup minced steamed mushrooms when pureeing the bean mixture.

SERVES 4 TO 6

$1/4$ cup chopped green onion with tops	1 tablespoon butter and/or rendered chicken fat
1 large garlic clove, minced	$1/4$ teaspoon crumbled dried tarragon

1	tablespoon unbleached flour	$^1/_2$	cup half-and-half cream or milk
$1^1/_2$	cups chicken, turkey, or pork stock		Herb seasoning and freshly ground white pepper to
$2^1/_2$	cups chopped steamed green beans		taste Crème Fraîche or sour cream

In a covered nonstick skillet cook onion and garlic in butter until softened. Sprinkle with tarragon and flour and cook, stirring occasionally, 2 minutes. Remove skillet from heat and gradually blend in stock. Return to heat; cook and stir until smooth and slightly thickened. Stir in beans and puree mixture in a blender or food processor. Transfer to a saucepan and add half-and-half. Reheat gently (do not boil) and season with herb seasoning and pepper. Ladle into heated soup cups and garnish each serving with a dollop of Crème Fraîche.

Pumpkin Soup

For a thicker, smoother soup, add 1 cup diced cooked potato when pureeing the pumpkin mixture.

SERVES 8

$^1/_4$	cup minced leek, white and a little green	$^1/_2$	teaspoon granulated sugar
3	tablespoons minced onion	$^1/_4$	teaspoon ground ginger
3	tablespoons minced celery with some leaves	3	cups pumpkin puree
2	tablespoons chopped fresh parsley	3	cups chicken stock
1	teaspoon minced fresh thyme	1	cup half-and-half cream or milk
2	tablespoons butter and/or rendered chicken fat		Herb seasoning and freshly ground white pepper to taste
			Freshly grated orange peel
			Freshly grated nutmeg

In a covered nonstick skillet cook leek, onion, celery, parsley, and thyme in butter until softened. Sprinkle with sugar and ginger and cook 1 minute. Add pumpkin puree and 1 cup of the stock. Puree mixture in blender or food processor and transfer to a saucepan. Stir in remaining stock and half-and-half. Reheat gently (do not boil) and add herb seasoning and pepper. Ladle into heated soup cups and garnish each serving with grated orange peel and a few gratings of nutmeg.

BREADS AND DUMPLINGS

Pumpkin Oatmeal Bread

Spicy Date Bread

Fresh Fruit Bread

Cornmeal Bread

Boston Brown Bread

Spinach or Parsley Dumplings

Stew Dumplings

Corn Dumplings

Breads and Dumplings

Almost any quick bread recipe that is normally baked can be steamed. The flavor is a tiny bit more pronounced and the loaf is usually a bit more moist, with a slightly more cakelike texture. Ingredients such as molasses, pumpkin, cornmeal, and dark spices offset the paleness that results from steaming, but the top crust does not develop a golden color or the characteristic cracking that results with baking. You can mask this by slicing the bread before serving.

Here you will find three examples of quick breads to steam: pumpkin oatmeal, spicy date, and fresh fruit. The spices in each are similar because they are the ones generally associated with sweet breads. The other ingredients are different—thus each bread is unique in taste and texture.

Quick breads should be completely cool before serving. The flavor improves if they are allowed to stand several hours after cooking. To keep them fresh, wrap in plastic and store in a cool, dry place for up to two days.

Offer quick breads at breakfast or brunch, at tea time, or as a light finish to a meal. They are all complemented by cream cheese or unsalted butter, or a dollop of whipped cream if serving as a dessert. These breads, however, are also delicious without any adornment.

Most yeast breads that are customarily baked are not good candidates for steaming. Not only is the glorious aroma of baking bread absent, but the cooked loaf is unappetizingly pale and the surface often has a pock-marked look. I tried steaming my favorite currant-and-cinnamon-streaked coffeecake. When I removed it from the steamer it was so snowy white it looked as if it had never been cooked. The flavor and the texture were passable, but there was no eye appeal. It had to be toasted to make you want to eat it.

And then there are the breads that are traditionally steamed: Boston's famous brown bread, a moist and richly colored loaf, and the *baos* of China, springy white buns often filled with a savory or sweet mixture (*baos* can be found in Appetizers and First Courses and in Desserts). Two additional steamed breads, *putus,* rice flour muffins of the Philippines, and East Indian *idlis,* savory cakes of rice and legume flours, do not appear here. To prepare them authentically requires special ingredients and equipment not easily available.

Though you may only have thought of dumplings dropped into a bubbling stew, they can be successfully steamed. The three distinctive recipes included here illustrate how any conventional dumpling recipe may be adapted to the steamer.

Pumpkin Oatmeal Bread

Bake this nutritious bread in small loaf pans so that you can easily share it with your friends. You will need a large steamer or a two-tiered steamer in order to cook all the loaves at once. Winter squash or yam puree may be substituted for the pumpkin, and chopped dates can replace the raisins.

MAKES 3 SMALL LOAVES

³/₄ cup unbleached flour	¹/₂ cup firmly packed dark brown sugar, sieved
³/₄ cup whole-wheat flour	
1¹/₄ teaspoons baking powder	4 tablespoons butter, melted and cooled
¹/₂ teaspoon salt	
¹/₂ teaspoon ground cinnamon	¹/₄ cup sour cream, combined with ¹/₄ teaspoon baking soda
¹/₂ teaspoon ground ginger	
¹/₄ teaspoon ground cloves	1 cup pumpkin puree
¹/₄ teaspoon freshly grated nutmeg	3 tablespoons freshly grated orange peel
¹/₂ cup unproccessed rolled oats	¹/₂ cup chopped raisins
2 eggs	¹/₂ cup chopped pecans, walnuts, or almonds

Oil three 5¹/₂ × 3 × 2-inch loaf pans with lecithin oil. Set aside. Wrap steamer lid in a towel. Bring water in steamer almost to a boil.

Sift flours, baking powder, salt, and spices into a bowl. Toss in oats and set aside. In a separate large mixing bowl beat eggs lightly, then stir in sugar until well blended. Add butter, sour cream–soda mixture, pumpkin puree, and orange peel. Mix well and add dry ingredients. Stir just until dry ingredients are moistened. Fold in raisins and nuts.

Divide batter among the 3 prepared pans. Place pans on rack over gently boiling water, cover pot, and steam 30 minutes, or until cake tester inserted in center comes out clean and loaves have pulled slightly away from sides of pans.

Remove pans to cooling rack and let stand 10 minutes. Invert pans onto rack, turn loaves right side up, and let cool.

Spicy Date Bread

MAKES 1 ROUND LOAF

1 cup chopped dates	1 egg
1 teaspoon baking soda	1¼ cups unbleached flour
Freshly grated peel of 1 large orange	½ teaspoon ground cinnamon
¾ cup low-fat milk	½ teaspoon ground cloves
¼ cup fresh orange juice	½ teaspoon freshly grated nutmeg
3 tablespoons butter, softened	¼ teaspoon ground coriander
½ cup granulated sugar	⅔ cup chopped pecans, walnuts, or almonds
½ cup firmly packed dark brown sugar	

Place dates, baking soda, and grated orange peel in a medium mixing bowl. In a covered nonstick saucepan bring milk and orange juice to a boil over medium heat. Pour over date mixture and let stand 15 minutes.

Oil a 6-cup soufflé dish or bundt pan with lecithin oil; set aside. Wrap steamer lid in a towel. Bring water in steamer almost to a boil.

Cream butter and sugars in a large mixing bowl. Beat in egg until mixture is fluffy. Blend in date mixture. Combine flour and spices in a sifter; sift into date mixture and stir just until dry ingredients are moistened. Fold in nuts and spoon into prepared basin.

Place basin on rack over gently boiling water, cover pot, and steam 40 minutes, or until cake tester inserted in center comes out clean and bread has pulled slightly away from sides of basin. Remove basin to cooling rack and let stand 15 minutes. Invert basin onto rack, turn loaf right side up, and let cool.

Fresh Fruit Bread

MAKES 1 ROUND LOAF

4 tablespoons butter, softened	1 cup unbleached flour
½ cup firmly packed brown sugar	½ teaspoon baking powder
1 egg	¼ teaspoon baking soda
1 teaspoon freshly grated lemon peel	½ teaspoon ground cinnamon
¼ teaspoon almond extract	¼ teaspoon ground cloves
½ cup peeled grated Granny Smith or other tart apple, or chopped pear, or a combination of apple and pear	¼ teaspoon freshly grated nutmeg
	¼ teaspoon ground cardamom
	1 tablespoon cultured buttermilk powder (see Note)
	⅓ cup finely chopped pecans

Butter a 7-inch round cake pan with lecithin butter; set aside. Wrap steamer lid in a towel. Bring water in steamer almost to a boil.

Cream butter and sugar in a large mixing bowl. Beat in egg, mixing well. Stir in lemon peel, almond extract, and apple. Combine dry ingredients in a sifter and sift into apple mixture. Mix just until dry ingredients are moistened. Fold in nuts and spoon into prepared pan.

Place pan on rack over gently boiling water, cover pot, and steam 30 minutes, or until cake tester inserted in center comes out clean and bread has pulled slightly away from sides of pan.

Remove pan to cooling rack and let stand 15 minutes. Invert pan onto rack, turn loaf right side up, and let cool.

Note: Cultured buttermilk powder, available in 12-ounce cans, is sold in supermarkets. Like dried milk, once opened it must be refrigerated. It is good to have on hand if you only occasionally cook with buttermilk, or if you want the buttermilk flavor but not the liquid.

Cornmeal Bread

This cornmeal bread steams beautifully. The texture is solid yet light and the yellow grain imparts a warm color. Serve warm, cut in wedges with jalapeño jelly for breakfast, or offer as an accompaniment to Iberian Pollock with Tomatoes.

MAKES 1 ROUND LOAF

1¼ cups nondegerminated
   yellow cornmeal
⅓ cup unbleached flour
¼ cup granulated sugar
½ teaspoon baking soda

½ teaspoon salt
2 tablespoons butter, melted
   and cooled
1 cup buttermilk

Oil a 4-cup soufflé dish with lecithin oil. Set aside.

Combine all dry ingredients in a large mixing bowl. Add butter and buttermilk and, with a wooden spoon, beat to mix well. Pour batter into prepared basin, cover tightly (see Improvised Lids), place basin on rack over gently boiling water, cover pot, and steam 45 minutes, or until cake tester inserted in center comes out clean.

Remove bread from steamer, uncover, and let stand 5 minutes. Invert dish onto a wooden board to remove bread, turn loaf right side up, and cut into wedges.

Boston Brown Bread

Prepare this classic steamed bread for serving with a New England boiled dinner, Boston baked beans, or a corned beef brisket. It is also good at teatime, spread with unsalted butter or cream cheese.

MAKES 1 LOAF

½ cup rye or whole-wheat
   flour
½ cup unbleached flour
1 teaspoon baking powder
1¼ teaspoons baking soda
¾ teaspoon salt

½ cup nondegerminated
   yellow cornmeal
1 cup buttermilk
6 tablespoons dark molasses
¾ cup chopped raisins

Oil a 1-pound coffee can with lecithin oil. Set aside.

Into a large bowl sift together flours, baking powder, soda, and salt. Mix in cornmeal, then stir in buttermilk and molasses. Blend just until dry ingredients are moistened. Fold in raisins.

Spoon batter into prepared coffee can, cover tightly (see Improvised Lids), and place on low rack in steamer. Add boiling water to come ¾ up sides of can. (This steaming method is the same as for a pudding. See Basic

Instructions for Steaming Puddings in the Desserts chapter.) Cover pot and steam with water at gentle boil for 3 hours, checking water level occasionally and replenishing if needed to maintain original level.

Remove can from steamer and uncover. Slip a thin-bladed knife down along inside edge of can to loosen bread. Turn can upside down over cooling rack and ease bread out of can by shaking gently. Cool 10 minutes before slicing.

Basic Instructions for Dumplings

Dumplings that are customarily cooked in bubbling broth or on top of a simmering stew may be cooked in the juices of a meat or poultry dish as it steams. They may also be steamed in a well-buttered shallow dish placed on a rack over boiling water.

With a small spoon, drop the dumplings at least one inch apart to allow for expansion during cooking. Check for doneness by breaking a dumpling apart with a fork and sampling a small center portion. It should be light and fluffy; if overcooked, the dumplings will become tough and rubbery.

Spinach or Parsley Dumplings

These dumplings will complement such dishes as Basic Herb Chicken and Mustard Rabbit.

SERVES 4

1 egg	¼ teaspoon salt
2 tablespoons butter, melted and cooled	¼ teaspoon freshly grated nutmeg
⅓ cup sour cream	⅔ cup well-drained chopped steamed spinach or minced fresh parsley
2 tablespoons freshly grated Parmesan cheese, or ½ teaspoon freshly grated lemon peel	
1 cup cake flour	2 to 3 tablespoons rich stock and/or butter, or juices from steamed dish being prepared, heated
1 teaspoon baking powder	

Lightly beat egg in a mixing bowl. Stir in butter and sour cream until well blended. Add cheese. In a sifter, combine the flour, baking powder, salt, and nutmeg and sift into egg mixture. Stir well and then add spinach, mixing until just combined. Drop by teaspoonfuls into lightly buttered large shallow dishes.

Set dishes on rack over boiling water. Wrap steamer lid in a towel, cover pot, and steam 10 minutes, or until dumplings are done. Pour heated stock over and serve immediately.

Stew Dumplings

Drop these onto any stock-based "stew" as it steams.

SERVES 3 OR 4

1 cup unbleached flour	1/4 teaspoon ground oregano, marjoram, or thyme
1 1/2 teaspoons baking powder	
1/2 teaspoon granulated sugar	2 tablespoons butter, cut into bits and chilled
1/2 teaspoon herb seasoning or salt	3/4 cup milk

In a sifter, combine all dry ingredients and sift into a mixing bowl. Crumble in butter with fingers until mixture has the consistency of coarse cornmeal. Just before ready to steam, stir milk in with a fork to form a soft dough.

Drop dough by rounded teaspoonfuls into liquid of steaming dish. Re-cover pot and steam 20 minutes, or until dumplings are done.

Corn Dumplings

For that little portion of corn you've cut off your steamed corn on the cob. These dumplings are delicious with South American-style Chicken.

SERVES 4 TO 6

1/3 cup nondegerminated yellow cornmeal	2 tablespoons butter, cut up and chilled
3/4 cup unbleached flour	2/3 cup milk
2 1/2 teaspoons baking powder	1/3 cup cooked corn kernels
1/2 teaspoon salt	
1/4 teaspoon ground sage	
Pinch granulated sugar	

Place cornmeal in a mixing bowl. In a sifter, combine all remaining dry ingredients and sift into cornmeal. Stir to mix well. Crumble in butter with fingers until mixture has the consistency of coarse cornmeal.

Just before ready to steam, stir in milk with a fork until dry ingredients are moistened. Stir in corn kernels. Drop by rounded teaspoonfuls into liquid of steaming dish, re-cover pot, and steam 10 minutes, or until dumplings are done.

EGGS AND TOFU

Savory Egg Custard

Chawan Mushi

Vietnamese Eggs with
   Crabmeat

Oeufs en Cocotte

Gado Gado

Timbales

Crab Mousse

Squash and Yam Pudding

Tofu with Chinese
   Seasonings

Tofu "Omelet"

Chicken and Tofu,
   Japanese Style

Tempeh

Eggs and Tofu

In this chapter eggs assume many roles. They are the base of steamed savory custards, which have a more delicate and silkier texture than baked ones. The custards range from the classic Japanese preparation called *chawan mushi* to a Vietnamese crab-flecked dish that is served with a pungent fish sauce.

Eggs form the wrappers that encase a variety of fillings, and star in the steamed version of traditionally baked shirred eggs. They bind pureed squash and yams in a smooth pudding that is the perfect accompaniment to a roast turkey, and are combined with vegetables or seafood in mousses and timbales. Hard-cooked eggs join with a variety of steamed vegetables in the Indonesian dish called *gado gado*, which is blanketed with a peppery peanut sauce.

Steam eggs you would normally boil in water along with a dish you are already steaming. Place room-temperature eggs directly on the steamer rack. Soft-cooked eggs require some trial and error to steam them exactly to your liking. The classic 3-minute egg will take about 5 minutes. Eggs will hard-cook in about 20 minutes.

There have been electric egg cookers on the market for a number of years. Operating on the steaming principle, they soft boil, hard boil, and poach eggs beautifully.

The best way to cook an unbeaten whole shelled egg is to break it into a lightly buttered or oiled small dish and steam it above gently boiling water. This method requires less of the cook's attention and less fat than preparing fried eggs. The steamed eggs are never rubbery and they have a particularly attractive appearance because the dish nicely shapes them.

Some cooks recommend steaming scrambled eggs. The process is quite tedious, though—steam a few minutes, stir, steam a few minutes, stir again, and so on—and the results are not worth the effort.

Following the egg dishes are three recipes that feature highly nutritious bean curd cakes, one with Chinese seasonings, one with Japanese seasonings, and the third a simple breakfast dish. Tofu also appears in several recipes in other chapters, and information on how it is packaged can be found in Terms and Ingredients. The final recipe in this section explains a number of ways to prepare tempeh, an extremely healthful soybean product that is formed by introducing a mold onto whole soybeans.

Savory Egg Custard

Use all those bits of leftover meats, poultry, fish, and/or vegetables in this versatile main dish for lunch or supper. Serve hot with a spinach salad dressed with Herb Vinaigrette and whole-grain toast.

SERVES 2

4	eggs, at room temperature	1	teaspoon safflower oil
2/3	cup hot (not boiling) water	1/8	to 1/4 teaspoon herb
1/4	cup minced green onion		seasoning
	with tops, or finely chopped	1/2	cup shredded cooked
	and well drained steamed		chicken
	spinach or Swiss chard		

With a whisk, lightly beat eggs and then beat in water until eggs are frothy. Add all remaining ingredients and pour into a 3-cup soufflé dish. Place on rack over *gently* boiling water, wrap lid in a kitchen towel, cover pot, and steam 30 minutes.

Variation: For a Chinese-style custard, add a few drops of Oriental sesame oil to the egg mixture. Steam 1½ ounces or 1 sausage lop chiang 5 minutes, mince, and use in place of the chicken. Just before serving, drizzle with a little oyster sauce. Serve with unfilled Chinese Buns (see Appetizers and First Courses).

Chawan Mushi (Japanese Custard Soup with Shrimp and Chicken)

This beautiful Japanese egg custard soup is steamed in specially designed covered bowls. If you do not have these bowls, custard cups or coffee cups covered with foil can be used.

Offer a side dish of lightly steamed green beans marinated in Oriental Dressing. Pass the soy sauce.

SERVES 5

3 small dried shiitake mushrooms	5 raw shrimp, shelled and deveined
1/3 cup warm water	1 tablespoon sake or dry sherry
3 water chestnuts	
3 small bamboo shoots	2 1/2 cups dashi or chicken stock
1/2 teaspoon granulated sugar	2 spinach leaves, finely shredded
1 tablespoon soy sauce	
1 small raw chicken breast half, skinned and boned (approximately 4 ounces)	3 eggs
	5 tiny watercress or parsley leaves
1/4 teaspoon salt	

In a small dish soak mushrooms in warm water 30 minutes or until softened. Drain, reserving soaking water. Discard stems and slice each mushroom cap into 5 strips. Place in a shallow dish. Cut each water chestnut into 5 slices and add to dish. Cut each bamboo shoot into 5 strips and add to dish. Combine sugar and 2 teaspoons of the soy sauce and pour over vegetables in dish. Place dish on rack over boiling water, cover pot, and steam 10 minutes.

Meanwhile, slice chicken breast into 15 thin strips. Combine with remaining soy sauce and salt; set aside.

Toss shrimp with *sake* and let stand 10 minutes. Place a shrimp in each of 5 *chawan mushi* bowls. Top with 3 strips of chicken, 3 mushroom strips, 3 water chestnut slices, and 3 bamboo-shoot strips. Add any juices in dish and reserved mushroom soaking water to *dashi*. Evenly divide shredded spinach among bowls.

With chopsticks or fork, beat eggs well but do not allow them to become frothy. Heat *dashi* to lukewarm and beat into eggs. Ladle mixture into bowls, cover bowls, and place on rack over gently boiling water.

Cover pot and steam 15 to 20 minutes, or until egg mixture is set. Garnish each serving with a watercress leaf.

Vietnamese Eggs with Crabmeat

In Vietnam, where they are plentiful, crabs are served in a variety of ways: grilled whole, quartered and deep fried, or the meat flaked and added to soups or used in the stuffing for imperial rolls. Here, crabmeat is combined with eggs and bean thread noodles to create a dish with the texture of an omelet. If crabmeat is not available, an equal measure of minced prawns and/or cooked pork can be used.

Serve with shredded cabbage or lettuce and steamed white rice. Provide each guest with a small bowl of *Nuoc Cham*, the chile-spiked sauce that accompanies virtually every Vietnamese meal.

SERVES 4

1	*ounce bean thread noodles*	1½	*teaspoons fish sauce*
6	*eggs*	¼	*teaspoon black pepper*
3	*green onions, minced*		Nuoc Cham *(recipe*
6	*ounces cooked crabmeat,*		*follows)*
	flaked		

In a saucepan soak bean threads in hot water to cover for 1 minute, or until flexible. Drain off water and, with scissors, cut bean threads into 2-inch lengths to measure about ¾ cup. Return bean threads to saucepan and add water to cover by 1 inch. Bring to a boil, reduce heat, and simmer 2 minutes, or until noodles are transparent. Remove from heat, drain, and set aside.

Beat eggs in a mixing bowl until well blended but not frothy. Add reserved noodles and all the remaining ingredients and stir to distribute ingredients evenly. Lightly oil a 1-quart basin with peanut oil. Pour egg mixture into basin, set on rack over boiling water, cover pot, and steam 20 minutes, or until eggs are set. Serve immediately with *Nuoc Cham*.

Variation: Soak 3 dried shiitake mushrooms 30 minutes in warm water to cover until softened. Drain, discard tough stems, and cut caps into slivers. Add to beaten eggs with crabmeat.

Nuoc Cham
(Vietnamese Fish Sauce with Seasonings)

MAKES APPROXIMATELY ²/₃ CUP

3 tablespoons fish sauce
1½ tablespoons distilled white
   vinegar
1½ tablespoons water
2 teaspoons granulated sugar

1 small hot chile pepper, very
   thinly sliced (see Note)
1 large garlic clove, finely
   minced
1 teaspoon fresh lime juice

Combine all ingredients and stir well to dissolve sugar. Sample the sauce and adjust according to your taste.

If not using immediately, pour into jar, cover, and refrigerate for up to 2 days.

Note: Any small red, green, or yellow chile pepper may be used in this sauce.

Oeufs en Cocotte (Eggs in a Dish)

This is a versatile preparation. The eggs can be the topping for almost anything, from cooked grains or vegetables to bean curd and meats. A simple version is to drizzle a little soy sauce over tofu arranged on the bottom of a small dish and then break an egg over the top. The egg will steam in a short time to a delicate finish; at the same time the tofu will heat through. Additional ideas follow the basic recipe.

Toasted English muffins or biscuits are good accompaniments to this brunch or luncheon dish, with perhaps a fruit salad or broiled tomato halves on the side. For a special occasion, top each serving with a teaspoon or so of Hollandaise Sauce.

SERVES 4

4 to 6 thin slices cooked ham,
   cut into narrow strips
1 cup spinach or Swiss chard
   puree (see Vegetable
   Steaming Methods)

8 eggs, at room temperature
   Herb seasoning
   Freshly ground white pepper
   Paprika

Lightly butter or oil four 1½-cup soufflé dishes. Evenly divide ham among the dishes and top each with ¼ cup of the spinach puree. Wrap steamer lid in a kitchen towel. Set dishes on rack over boiling water, cover pot, and steam 5 minutes until mixture is heated through. Break 2 eggs over each filled dish and sprinkle lightly with herb seasoning, pepper, and paprika. Re-cover pot and steam eggs 7 to 10 minutes, or until whites are set and yolks are still soft or eggs are cooked to taste.

Variations:

Substitute 1½ cups sliced mushrooms steamed with 2 tablespoons minced shallots (see Vegetable Steaming Methods) for the ham slices and spinach puree. Divide mixture evenly among the 4 dishes. Sprinkle each dish with 1 tablespoon freshly grated Parmesan cheese. Heat 5 minutes as directed, break in eggs, and then steam as directed.

Omit ham slices and spinach puree. Pour 2 tablespoons rich stock, half-and-half, or Béchamel Sauce (see Basic Savory Sauces) mixed with 1 tea-spoon Dijon-style mustard into each dish. Heat 5 minutes as directed. Break in eggs, sprinkle with herb seasoning and pepper, and then strew 2 tablespoons finely shredded Monterey Jack cheese over. Sprinkle with paprika. Steam as directed.

Omit ham slices and spinach puree. Chop 2 medium-size ripe tomatoes and drain well. Combine with 2 tablespoons minced fresh parsley, 2 tea-spoons minced fresh oregano, and 1 to 2 garlic cloves, minced. Divide evenly among the 4 dishes and heat 5 minutes as directed. Break in eggs and steam as directed.

Strew 1 tablespoon diced firm bean curd and ½ teaspoon minced fresh chives on the ham and spinach in each dish. Drizzle a little soy sauce and a few drops of Oriental sesame oil over the tofu. Omit herb seasoning and paprika. Heat 5 minutes as directed. Break in eggs and steam as directed.

Gado Gado
(Indonesian Vegetables with Peanut Sauce)

This mixed-vegetable salad, eaten principally in Indonesia and on the Malay peninsula, has many variations. Make it the centerpiece of your meal, with steamed rice or whole-wheat rolls on the side.

Prepare a wide selection of lightly steamed and raw vegetables and arrange them attractively on a bed of shredded spinach. Garnish the platter with quartered hard-cooked eggs, small squares of tofu and/or tempeh (see tempeh description later in this chapter) and grated raw carrot. Serve a bowl of Peanut Sauce on the side.

To serve 4 persons, you will need approximately 2 pounds of vegetables, 3 hard-cooked eggs, and 1 recipe of Peanut Sauce. The lightly steamed vegetables may include: shredded cabbage; sliced carrots and celery; whole green beans and Brussels sprouts; broccoli stalks, cut into strips; new potatoes, peeled and sliced; and green or red bell peppers, cut into eighths. The vegetables should be at room temperature before assembling the salad. Whole or slivered green onions, sliced cucumbers, sliced zucchini, and bean sprouts are good choices for the raw vegetables.

Timbales

Timbales, soufflélike purees, are classically prepared with egg yolks and heavy cream. To reduce calories and fats in your diet you can use whole eggs and half-and-half, but the texture will not be as rich and dense. The recipes that follow are examples of how timbales can be made with whole eggs or with egg yolks and light cream (half-and-half).

Create your own variations using the proportions given in these recipes. Start from scratch or use vegetables you have already oversteamed for purees or soups. One-half pound of trimmed raw vegetables such as green beans, carrots, asparagus, broccoli, or cauliflower will yield the correct amount for 6 timbales. Pound measurements for greens such as Swiss chard and spinach can only be approximate. Plan for about 3 cups firmly packed chopped raw greens. Zucchini, because of its high water content and delicate flavor, is not suitable for making this dish.

Six timbales will serve 6 as an accompaniment to a fish, meat, or poultry dish, in which case they need not be topped with a sauce. When serving 3 as a lunch or supper dish with rolls and a salad, the timbales are enhanced by a light sauce, such as mustard-seasoned Béchamel Sauce garnished with cooked tiny shrimp; Sorrel, Mushroom, or Oyster Sauce; or Basic Tomato Sauce with a sprinkling of freshly grated Parmesan cheese.

Timbale molds hold about ½ cup of egg mixture. If you do not have the classic form, use any half-cup or larger custard or soufflé dish. Larger vessels will take more egg mixture than the half cup specified in the recipes, so adjust the amount put in each accordingly. Or use one large basin and slice the timbale into wedges to serve.

Oil the timbale molds with lecithin oil. Fill the molds and cover tightly (see Improvised Lids). To steam, place filled molds on rack over *gently* boiling water, cover pot, and steam 18 to 20 minutes, or until set. If using one large basin, increase steaming time by 5 to 7 minutes.

Remove basins from steamer and let stand on cooling rack 10 minutes. With a thin-bladed knife, loosen edges of timbales and then invert on heated individual plates or on a platter.

Green Bean Timbale

Serve this subtly flavored timbale to accompany leg of lamb and roast potatoes.

MAKES 6 TIMBALES

¼ cup minced green onion with tops	2 tablespoons minced fresh parsley
1 large garlic clove, minced (optional)	¼ teaspoon ground sage
1½ teaspoons butter and/or rendered chicken fat	¼ teaspoon herb seasoning, celery salt, or salt
1⅓ cups chopped steamed green beans	⅛ to ¼ teaspoon freshly ground black pepper
½ cup half-and-half cream	⅓ cup fine dry breadcrumbs (optional)
2 eggs	Watercress or parsley sprigs

Prepare 6 timbale or similar molds as directed and set aside.

In a covered nonstick skillet cook onion and garlic in butter until softened. Puree in blender or food processor with the beans, cream, and eggs; do not allow mixture to become frothy. If it should, set it aside for 30 minutes or so until froth subsides; stir occasionally.

Transfer puree to mixing bowl and stir in minced parsley, seasonings, and breadcrumbs. Fill prepared molds and steam as directed. Garnish with watercress sprigs.

Nutty Watercress Timbale

Simply steamed fish fillets are complemented by this rich-tasting dish. The timbale can also be sliced thinly and served as an appetizer; accompany with French bread rounds.

MAKES 4 TIMBALES

1 7- to 8-ounce bunch watercress
1¼ cups half-and-half cream
3 egg yolks
½ teaspoon herb seasoning
¼ teaspoon freshly ground white pepper
Pinch of cayenne pepper

1 teaspoon prepared horseradish
½ cup finely chopped pecans or lightly toasted slivered blanched almonds
Thin slivers of sun-dried tomatoes
Thin slivers of lemon peel

Prepare 4 timbale or similar molds as directed and set aside.

Remove watercress leaves from stems to measure 2½ to 3 cups firmly packed leaves. Reserve stems and place leaves in collapsible steamer rack over boiling water. Cover pot and steam 2 to 3 minutes until limp. Drain well in sieve, pressing out all moisture with the back of a spoon. Let stand in strainer while continuing.

Coarsely chop the reserved watercress stems and place in a heavy saucepan with the half-and-half. Cover, slowly bring to a boil, lower heat, and simmer 10 minutes. Strain and cool, discarding stems. In a blender or food processor fitted with metal blade, puree watercress leaves with a little of the strained half-and-half. Return to remaining half-and-half; whisk in yolks, seasonings, and horseradish.

Place 2 tablespoons of the chopped nuts into each prepared mold; tilt the molds to coat the sides and bottoms evenly with nuts. Fill the molds and steam as directed. Garnish each timbale with alternating slivers of sun-dried tomato and lemon peel, arranged in a spoke pattern.

Crab Mousse

Subtly flavored with mustard, this mousse is delicate in both taste and texture, much like a soufflé. Your guests will have to wait for it, because it will not hold its airiness once out of the steamer. Timing is exact, so follow the directions closely.

The mousse is very rich, so mask it sparingly with a thin Béchamel Sauce made with fish stock to which you have added minced fresh chives or parsley. A butter lettuce salad dressed lightly with Herb Vinaigrette and small rolls will complete this lunch or supper presentation.

SERVES 4

1/4 cup fine fresh breadcrumbs
1/3 cup heavy cream
2   eggs, separated, at room
     temperature
1/3 cup milk
1   teaspoon finely minced fresh
     chives
1   tablespoon fresh lemon juice
1   teaspoon dry mustard
4   drops Tabasco, or to taste

1/2 teaspoon salt
1/4 teaspoon freshly ground
     white pepper
1/4 cup minced shallots
1   teaspoon minced fresh
     tarragon
7   ounces crabmeat, flaked and
     well drained (approximately
     1¾ cups)
     Pinch of cream of tartar

Using a 6-cup soufflé dish, follow Basic Instructions for Steaming Puddings.

In a large mixing bowl combine breadcrumbs and cream. Let stand 5 minutes until breadcrumbs have softened. Stir in egg yolks, milk, chives, lemon juice, mustard, Tabasco sauce, salt, and pepper. Finely mince shallots and tarragon in a blender or food processor. Add crabmeat and puree just to mix and finely grind the crab.

With a fork, stir crab mixture into egg mixture just to blend. Beat egg whites and cream of tartar until stiff peaks form. Stir about ¾ cup of the egg whites into the crab mixture to lighten it, then fold in remaining egg whites.

Spoon crab mixture into prepared basin, leveling gently with the back of a wooden spoon or a spatula. Cover basin tightly as directed and place on rack in boiling water. Cover pot and steam, with water boiling gently, exactly 45 minutes.

Remove mousse to work surface, uncover, and serve immediately directly from the basin.

Squash and Yam Pudding

Pureed yams give this spicy egg-based vegetable side dish its rich, full-bodied quality. It is the perfect accompaniment to your holiday turkey or ham in place of the usual squash puree and candied yams.

SERVES 6

1   piece Hubbard squash
     (approximately 8 ounces)

1   to 2 yams (approximately 8
     ounces)
3   eggs, at room temperature

2 teaspoons fresh lemon juice	¼ teaspoon freshly grated
¼ cup firmly packed dark	nutmeg
brown sugar	¼ teaspoon salt
1 tablespoon freshly grated	1 cup half-and-half cream
orange peel	Lightly toasted finely
¾ teaspoon ground cinnamon	chopped pecans
¼ teaspoon ground cloves	

Steam squash and yams until tender (see Vegetable Steaming Methods). When cool enough to handle, discard any seeds and stringy pulp from the squash, peel, and puree in a blender or food processor. Measure ¾ cup and set aside. Peel and puree yams; measure ¾ cup and set aside. Using a 4-cup soufflé dish, follow Basic Instructions for Steaming Puddings (see Desserts).

In a large mixing bowl beat eggs lightly. Stir in lemon juice, sugar, spices, salt, reserved pureed squash and yam, and cream. Mix well and pour into prepared dish. Cover as directed and steam 1 hour and 20 minutes.

Transfer pudding to cooling rack and remove cover. Sprinkle with pecans and serve warm.

Tofu with Chinese Seasonings

Serve this healthful dish with steamed rice and snow peas marinated in Oriental Dressing.

SERVES 2

2 or 3 Napa cabbage leaves	water 30 minutes to soften,
2 or 3 firm tofu cakes	drained, stemmed, and cut
(approximately 12 ounces)	into very fine slivers
2 large garlic cloves, finely	2 green onions with tops, cut
minced	into very fine slivers
2 or 3 slices ginger root, cut	2 to 3 teaspoons soy sauce
into very fine slivers	½ teaspoon Oriental sesame
3 or 4 dried shiitake	oil
mushrooms, soaked in warm	Fresh coriander sprigs

Line a shallow dish with cabbage leaves. Cut bean curd cakes in half and arrange in a single layer on top of cabbage. Strew garlic, ginger root, mushrooms, and green onions over cakes. Drizzle with soy sauce and sesame oil.

Place dish on rack over boiling water, cover pot, and steam 10 minutes. Remove dish from steamer and garnish with coriander. Serve immediately.

Variations:

Reduce soy sauce to 1 teaspoon and combine with 1 teaspoon dry sherry and 2 teaspoons oyster sauce. Use in place of the soy sauce and omit sesame oil.

Add ¼ cup each very finely slivered bamboo shoots and water chestnuts with the green onions.

Omit sesame oil. Drizzle with hot chile oil to taste.

Tofu "Omelet"

For an extra measure of protein in the morning, make this simple dish, similar in texture to an omelet, and accompany it with fresh fruit and blueberry muffins.

To turn this breakfast fare into a light dinner, add minced green onions to the egg mixture, steam as directed, and serve with new potatoes sprinkled with chives and bean sprouts dressed with soy sauce. Pass a small bowl of Peanut Sauce.

SERVES 2

¼ cup soft tofu (see Note)
½ teaspoon herb seasoning
¼ teaspoon freshly ground
    white pepper

½ teaspoon light soy sauce
4 eggs

With a fork mash together tofu, herb seasoning, pepper, and soy sauce. Add eggs and beat well with whisk or fork. Pour into a shallow dish and place on rack over boiling water. Wrap lid in a towel, cover pot, and steam 15 to 18 minutes until eggs are set.

Note: Soft tofu is so soft that it can easily be spooned into a measuring cup. The measurement in this recipe, however, is not critical; a little more or less tofu will not ruin the final result.

Chicken and Tofu, Japanese Style

Use attractive individual serving dishes that can go from the kitchen to the dining table for steaming this combination of velvety tofu and delicate chicken.

Nori, dried seaweed (laver) squares or sheets packaged in cellophane or tins at Japanese markets and many supermarkets, are available toasted or untoasted. To toast a sheet, hold it over an open flame until it curls slightly, or place the sheet in a heated cast iron skillet a few seconds.

Spinach topped with crushed lightly toasted sesame seeds and steamed short-grain white rice are perfect accompaniments.

SERVES 4

1 *whole chicken breast (approximately 12 ounces), skinned, boned, and cut into thin strips about 1½ inches long*	1 *block soft tofu (approximately 14 ounces) Japanese Miso Sauce (see Japanese Miso Sauce for steamed shrimp)*
2 *tablespoons soy sauce*	*Thin slivers of lightly*
2 *teaspoons sake*	*toasted nori*
½ *teaspoon grated ginger root*	*Thin slivers of lemon peel*

In a mixing bowl combine chicken, soy sauce, sake, and ginger root. Toss to mix and let stand 30 minutes.

Cut the tofu block into quarters and divide pieces among 4 small shallow dishes. Spoon one-fourth of the chicken mixture over each tofu portion. Wrap steamer lid in a kitchen towel. Set dishes on racks over boiling water, cover pot, and steam 10 minutes. Prepare miso sauce while chicken cooks.

Remove dishes from steamer and garnish with nori and lemon peel. Pass the miso sauce separately.

Tempeh

This Indonesian-originated "wonder food" contains a third more protein than bean curd or soybeans and has considerably more thiamin, niacin, and riboflavin. It is low in calories and, unlike bean curd, is a source of fiber. Tempeh is available in 8-ounce rectangular cakes or in a variety of already seasoned "burger" preparations.

Many find this healthful food an acquired taste, as it has a somewhat yeasty flavor. These qualities are masked when tempeh is fried but are not as easily hidden when it is steamed. I have found that the best way to steam it is to cut it into ¼-inch-wide strips, sprinkle it with soy sauce and a few drops of Oriental sesame oil, and steam it in a shallow dish for 20 minutes. It can then be dressed with a highly seasoned sauce such as Curry Sauce, Basic Tomato Sauce, or Caribbean Spicy Sauce.

VEGETABLES AND GRAINS

75

Vegetables and Grains

Vegetables

The advantages of steaming vegetables have long been touted by nutritionists, food writers, and home cooks. Steamed vegetables retain their natural flavors and colors, vitamins and minerals are not boiled away, and there is no need for the addition of butter or oils during cooking. Moreover, steaming makes it possible for the cook to remove the vegetables at the optimal point of doneness.

This is a how-to chapter. First, vegetables are listed alphabetically, with directions on how to ready them for steaming, cooking times, and serving suggestions. Suggestions with capitalized initial letters refer to recipes in Basic Savory Sauces or in this chapter.

Some vegetables do not appear in the listings. In my opinion, celery, cardoon, and fennel are better suited to boiling and braising because they need more direct heat to cook properly. Others, like daikon, I prefer raw or added to a soup or simmered stew. Legumes require a generous measure of water and long cooking, which are not practical with steaming. Dried lentils and split peas, if almost completely precooked, can be finished in a covered stewlike steamed dish; other legumes must be completely cooked and only reheated in the dish.

Following the vegetable listings are four sections: Vegetable Purees, Marinated Vegetables, Fillings for Stuffed Vegetables, and Toppings for Vegetables. The first two give general directions on how to create these popular preparations. The stuffing recipes can be used to fill a variety of vegetables for steaming, and the toppings are suggestions for garnishing dressed or plain steamed vegetables. Directions for preparing light pureed-vegetable soups appear in Appetizers and First Courses.

VEGETABLE STEAMING METHODS

In general, the best way to steam vegetables is to place them directly on the perforated level of a tiered steamer, a collapsible basket, a colander, or a rack one inch above water. Any recommended departure from this method is described in the individual listings. As with all steaming, it is important that the cooking time be counted from the moment rising steam is first visible and that the vegetable not touch the water.

Some vegetables steam best when stood upright, and I have indicated these. These vegetables have either large bases and small tops or the lower portion is tougher than the upper portion. The part of the vegetable that is closest to the steaming water will cook more quickly. When I suggest a spoke arrangement, it is for a similar reason. The larger or tougher vegetable sections need the more intense heat at the center of the rack. If it is impossible for you to position the vegetables as suggested, they will steam anyway, but may cook unevenly.

Always test for desired doneness by piercing the vegetable with a cake tester, a slender metal or bamboo skewer, or the point of a thin-bladed knife. And don't discard the water; save it for adding to soups and stocks.

The steaming times are only general guidelines; they will vary according to the size, freshness, and age of the vegetable, and how crowded the steamer is. For instance, if broccoli florets are placed 1 or 2 inches apart on the rack, the steam will circulate more efficiently than if the florets are touching. Vegetables will also take longer to cook if they are combined in a dish with meats or poultry, or if they are on a rack 4 or 5 inches rather than 1 inch above the boiling water.

Undercook vegetables that are to be marinated and/or added to a salad. Remove them from the steamer when they are still quite firm and immerse them in cold water immediately to arrest the cooking. Steam a vegetable until it is very soft if it is to be pureed for a side dish or a soup.

If you want to cook vegetables in an electric steamer, such as Hitachi's Chime-o-matic or Rival or Waring's popular model, follow the manufacturer's instructions. You may trim, cut, and season the vegetables in the manner described for stovetop steaming, but the amount of water and the timing may be different.

Artichokes

To Prepare and Steam: Directions are for medium or large globe artichokes. I prefer the tiny ones sautéed or French fried, but they may be steamed in the same way as the larger ones; simply reduce the cooking time. Wash each artichoke well; with a sharp knife, cut ⅓ off the top and trim the stem end even with the bottom. Discard any tough outer leaves and, with scissors, snip off ½ inch of the remaining leaf tips. As each artichoke is trimmed, place it in acidulated water to prevent discoloration and to rid it of insects that may be hiding between the leaves.

Place a rack on the bottom of a stainless steel pot (do not use an aluminum or iron pot or the artichokes will discolor) and stand the artichokes, stem ends down, on the rack. For added flavor, use chicken, vegetable, or other stock instead of water as the steaming liquid. Add enough stock to the pot to cover the bottom third of the artichokes. Strew chopped onion, crushed garlic, black peppercorns, and fresh oregano or basil leaves over the artichokes and drizzle with olive oil to taste. Top each with a lemon slice. Cover pot and steam for 25 to 40 minutes. Test for doneness by piercing the base or sampling the edible bottom portion of a leaf pulled from the center.

To Serve: Serve artichokes hot with melted butter and a little of the cooking stock, or with any of the following: Brown, Lemon/Lime, Garlic/Shallot, or Herb Butter Sauce. Serve hot or cold with various Mayonnaises or Vinaigrettes.

To serve cold artichoke "salad bowls," remove the center chokes. This may be done before or after steaming by pulling apart the leaves and scraping the fuzzy center ("choke") out with a melon baller or a grapefruit spoon. Fill the "bowls" with your favorite chicken, shrimp, or turkey salad.

Asparagus

To Prepare and Steam: Thoroughly wash the asparagus, being careful to remove any dirt clinging to the tips or trapped under the scales. Snap off the stems where they break easily (save the tough portions for adding to the stockpot) and lightly peel the ends so that the spears will cook evenly. Remove the scales if you feel the appearance is more pleasing.

If desired, tie the asparagus in serving portions with kitchen string. To assure even cooking, stand them, stem ends down, in the basket insert of an asparagus steamer. If you do not have an asparagus steamer, make one by piercing holes in the bottom of a topless coffee can. Place the can on a rack over boiling water in a large pot and stand the asparagus in the can. Cover pot and steam 4 to 8 minutes, or until asparagus is just cooked. Alternatively, arrange the bundled or unbundled asparagus in a spoke pattern, with tips facing out, on a collapsible basket or any steamer rack over boiling water. Cover pot and steam for 4 to 8 minutes. For added flavor, put a few tarragon leaves or one or two slices of ginger root on the asparagus as it steams.

To Serve: Serve asparagus hot with fresh lemon or lime juice, or with any of the following: Butter Sauces, Sliced Almond Butter Sauce, any of the Mayonnaises (especially Garlic Mayonnaise, then top with lightly toasted pine nuts), Hollandaise Sauce, or Toppings for Vegetables. To serve cold, see Marinated Vegetables.

Beets

To Prepare and Steam: If the beets have fresh greens intact, cut off the greens, leaving a 2-inch stem, and reserve them for cooking (see Greens). If the roots are long, trim them to within 2 inches of the bottom. It is important that you not cut into the beets or they will bleed during cooking.

Scrub the beets well but gently under cold running water and place directly on rack over boiling water. Cover pot and steam for 25 to 40 minutes. Remove from the steamer and let stand until cool enough to handle, then trim, slip peel off, and slice or dice. Beets can also be arranged on a rack around a long-steaming dish to cook at the same time.

To Serve: Reheat the sliced beets over low heat in a covered nonstick skillet. Serve hot with melted butter and minced fresh parsley or chives; or with fresh lemon juice or white vinegar and a few dabs of prepared horseradish, sour cream, or Crème Fraîche; or with melted butter, fresh lime juice, grated orange peel, and a sprinkling of granulated sugar. To serve cold, see Marinated Vegetables.

Broccoli

To Prepare and Steam: Wash the broccoli, slice off and discard the tough ends, and lightly peel the stalks. For even cooking, slit the thick stalks from the bottom up to the top, or divide the heads into florets and cut the stems into thin slices.

To assure even cooking, stand large broccoli stalks upright in an asparagus or equivalent steamer (see information under Asparagus), or arrange the stalks or florets in a spoke pattern, with the flowers facing outward, on a collapsible basket or other steamer rack over boiling water. Scatter crushed garlic over the broccoli for added flavor. Cover pot and steam for 5 to 10 minutes.

To Serve: Serve broccoli hot with fresh lemon or lime juice and top with toasted sliced almonds or with any of the following: Mornay Sauce, Butter Sauces, Walnut Butter Sauce, Mayonnaises, Hollandaise Sauce, or Toppings for Vegetables. Or transfer to a saucepan and toss with Lemon/Lime Butter Sauce, minced garlic, and halved cherry tomatoes, then heat just until tomatoes are warmed. To serve cold, see Marinated Vegetables.

Brussels Sprouts

To Prepare and Steam: Remove any damaged outer leaves from the Brussels sprouts, trim stem ends even with bottoms, and wash well to remove any dirt trapped between the leaves. To assure even cooking, make shallow crosses in the stem ends. Place on rack over boiling water, cover pot, and steam for 10 to 15 minutes.

To Serve: Serve Brussels sprouts hot with fresh lemon or lime juice and freshly ground black pepper or freshly grated Parmesan cheese; tossed with steamed julienned carrots, butter, salt, freshly ground black pepper, and minced fresh parsley; tossed and heated with halved seedless grapes in melted butter; or with any of the following: Lemon/Lime Butter Sauce, Walnut, Hazelnut, Pecan, or Chestnut Butter Sauce, or Mustard Sauce. To serve cold, see Marinated Vegetables.

Cabbage

To Prepare and Steam: The term cabbage includes a number of varieties. Only the firm, round red and green head cabbages are discussed here. I have included the long, thin Napa cabbage and leafy bok choy with the greens listing, since I treat them in the same manner as I do greens.

Discard the outer leaves of red or green head cabbage and wash the heads well. Cut out the tough portion of the core and then cut the cabbage into four to eight wedges. Tie each wedge with kitchen string to keep it intact as it steams. Place on rack over boiling water, cover pot, and steam for 8 to 10 minutes. Alternatively, shred the cabbage coarsely and steam for 5 to 8 minutes. To steam cabbage leaves for use as wrappers, see Cabbage Rolls.

To Serve: Serve cabbage hot with melted butter; Crème Fraîche and caraway seeds; white or cider vinegar, sour cream, and dill; or Basic Tomato Sauce. Or reheat in a little rich stock with slivered softened shiitake mushrooms, or with sliced water chestnuts and cooked peas. Steamed shredded cabbage and lettuce, with or without cooked peas, is a good combination.

Carrots, Parsnips, and Salsify (Oyster Plant)

To Prepare and Steam: Because these three root vegetables are trimmed and steamed in much the same way, they have been grouped together. Salsify is a little-known vegetable that is cream-colored and looks somewhat like a long, thin parsnip. It has a slight oyster flavor.

Trim off the stems and root ends and, if the vegetable is young, simply scrub hard under running cold water. More mature carrots, parsnips, and salsify need to be lightly scraped, but be careful not to peel deeply or vitamins will be lost.

Cook these root vegetables whole (or halved lengthwise if large), arranging them stem end down in an asparagus or equivalent steamer. If precooking for adding to an oven roast, steam for 5 minutes; to cook carrots and parsnips completely, steam for 10 minutes, salsify a few minutes longer.

Alternatively, halve these root vegetables crosswise, slice, or julienne, and arrange on a steaming rack over boiling water. Cover pot and steam carrots and parsnips 4 to 8 minutes, salsify 8 to 10 minutes.

To Serve: Serve carrots, parsnips, and/or salsify hot with fresh lemon juice and minced fresh herbs; or reheat in a covered nonstick skillet with Crème Fraîche and minced green onion tops, or with butter and crumbled, crisply cooked bacon; or reheat with butter, honey, fresh lemon juice, grated lemon peel, and grated ginger root. These vegetables are also good tossed with Brown Butter Sauce; Slivered Almond Butter Sauce; Pecan Butter Sauce; melted butter and minced fresh mint; or melted butter, salt, and freshly ground black pepper with a sprinkling of freshly grated Parmesan cheese. Roll whole steamed parsnips or carrots in melted butter and then in brown or granulated sugar; place in a nonstick skillet and heat until glazed. Or combine carrots with peas or cauliflower and toss in Lemon/Lime Butter Sauce and minced fresh parsley. To serve cold, see Marinated Vegetables.

Cauliflower

To Prepare and Steam: Break off and discard the green leaves of the cauliflower and rinse the head under running water. To cook whole, cut up into the head and remove about 2 inches of the core. Place the head, stem end down, on a steaming rack over boiling water. Cover pot and steam a 1½-pound cauliflower (6 inches in diameter) for 12 to 15 minutes. Alternatively, cut or break the head into florets and steam for 5 to 8 minutes.

To Serve: Serve whole cauliflower hot drizzled with Brown Butter Sauce and sprinkled with crumbled blue cheese and lots of minced fresh parsley; or surround with cooked peas and pour Sliced Almond Butter Sauce over the top; or dress with fresh lemon juice and sprinkle with chopped fresh coriander. Serve florets hot with Tahini Dressing or Avocado Tahini Dressing, or with Anchovy Butter Sauce made with garlic. See the broccoli listing for additional suggestions. To serve cold, see Marinated Vegetables.

Celeriac (Celery Root)

To Prepare and Steam: Though boiling is the most common and most fuel-efficient method for cooking celeriac, it is appropriate to steam it when you are already using the steamer for a long-cooking dish. Trim the root ends and scrub the celeriac well under running water, but do not peel. Place celeriac on rack over boiling water, cover pot, and steam a 12-ounce celeriac for 40 to 50 minutes. Remove from the steamer, peel, and cut into julienne.

To Serve: Serve julienned celeriac hot with Lemon/Lime or Herb Butter Sauce or Crème Fraîche and thin strips of roasted pepper. Or combine the celeriac with steamed julienned carrots and/or cooked peas and dress in the same manner. To serve celeriac cold, see Marinated Vegetables.

Corn

To Prepare and Steam: Husk the corn, snapping off the stems as you pull away the leaves. Remove any silk clinging to the ears by twisting them in your hands. Wash the corn and place stem end down in an asparagus or equivalent steamer. Steam for 3 to 4 minutes for young corn and 8 to 10 minutes for more mature ears. To keep ears warm until they are served, wrap them in an attractive kitchen towel that can be brought to the table. The towel traps heat so well that the corn continues to cook, so take this into consideration when timing.

If you have no asparagus or equivalent steamer, simply put the corn on a rack over boiling water, cover pot, and steam as directed.

Corn is a seasonal vegetable that holds up well when frozen. Steam extra ears, cut off the kernels, and freeze them for up to 3 months. The corn can, of course, be frozen on the cob, but that would take up freezer space unnecessarily.

To Serve: Serve corn on the cob hot with butter, freshly ground black pepper, and/or herb seasoning. Warm corn kernels in a little stock and/or butter, or use the kernels in all sorts of dishes such as soups and chowders, casseroles, tamales, and vegetable stuffings.

Eggplant

To Prepare and Steam: Trim the stem end, including the green cap, from the eggplant and rinse under cold water. Leave whole, especially if cooking the slender Japanese variety, or halve or cut into wedges. Place on rack over boiling water and steam whole globe eggplants for 15 to 20 minutes, whole slender ones for 10 to 12 minutes, and eggplant pieces for 5 to 8 minutes.

To Serve: To serve eggplant hot, cut into cubes and toss with sautéed onion and garlic, chopped fresh tomatoes, and shredded mozzarella cheese; or heat in Curry Sauce; or sprinkle with minced fresh parsley and pass freshly grated Parmesan cheese; or sauce with Tahini Dressing. To serve cold, see Marinated Vegetables.

Green Beans and Yellow Wax Beans

To Prepare and Steam: The Kentucky Wonder, the Blue Lake, the Romano, and the long bean (a very long, thin popular Asian variety) are the most common types of green bean. Trim the ends of these and the yellow wax variety, remove any strings, and wash the beans well. All of these, with the exception of the long bean, may be cooked whole, cut in half lengthwise, snapped or cut into pieces, or thinly sliced on the diagonal. The long bean should be cut into 4- to 5-inch lengths. Place on rack over boiling water, cover pot, and steam for 4 to 12 minutes, depending upon the variety.

To Serve: Serve beans hot with fresh lemon or lime juice and toasted chopped walnuts, or with any of the following: Butter Sauces, Nut Butter Sauces, Hollandaise Sauce, Mustard Sauce, Vinaigrettes, or Toppings for Vegetables. To serve cold, see Marinated Vegetables.

Greens: Mustard, Collard, Turnip, Beet, Kale, Dandelion, Swiss Chard, Spinach, Bok Choy, Sorrel, Napa Cabbage, Lettuces

To Prepare and Steam: Wash all greens well to remove any dirt and sand trapped in the leaves and trim off the tough stem ends. Cut away the central ribs of large-leaved greens, such as those of mustard and collard, for they do not become tender when cooked. In the case of greens with broad, edible stems, such as Swiss chard and bok choy (a vegetable with dark green leaves and broad white stalks), separate the stems from the leaves, slice or mince the stems, and steam them for 2 minutes before adding the quicker-cooking leaves.

Cook halved or quartered Swiss chard leaves, whole or halved spinach or bok choy leaves, whole dandelion greens, and shredded kale and beet greens in one of two ways: place in a colander one inch above water, or put in a large covered pot with only the washing water that clings to the leaves. If desired, put a couple of crushed garlic cloves in the bottom of the pot and drizzle the leaves with a little olive oil. Steam these greens for 4 to 6 minutes.

Mature collard, mustard, and turnip greens are quite sharp-flavored and taste best when long-cooked in bacon fat or with salt pork. They should be steamed in the same manner as the above greens only when they are *very* young and tender.

Sorrel is used as a flavoring more than as a vegetable. The light green leaves, similar in appearance to spinach, have a tangy lemony taste. Place leaves on a rack over boiling water and steam until they have softened and darkened.

Cut Napa or celery cabbage and romaine or iceberg lettuce heads into 4 to 8 wedges, secure the wedges with kitchen string, place wedges on rack over boiling water, cover pot, and steam for 3 to 6 minutes. Napa cabbage and lettuce may also be coarsely shredded and steamed for 2 to 3 minutes.

Romaine, butter, and iceberg lettuce, spinach, and Swiss chard leaves can be used as wrappers for various fillings. To make the leaves pliable, separate them and steam flat on a rack over boiling water for 1 minute or until just limp. Immediately immerse in ice water and drain on paper toweling.

To Serve: Serve Swiss chard; spinach; dandelion and beet greens; young collard, mustard, and turnip greens; and kale hot without additional dressing if they have been cooked with olive oil and garlic. If they have been prepared plain, drizzle them with garlic olive oil, Lemon/Lime Butter Sauce, or Sesame Seed Butter Sauce. Bok choy is especially good dressed with a little soy sauce, a few drops of Oriental sesame oil, and toasted sesame seeds.

Chop or mince steamed sorrel leaves and add to soups and steamed eggs, or use to make a compound butter.

Serve Napa cabbage and lettuce wedges hot with melted butter, fresh lemon juice, and freshly ground white pepper, or see the cabbage listing for more suggestions.

Kohlrabi, Rutabagas, Sunchokes, and Turnips

To Prepare and Steam: Kohlrabi and sunchokes (Jerusalem artichokes) are grouped here with two root vegetables, turnips and rutabagas, because they are trimmed and steamed in a similar manner.

Kohlrabi must be washed, then peeled and the stalks and base trimmed. Rutabagas, called yellow turnips in Britain, have coarse skin that must always be pared regardless of their size. If you are cooking them whole for pureeing, wait to peel them until after they are steamed; the skins will pull away as easily as those on cooked beets. Although some recipes say to peel sunchokes, I find they need only a good scrubbing. If turnips are quite young, they need only to be scrubbed well under running water and the stem and root ends removed. More mature ones, however, must be peeled.

All of these vegetables can be steamed on a collapsible basket or any rack-type steamer, or if whole can be placed directly on the rack around a long-steaming dish. Steam whole kohlrabi for 10 to 14 minutes, ¾-inch pieces (sliced or diced) for 4 to 7 minutes. Whole turnips will cook in 20 to 25 minutes, ¾-inch pieces in 7 to 10 minutes. Rutabagas take longer: 40 to 45 minutes when whole and 10 to 12 minutes when cut into ¾-inch pieces. To precook rutabagas and turnips for adding to an oven roast, steam the former about 15 minutes and the latter about 10 minutes. Sunchokes are the quickest cooking: whole ones take about 7 minutes, halved ones about 4 minutes, and slices about 2 minutes.

To Serve: Serve these vegetables hot drizzled with Garlic/Shallot or Herb Butter Sauce and topped with freshly grated Gruyère cheese; or with browned onions and a sprinkling of paprika. Or reheat them in a covered nonstick skillet with a little rich stock and sprinkle with minced fresh parsley or chives. To serve cold, see Marinated Vegetables.

Mushrooms

To Prepare and Steam: Trim off the dry ends of mushroom stems and then clean the mushrooms with a soft-bristled brush. Do not wash; the moisture will soften them and ruin their crisp texture. Slice ¼ inch thick and place in a shallow dish. Drizzle mushrooms with a little garlic olive oil, fresh lemon juice, and herb seasoning. Set dish on rack over boiling water, cover pot, and steam for 3 to 5 minutes. Whole or halved mushrooms will take a few minutes longer; watch carefully so they don't overcook.

To prepare mushrooms for stuffing, pull the stems from the caps, trim off the tough ends, and mince the remaining tender portion for adding to the filling. Steam the minced stems in the same manner as mushroom slices, 2 to 3 minutes, then combine them with the filling ingredients. Fill (see Stuffed Mushrooms) and steam for 7 to 10 minutes.

To Serve: Serve mushrooms hot as a side dish without any additional seasoning, combine with steamed greens, spoon over cooked poultry or meats, or add to casseroles.

Onions: Globe Onions, Boiling Onions, Leeks

To Prepare and Steam: To prepare onions for stuffing, peel large white or yellow onions, cut a ½-inch slice off the tops, and place on rack over boiling water. Cover pot and steam for 4 to 5 minutes until just tender. Remove the centers to form a shell about ⅓ inch thick. Sprinkle onion cavities with salt and turn upside down on wire rack. Fill (see Fillings for Stuffed Vegetables), stand on rack over boiling water, cover pot, and steam for 15 to 20 minutes. To precook large onions for adding to an oven roast, peel and steam for 10 minutes.

Steam unpeeled small boiling onions (about 1½ inches in diameter) on rack over boiling water for 2 minutes. Remove from the steamer, peel, and cut a shallow cross on the stem ends to assure even cooking and help keep them from falling apart. Return the onions to the steamer and cook an additional 7 to 8 minutes.

Trim off the root ends and all but ½ inch of the green stalks from young leeks. (Large, mature leeks are not suitable for steaming; they must be braised to become tender.) As there is usually a great deal of sand caught between the leaf layers, wash thoroughly under running water, pulling the leaves apart slightly to rinse away the trapped sand. If the leeks are quite slender, leave them whole; halve large ones lengthwise. If desired, tie into serving portions with kitchen string. Arrange them on a rack over boiling water, cover pot, and steam for 6 to 8 minutes.

To Serve: Serve boiling onions hot tossed in melted butter and sprinkled with minced fresh parsley; or reheat in Béchamel or Mornay Sauce with cooked peas; or toss with broccoli florets in Herb Butter Sauce.

Serve leeks hot with Brown or Anchovy Butter Sauce. To serve cold, see Marinated Vegetables.

Peas: Garden, Snow, Sugar Snap

To Prepare and Steam: Though common garden peas can be steamed, I prefer to cook them quickly by immersing in boiling water, thus brightening their color and assuring crisp texture. If you want to steam peas, put them in a shallow bowl, set bowl on rack over boiling water, cover pot, and steam 2 minutes, or until peas are just barely done. Strew peas over chicken pieces or meats that are being steamed in a shallow dish or Yunnan pot the last few minutes of steaming.

Snow peas (Chinese peapods) and sugar snap peas, however, are good candidates for steaming. Trim the ends and pull away any strings, then wash well. Place them on a rack over boiling water, cover pot, and steam for 2 to 5 minutes, or until barely cooked.

To Serve: Crunchy garden peas are good with chopped fresh mint and freshly grated orange peel or with Slivered Almond Butter Sauce. Combine them with brown rice, slivered cooked ham, chopped fresh parsley, and freshly grated Parmesan cheese; or toss with white rice, ground cumin, ground turmeric, and chopped fresh coriander. Heat minced garlic and shredded prosciutto in a little butter and toss in peas.

Snow peas and sugar snap peas combine well with sliced water chestnuts and/or bamboo shoots, softened and slivered shiitake mushrooms, or steamed shredded lettuce. They are also good served alone with any of the Butter Sauces or Sesame Seed Butter Sauce. To serve cold, see Marinated Vegetables.

Peppers: Sweet Green and Red Bell

To Prepare and Steam: To prepare whole peppers for stuffing, wash peppers and stand them upright on rack over boiling water. Cover pot and presteam for 2 minutes. Remove peppers from the steamer, cut off 1 inch of the stem end, and remove the ribs and seeds. Invert peppers on a wire rack to drain well. Finely dice the flesh around the stem and sauté with filling ingredients (see Fillings for Stuffed Vegetables). Fill pepper cavity and steam for 15 minutes.

To Serve: The presteamed peppers may also be cut into julienne (steam them a bit longer if you prefer them softer) and dressed with melted butter; combined with steamed green beans or sugar snap or snow peas and drizzled with any of the Butter Sauces; added to tomato sauces; or cut into very thin strips and used as a garnish for cauliflower.

Potatoes, Yams, and Sweet Potatoes

To Prepare and Steam: Steaming is the best way to bring out the flavor and preserve the texture of the thin-skinned white or red new potatoes and of yams and sweet potatoes. Thick-skinned white potatoes such as russet and Idaho can be steamed, but unless you are already using the steamer, it is better to boil them so that the cooking liquid can be saved for making breads and for adding to soups.

Scrub new potatoes well but do not peel. Place on rack over boiling water, cover pot, and steam for 25 minutes for 3-inch potatoes, 15 to 18 minutes for 2-inch potatoes, and 10 to 14 minutes for 1½-inch ones. Add pickling spices, garlic, or herbs such as basil or rosemary to the steaming water, if desired. These seasonings will permeate the potato skins and delicately infuse the potatoes with flavor.

Scrub thick-skinned potatoes and yams or sweet potatoes and place unpeeled on a rack over boiling water. Cover pot and steam a 6-ounce white or sweet potato about 45 minutes, a yam about 35 minutes. Potatoes will not feel soft to the touch as they do when baked, so test by piercing with a cake or other tester. Remove from heat and peel. Mash, rice, slice, or dice them as you would had they been boiled.

If you are long-steaming another dish, cook the potatoes or yams around the edge of it. Alternatively, start them first, and then put the quicker-cooking dish that is to accompany them in the steamer.

To precook thick-skinned potatoes for adding to an oven roast, steam 10 to 15 minutes. Undercook yams slightly if they are to be sliced for adding to casseroles.

To Serve: Serve whole new potatoes or peeled and sliced thick-skinned potatoes hot with Crème Fraîche, sour cream, or cottage cheese and a sprinkling of chopped fresh chives; or with Lemon/Lime, Garlic/Shallot, Herb, or Anchovy Butter Sauce, or with Pesto Sauce; or tossed with green beans, melted butter, and chopped fresh mint.

Serve yams or sweet potatoes hot with Lemon/Lime Butter Sauce, minced fresh parsley or chives, and freshly ground black pepper; Pecan or Hazelnut Butter Sauce; or Peanut Sauce.

Pumpkin

To Prepare and Steam Whole Pumpkin: Wash and then cut a 4-inch cap from the stem end of a 5-pound pumpkin. With your hand, pull out the seeds and fibers, then finish the job with a melon baller. (Reserve the seeds for roasting.*) Place a rack with 2-inch legs in the bottom of a deep pot. (If you do not have such a rack, stack two racks and place a jar-lid ring between them to add height.) Replace the cap and tie a cheesecloth sling around the pumpkin to facilitate removing it from the pot. Place the pumpkin on rack over boiling water, cover pot, and steam for 30 to 45 minutes.

To Serve Whole Pumpkin: Fill a steamed whole pumpkin with your favorite thin-gravied beef, lamb, pork, or goat stew for an attractive dinner presentation. For a vegetable stew, combine a well-seasoned stock with any combination of steamed yams, carrots, turnips, potatoes, rutabagas, zucchini, and corn. Or use the pumpkin to hold chicken-rice soup made with snow peas and mushrooms or even a cream of pumpkin soup. The tender flesh of the pumpkin then becomes part of the meal.

A 5-pound pumpkin, about 25 inches in circumference and 7 to 8 inches high, will hold 3 to 4 cups of stock and solid ingredients, an amount sufficient for four servings. The dish must be completely cooked and at serving temperature before adding it to the pumpkin. Begin steaming the pumpkin, and then halfway through the cooking time, ladle in the stew

---

*Remove any fibers from the pumpkin seeds, then rinse, dry with paper toweling, and place in a single layer on a baking sheet. Sprinkle lightly with salt and bake in a 325° F oven for 20 to 25 minutes, or until lightly browned and toasted, stirring often. Toss with melted butter and store in a jar with a tight-fitting lid. If not eating within 2 days, refrigerate up to 1 week.

or soup. Judge the halfway point by pressing gently against the walls of the pumpkin. If they give slightly, it is time to add the stew or soup. Be careful not to overcook the pumpkin, or it will fall to pieces when the cheesecloth sling is removed.

To Prepare and Steam Pumpkin Pieces: Cut pumpkin into 6 or 8 pieces, scrape out stringy pulp and seeds, and place pieces skin side down on rack over boiling water. Steam for 20 to 25 minutes, or until flesh is tender when pierced with a fork.

To Serve Pumpkin Pieces: Peel pumpkin pieces and cut into 1- to 2-inch chunks. Heat pumpkin chunks in a covered nonstick pan with Lemon/Lime or Herb Butter Sauce; any of the Nut Butter Sauces; Sesame, Sunflower, or Pumpkin Seed Butter Sauce; or a little rich stock seasoned with ground ginger or nutmeg.

Summer Squash: Zucchini, Pattypan, Chayote, Yellow Crookneck and Straight-neck, Young Kuta

To Prepare and Steam Stuffed Summer Squash: Zucchini, pattypan (scallop or cymling), and chayote (mirliton or christophene) squash are especially good stuffed and then steamed (see Fillings for Stuffed Vegetables).

Select a 6- to 7-inch zucchini for stuffing. Wash, cut off the stem and blossom ends, and halve lengthwise. Remove and discard any large seeds and scoop out the pulp to form a ¼-inch shell. Dice the pulp and add it to the filling. Stuff the zucchini halves and steam for 15 to 20 minutes.

Unlike zucchini, pattypan squash must be precooked before stuffing. Wash, place on a rack over boiling water, cover pot, and steam for 3 minutes. Then, with a sharp knife, slice a 1½-inch disc from the rounded top of each squash, cutting it in the style of a cap for a jack o' lantern. Scoop out and discard any large seeds and remove enough pulp to form a ¼-inch shell. Reserve the pulp for adding to the filling. Stuff the squash, replace the caps, and steam for 15 to 20 minutes. Whole pattypan squash can also be steamed 40 to 45 minutes, or until tender, then cut and hollowed out as described, and filled with a hot stuffing, such as pureed pumpkin, beet greens, or kale (see Vegetable Purees), just before serving.

Wash chayote and halve lengthwise, place cut side up on rack over boiling water, cover pot, and steam for 35 minutes, or until fork tender. Discard the seeds and stringy pulp and scoop out halves to form a ¼-inch shell. Dice the pulp and add it to the filling. Stuff the chayote halves and steam for 15 to 20 minutes.

To Prepare and Steam Plain Summer Squash: I prefer to butter-steam or quickly sauté all of the summer squash. They may be steamed, however, with good results. Leave them whole; wash and place them directly on a rack over boiling water. Cover pot and steam until tender.

A 1-pound zucchini or young kuta (a new variety similar to a zucchini when young and a winter squash when mature) about 7 inches long and 2 inches in diameter will cook in 10 to 15 minutes. Steam 3-ounce pattypans for about 6 minutes, and 5-ounce yellow crookneck or straight-neck squash for 6 to 8 minutes.

To Serve: Slice or cut steamed squash into chunks and serve hot with fresh lemon juice and herb seasoning, or with any of the following: Lemon/Lime, Garlic/Shallot, or Herb Butter Sauce; Pesto Sauce; melted butter and freshly grated Parmesan cheese; or Toppings for Vegetables.

Winter Squash: Spaghetti, Dumpling, Acorn, Hubbard, Banana, Butternut, Mature Kuta

To Prepare and Steam Spaghetti Squash: The flesh of this squash will come out better in strands if it is steamed whole. Wash a spaghetti squash (about 2½ pounds), place on rack over boiling water, cover pot, and steam for 1 hour. Halve and scoop out and discard the seeds and stringy pulp. With a fork, pull out the flesh; it will form strands that resemble very fine spaghetti.

To Serve Spaghetti Squash: Reheat strands gently in a covered nonstick skillet with a little rich stock, herb seasoning, and ground ginger or freshly grated nutmeg; or with shredded mozzarella cheese, tossing until cheese is just melted; or in Basic Tomato Sauce. Alternatively, reheat squash strands in butter and pass freshly grated Parmesan cheese at table.

To Prepare and Steam Other Winter Squash: Dumpling squash, a pretty green and white squash named for its shape, may be steamed whole. A 1-pound squash will cook in 35 to 40 minutes. When tender, halve and discard seeds and fibers. Peel and cut into 1- to 2-inch chunks.

Scrub acorn, hubbard, banana, mature kuta (for description, see summer squash entry), and butternut squash. Place squash on a steady surface and with a large knife cut in half lengthwise. Remove seeds and fibers, and place skin side down on a rack over boiling water. (If squash is very large, cut into quarters or eighths.) Cover pot and steam for 20 to 25 minutes. Remove the squash from the steamer, peel, and cut into chunks. (If the acorn squash is small, do not peel or cut up.)

To Serve: Gently reheat squash chunks in a covered nonstick skillet and toss with any of the following: stock, herb seasoning, and ground ginger or freshly grated nutmeg; Lemon/Lime or Herb Butter Sauce; or any of the Nut Butter Sauces. (All of these may be spooned into the acorn squash halves.)

Vegetable Purees

This section explains how to transform some of the vegetables you have steamed into purees. It is not intended to be a complete chapter on purees, nor are the yields and measurements meant to be exact. The yields are determined by how many purees you are serving at a meal, and how rich and filling each puree is.

A vegetable puree served as a side dish is an excellent way to dress up a meal. This colorful, delicious addition to the table is also a boon to the busy chef, as the puree can be prepared ahead of time and then reheated with seasonings just before serving. These same pureed vegetables may be used as the base for an elegant soup (see Appetizers and First Courses), a timbale or vegetable pudding (see Eggs and Tofu), or for other non-steamed creations such as soufflés, crêpes, or omelets.

Vegetable weights vary. As a general rule, allow 1 to 1½ pounds vegetables to measure 2 cups puree, generally enough to serve 4 persons as a side dish. Steam the vegetables until they are quite soft. To economize on fuel, put them in with a dish you are already cooking, or steam more than you need for a meal and let the portion to be pureed cook longer.

Put the steamed vegetables in a blender or food processor fitted with metal blade. Puree, adding a little stock if vegetables are too dry to puree smoothly. Stop once or twice to scrape down sides of container with a spatula. Do not puree to the extent that the mixture becomes mushy. In general, a blender makes a very smooth puree and a processor a coarser one. The only vegetable that should be handled differently is the potato. It becomes gummy in these appliances and should therefore be mashed or riced.

Transfer the pureed vegetable to a skillet or saucepan and heat gently. For 2 cups of puree, add 2 tablespoons butter and enough heavy cream, Crème Fraîche, or Béchamel Sauce to make a smooth consistency. Only with heavy cream will you achieve the classic result. Half-and-half, dairy substitutes, or rich stock can be used, but the result will be less spectacular. Season to taste with herb seasoning, salt, and/or freshly ground white or black pepper, or add finely minced garlic, grated onion, chopped fresh herbs, dry sherry, curry powder, or spices such as freshly grated nutmeg or ground ginger.

If desired, press the puree briefly into individual cups or timbale forms and invert on serving plates. This should only be attempted with a puree that is thick and rather stiff; very soft purees will not keep their shape.

For extra flavor and eye appeal, garnish purees with minced fresh parsley, chives, or mint; tiny slivers of sun-dried tomato; thin strips of roasted pepper or pimiento; lightly toasted slivered blanched almonds; crumbled, crisply cooked bacon; or freshly grated cheese.

Artichokes, asparagus, broccoli, cauliflower, green beans, greens, leeks, peas, potatoes, yams, winter squashes, and root vegetables all lend themselves to pureeing. Following are a few vegetable puree recipes that will serve 4. At the end of the recipes is a short list of some complementary combinations to guide you in creating your own purees.

Beet Puree: 2 cups pureed beets, 2 to 3 teaspoons fresh lemon juice, ½ cup Crème Fraîche (or as needed), and salt and freshly ground black pepper to taste.

Beet and Potato Puree: 2 cups pureed beets, ½ cup mashed or riced potato, 4 teaspoons butter, 4 teaspoons heavy cream (or as needed), 2 teaspoons fresh lemon juice, and freshly grated nutmeg, salt, and freshly ground black pepper to taste.

Yam and Apple Puree: 2 cups pureed yams, ½ cup pureed tart apple (steam along with the yams), 4 teaspoons butter, ⅓ cup heavy cream (or as needed), and ground ginger, salt, and freshly ground black pepper to taste. Especially good with Thanksgiving turkey or ham.

Celeriac and Potato Puree: 1½ cups pureed celeriac, ¾ cup mashed or riced potato, 4 teaspoons butter, ⅓ cup half-and-half cream (or as needed), 4 teaspoons fresh lemon juice, and celery salt, salt, and freshly ground white pepper to taste.

Turnip and Pumpkin Puree: 1⅓ cups pureed turnip, ⅔ cup pureed pumpkin, 1 tablespoon butter, 3 tablespoons heavy cream (or as needed), ¼ teaspoon ground thyme, or to taste, and salt and freshly ground black pepper to taste. Especially good with goat or lamb.

Kale or Other Greens Puree: 2 cups pureed kale, 1 teaspoon fresh lemon juice, ⅔ cup Béchamel Sauce, and freshly grated nutmeg, salt, and freshly ground black pepper to taste. Especially good mounded in cooked artichoke bottoms; sprinkle with freshly grated Parmesan cheese and paprika, then broil to heat through.

SUGGESTED COMBINATIONS:

Artichokes and leeks seasoned with oregano or dill and fresh lemon juice.

Cabbage and potato seasoned with herb seasoning and freshly ground black pepper, sprinkled with caraway seeds.

Carrot and potato or onion seasoned with a little sugar and ground ginger.

Cauliflower and peas seasoned with curry powder; or cauliflower and grated Gruyère cheese.

Celeriac and potato with garlic and parsley; or celeriac and beet seasoned with freshly grated nutmeg.

Rutabaga with garlic and parsley, seasoned with herb seasoning and freshly ground white pepper.

Rutabaga, parsnip, and carrot seasoned with fresh lemon juice, herb seasoning, and freshly ground white pepper.

Rutabaga and potato topped with crumbled, crisply cooked bacon.

Turnips, carrots, and broccoli with grated Parmesan cheese.

Winter squash seasoned with salt, freshly ground white pepper, and grated nutmeg or ground mace.

Marinated Vegetables

This section, like the one on vegetable purees, does not give full recipes. These directions are designed to help you turn your deliberately under-cooked vegetables into a main-meal or side-dish salad. There are a few recipe suggestions following a list of suitable vegetables and how to prepare them. Dressings and toppings that appear with capitalized initial letters can be found in Basic Savory Sauces and at the end of this chapter, respectively.

Asparagus, beets, broccoli, Brussels sprouts, carrots, cauliflower, eggplant, green beans, leeks, snow peas, bell peppers, and summer squashes are good choices for marinating. Don't let this list limit you; experiment with any vegetable you are steaming for dinner.

Steam the vegetables *just* until beginning to soften, remove from heat, and immediately immerse in ice water to retard further cooking. Drain and refrigerate, covered, up to 3 days. Some cooks recommend dressing vegetables while they are hot. I find that the vegetables stay crisper and have a cleaner taste and brighter color if the cooking is halted and the vegetables chilled. They will still absorb the dressing.

An hour or two before serving, toss the steamed vegetables with any vinaigrette-type dressing. Serve them alone or on a bed of lettuce. If you prefer, skip the marinating and add these crisp vegetables plain to a tossed salad; the salad dressing will flavor both the greens and the steamed vegetables.

When serving vegetables alone or on a bed of lettuce, garnish with toasted nuts, thin strips of roasted pepper or pimiento, chopped hard-cooked eggs, slivered or halved pitted ripe olives, tiny slivers of sun-dried tomato, or minced fresh herbs.

SALAD COMBINATIONS:

Asparagus with Garlic Mayonnaise, garnished with tiny strips of sun-dried tomato; or asparagus marinated in Mustard Vinaigrette, finely minced garlic, and a few drops of Oriental sesame oil.

Beets, chopped hard-cooked eggs, and grated onion tossed with Herb Vinaigrette, then topped with grated raw carrot.

Broccoli dressed with Oriental Salad Dressing which has been seasoned with oyster sauce and sprinkled with lightly toasted sesame seeds; or dressed with Anchovy or Blue Cheese Vinaigrette and garnished with halved cherry tomatoes or tiny strips of sun-dried tomato.

Brussels sprouts tossed with Lemon/Lime Vinaigrette and garnished with tiny balls of cream cheese and/or blue cheese.

Cauliflower with Avocado Tahini Dressing.

Celeriac tossed with Herb Mayonnaise thinned with fresh lemon juice and a little oil, chopped hard-cooked eggs, and lots of minced fresh parsley; or tossed with Lemon/Lime Mayonnaise and finely chopped fresh sorrel.

Eggplant tossed in Oriental Dressing and lightly toasted sesame seeds; or tossed with finely minced garlic and Herb Vinaigrette made with minced fresh dill. Garnish either with halved cherry tomatoes.

Sunchokes in Mustard Vinaigrette with a garnish of carrot curls.

Tiny new potatoes tossed with Anchovy Vinaigrette, shredded raw spinach, and bits of crisply cooked bacon.

Fillings for Stuffed Vegetables

Steamed stuffed vegetables served with a tossed salad and bread make an easy do-ahead meal. In the morning, or the night before, prepare the filling, stuff the vegetables, and refrigerate; bring to room temperature before steaming.

Leftover or freshly cooked grains such as brown, white, and wild rice; bulghur wheat; barley; wheat and triticale berries; and pastas such as orzo and tiny shells can form the bases of the fillings. To these can be added any of the following: cooked meats, poultry, and sausages; chopped tomato or tomato paste; small amounts of steamed vegetables, especially spinach and Swiss chard; chopped green onion tops; minced pimiento; chopped nuts; shredded or grated cheese; dried or fresh herbs; herb seasoning; fresh lemon juice.

Using the basic onion mixture (recipe follows), create your own fillings according to what you have on hand and/or your favorite flavor combinations. To this onion base, add ingredients to yield 2 to 2½ cups of filling, an amount sufficient to stuff two large bell peppers, six small to medium pattypan squash, two 6- to 7-inch zucchini, two 8- to 10-ounce chayote squash, or four medium-large onions. For directions on how to prepare these vegetables for stuffing and their steaming times, see the Onions, Peppers, and Summer Squash listings in Vegetable Steaming Methods.

Following the basic onion mixture are four stuffing recipes sufficient to fill the above-mentioned vegetables. (For fillings for steamed stuffed mushrooms, see Stuffed Mushrooms.) Each recipe will serve two or four persons, depending upon whether the stuffed vegetable is the centerpiece of the meal or a side dish.

Basic Onion Mixture: In a covered nonstick skillet, cook until softened 3 or 4 tablespoons minced onion, or onion and celery, 1 or 2 garlic cloves, finely minced, the reserved diced flesh of the vegetable being stuffed, and 1 tablespoon olive oil and/or butter. (If stuffing onions, omit the minced onion; replace with all of the reserved diced flesh.) Combine onion mixture with one of the filling mixtures specified below, following directions in the filling recipes. If the combined ingredients lack body, mix in a lightly beaten egg; if they are too wet, add fine dry breadcrumbs as needed. Fill the vegetable shells and steam as directed. Put any excess filling into a lightly buttered basin and steam along with the stuffed vegetables.

FILLINGS TO ADD TO BASIC ONION MIXTURE:

Veal and Bulghur Filling: Add ¾ cup shredded cooked veal roast or cooked ground veal to basic onion mixture and cook, covered, for 2 minutes. Remove from heat and with a fork stir in 1 cup cooked bulghur, ½ cup shredded Monterey Jack cheese, 2 tablespoons lightly toasted finely chopped pecans, 1 lightly beaten egg, 2 to 3 tablespoons tomato paste, ½ teaspoon crumbled dried basil, and fresh lemon juice, herb seasoning, and freshly ground black pepper to taste.

Italian Sausage and Orzo Filling: On rack over boiling water, steam 2 Italian sausages (approximately 8 ounces) 10 to 15 minutes, depending on size. When cool enough to handle, remove casings and crumble meat into a bowl. With a fork stir in basic onion mixture, 1 cup cooked orzo (small rice-shaped pasta), 1 medium-size ripe tomato, chopped and well drained, ½ cup freshly grated Parmesan cheese, ½ teaspoon each crumbled dried oregano and basil, 3 to 4 tablespoons fine dry breadcrumbs, and fresh lemon juice, herb seasoning, and freshly ground black pepper to taste.

Pork and Brown Rice Filling: Add ¾ cup shredded cooked pork roast or cooked lean ground pork to basic onion mixture and cook, covered, 2 minutes. Remove from heat and, with a fork, stir in 1 cup cooked brown rice, ½ cup shelled peas, blanched 30 seconds, 3 tablespoons minced green onion tops, 1 lightly beaten egg, 2 to 3 tablespoons fine dry bread-crumbs, ¼ teaspoon ground sage, and herb seasoning and freshly ground black pepper to taste.

Cheese and Wheat or Triticale Berry Filling: With a fork, stir into basic onion mixture 1¾ cups cooked wheat or triticale berries, ½ cup chopped cooked and well drained spinach or Swiss chard, ½ cup shredded Gouda or Edam cheese, and herb seasoning and freshly ground black pepper to taste.

Toppings for Vegetables

Steamed vegetables that have been simply dressed with fresh lemon or lime juice or a light coating of Lemon/Lime Butter Sauce are enhanced by the addition of toppings that add color, texture, and/or flavor. For example, decorate cauliflower with tiny strips of sun-dried tomato, or sprinkle toasted sesame seeds on spinach or broccoli.

Consider these toppings when serving hot or cold steamed vegetables: minced fresh herbs; chopped hard-cooked eggs; buttered coarse bread-crumbs and chopped hard-cooked eggs; hard-cooked eggs, yolks and whites sieved separately; lightly toasted chopped or slivered nuts; thin strips of sun-dried tomato; thin strips of pimiento or roasted pepper; thin bell pepper strips or rings; lightly toasted sesame or other seeds; freshly grated Parmesan, Romano, or other hard cheese; sliced pimiento-stuffed olives or sliced or slivered ripe olives.

Steaming Grains

Included here are some popular grains—rice, millet, bulghur, semolina—all of which can be steamed, in the strictest sense, with varying degrees of success. For example, rice combined with water will steam above boiling water, but a superior result is possible with a boil-and-steam method.

In some Asian countries, glutinous rice is traditionally steamed in a basket above water, a process explained in this section. It is an arduous procedure, however, and I have found that this type of rice can be prepared in the same way as white or brown rice with no discernible loss of the grain's identity.

Throughout the book I have recommended rice as an accompaniment, usually specifying both color and kernel length. These recommendations are based on the type of rice traditionally eaten in the dish's homeland or the type I think would best complement the dish. For example, I suggest short-grain white rice with Japanese preparations and long-grain white rice with Chinese ones. These serving suggestions are only guidelines. Those readers who prefer brown over white, or short-grain over long, may substitute their favorites.

Millet and bulghur fare better when simmered with liquid than when prepared by the boil-and-steam method, or in a bowl with water placed on a rack above boiling water. Barley, on the other hand, steams to a wonderful, chewy finish after it has been parboiled. Wheat and triticale berries may be parboiled and then steamed as for barley, but the cooking time is far longer than when these berries are boiled and the results are not discernibly better.

Semolina, or couscous as it is popularly known, is a star in the steaming world. The tiny pasta grains respond beautifully to the steam method, and cooking them in water rather than above it is not a workable substitute. Do not be discouraged by the length of the couscous steaming directions; this preparation is well worth your time and will bring much-deserved compliments for your efforts.

Apart from couscous, pasta is a "member" of the grain family that cannot be steamed—those hard noodles simply won't soften properly. They can, however, be cooked in the conventional way and then combined with other ingredients in a casserole that can be steamed rather than baked. The pasta retains its *al dente* texture without drying out as it would in the oven.

Because steaming keeps a casserole moist, the cream sauces that usually bind the noodles, such as in macaroni and cheese, can be omitted. For example, combine cooked pasta and a seasoned ground meat mixture and top it with mozzarella or another good melting cheese. The cheese won't brown as the casserole steams, but it will melt down into the pasta mixture to produce a smooth and unusual texture.

Fresh ravioli, tortellini, and other filled pastas can be steamed directly on a rack, but there is little difference in the texture. They must be steamed in a single layer and take about the same amount of time as when they are boiled. I usually find this impractical unless I already have my large steamer on the stove. Fresh noodles are impossible to arrange in a single layer and will stick together if the strands touch.

WHITE AND BROWN RICE

The method I recommend for cooking rice is not literally steaming, but rather a boil-and-steam method. It is possible to steam any rice above boiling water, combining the rice with water (measured as for the boil-and-steam procedure described below) in a bowl and placing the bowl on a steamer rack above boiling water. Testing has proved this an unsatisfactory method, as the steamer must be frequently uncovered and the rice stirred so that it will cook evenly. This stirring bruises the grains and makes the rice mushy.

The Rival and the Waring all-purpose electric steamers operate on this basic principle of steaming "in water, above water": a bowl containing rice and water sits above a reservoir filled with water. These manufacturers have eliminated the need to uncover and stir, but I find that rice cooked in these appliances isn't as good as that prepared by the boil-and-steam method, or by the electric rice cooker.

For no-fail, fluffy rice every time, purchase an electric rice cooker (see Specific-use Steamers in Equipment) and follow the manufacturer's instructions. The cookers are easy to use, require none of the cook's attention, and allow you to coordinate the timing of the rice with the other dishes you are serving.

The boil-and-steam method can be used for short- or long-grain white or brown rice. (It can also be used for glutinous rice, which is described in the following section. To prepare quick-cooking or converted rice, follow the package instructions.) For 3 cups of cooked rice, wash 1 cup raw rice until water runs clear. Place in a 1-quart saucepan and add water to ½ inch above level of rice. For brown rice, add 2 or 3 additional tablespoons water. No matter how much rice you decide to cook, always use this ½-inch measure for the water.

If time permits, cover pan and let rice stand for an hour. During this soaking period, the kernels begin absorbing the water; this absorption results in a more tender, more fluffy, drier grain once the rice is cooked.

Place saucepan with the soaked rice, uncovered, over medium-high heat. Bring to a boil and reduce heat slightly. Boil uncovered and without stirring until all water has disappeared from the surface and small craters have formed. Cover, turn heat to lowest level, and steam 20 minutes for white rice and 30 minutes for brown rice.

Remove saucepan from heat and let stand, covered, 5 minutes. Fluff with a fork just before serving.

MILLET AND BULGHUR

Both millet and bulghur may be cooked by the boil-and-steam method described for rice. For millet, use ½ cup of the grain and 1½ cups of water or stock. Millet takes about 45 minutes to cook and this amount will yield about 2 cups. For bulghur, the measures are 1 cup bulghur and 2 cups liquid; the cooking time is as for white rice and the yield is about 2 cups.

With this said, I must add that I prefer to cook these grains by methods other than the boil-and-steam one. I usually prepare millet by adding it to boiling stock and cooking it covered over low heat. Bulghur can be done this same way or as a pilaf, i.e., browned in oil or butter with seasonings before boiling water or stock is added. (Of course, seasonings can be added with the boil-and-steam method, but the results are not as flavorful because they are not sautéed.) I think these methods better retain the unique textures of these grains.

BARLEY

Following much kitchen testing, I have found that I prefer steamed barley over boiled, because the grains better retain their identity. For 2 scant cups of cooked barley, allow ½ cup raw barley and 2 cups water seasoned with ¼ teaspoon herb seasoning.

In a saucepan bring water and herb seasoning to a boil, add barley, and cook uncovered 20 minutes, or until almost all the water has evaporated. Spoon barley directly onto a rack with small perforations set over boiling water, cover pot, and steam 35 minutes, or until barley is done to your liking.

GLUTINOUS RICE

Glutinous rice, also known as sweet rice, is commonly eaten with daily meals in some areas of Southeast Asia, especially northeastern Thailand, Burma, and Laos, and is a popular specialty rice in other Asian countries. This creamy-colored, short-grain, pearllike rice has a sticky consistency when cooked, hence its third name, sticky rice. Health-food stores in the United States carry a brown glutinous rice as well.

In areas of Thailand and Laos this rice is traditionally steamed in a large basket. (A description of the basket can be found in the Equipment chapter.) Glutinous rice may also be steamed in the same manner as white or brown rice, but must be presoaked as described below and steamed for about 35 minutes. One cup of raw glutinous rice prepared by either method will yield 3 cups cooked.

Wash the rice until the water runs clear. Place in a saucepan, cover with cold water, cover the pot, and let stand at least 4 hours, but preferably overnight. Drain rice and place in the basket. Rest the basket on the rim of a large saucepan filled with 3 inches of boiling water; the base of the basket must not come in contact with the water. The top half of the basket will rise above the pan sides. To cover the rice, place the lid down into the basket. It will rest snugly some distance above the rice. Steam for 1 hour or until rice is tender.

COUSCOUS

Though most commonly thought of as a Moroccan specialty, couscous is also found in other North African countries, across the water in Trapani, Sicily, where it is called *cuscusu,* in Senegal, and even in Brazil, where it is known as *cuscuz* and was probably carried from West Africa by Portuguese slave traders.

The word couscous is used for both the semolina portion of the dish and for the complete dish, which includes the stew that is often prepared with it. To further confuse the description, in Brazil cornmeal, tapioca, or rice sometimes replaces the semolina, and throughout North Africa the preparation goes by different names, depending on the local dialect. Couscous, however, is the most commonly used term.

Couscous can be either savory or sweet. The basic steaming method can be adapted for a main dish, a side dish, or a dessert. For main-dish couscous, see Lamb Stew and Sicilian Fish Stew to Accompany Couscous; a sweet couscous can be found in Desserts. To serve couscous as a side dish, prepare it in the manner described here. Its neutral taste and fine, firm texture provide a good balance to rich dishes.

Packaged couscous can be found in specialty markets and some supermarkets. Imported couscous sold in bulk is the best to use but is difficult to find in some areas.

Do not follow the cooking instructions printed on the package. They direct you to cook the grains in water rather than above it, resulting in a mushy consistency. Also, never buy a box of couscous that is marked quick-cooking or precooked; the grains will not react correctly when prepared by the traditional steaming method.

The couscous steaming procedure is a complicated one, but well worth the effort for its delicious result. The grains must first be treated with water so that they swell, and then they are steamed twice. If you are steaming the grains above a stew, you will need a true *couscousière* or a three-piece steamer (see Specific-use Steamers and All-purpose Steamers, respectively, in Equipment). The upper pans of some three-piece steamers have fairly large perforations, so they will need to be lined with cheesecloth. If you are lucky enough to have a colander that fits snugly into the rim of a saucepan, this arrangement may also be used. Line the colander with cheesecloth.

If you will not be steaming the couscous over a stew, a cheesecloth-lined colander set inside a deep, wide pot can be used. Place a 2-inch-high rack or other platform on the pot bottom. Set the colander on the rack and add the water or other liquid to within 1 inch of the base of the colander. Line the colander with cheesecloth and steam couscous as directed. Traditionally, couscous is not covered as it cooks, but a lid is necessary with this improvised system.

One and a half cups of uncooked couscous will yield about 4 cups cooked, which is sufficient to serve 4 persons. Spread the grains evenly over the bottom of a large shallow pan. Add cold water to barely cover and let stand 5 minutes. With fingers, rub grains together to separate them into very tiny pellets; drain in a sieve.

Line the same shallow pan with a tea towel and spread drained couscous evenly over it. Let stand 10 minutes for grains to swell slightly. With fingers, again separate the grains. Spread grains evenly on the towel and let stand another 10 minutes.

The two pans of the *couscousière* (or three-piece steamer or colander set on rim of saucepan) must be sealed together where they meet so that the steam travels only through the perforated bottom of the upper pan. At this point, the bottom pan must contain at least 2 cups of boiling water or other liquid, or the bubbling prepared stew. Do not fill to the point that the liquid touches the upper pan. To form the seal, wrap the lip of the bottom pan with a strip of dampened cheesecloth dusted lightly with flour. Rest the top pan in the bottom one and press gently.

With fingers, gradually drop couscous into top pan and steam uncovered 20 minutes. (If you have improvised with a colander *inside* a pot, the pot will need to be covered.) Turn out onto a large shallow pan and sprinkle with ¼ cup cold water mixed with ½ teaspoon salt. With fingers, separate the grains, spreading evenly on pan. Leave grains to dry 10 to 15 minutes. If not completing the steaming at this point, cover with a lightly dampened cloth and let stand up to 2 hours.

Reseal the *couscousière* with the cheesecloth strip for the final steaming of the couscous. Make sure the liquid or stew in the bottom pan is at a boil. If the couscous has rested longer than 15 minutes, break up any lumps with wet fingertips. Slowly return couscous to top pan, separating grains as you work. Steam uncovered 20 minutes. For each 4 cups cooked couscous, toss in 2 tablespoons olive oil and/or softened butter.

FISH AND SHELLFISH

Chinese Whole Sea Bass with Brown Bean Sauce

Yucatecan Snapper with Orange Slices and Olives

Iberian Pollock with Tomatoes

Stuffed Whole Fish

Basic Fish Steaks or Fillets

Tarragon Salmon Steaks

Mediterranean Fish Steaks or Fillets with Smoked Ham

Italian Anchovy Fish Steaks or Fillets

Chinese Fish Steaks or Fillets with Three Sauces

Miso Fish Steaks or Fillets

Fish Steaks or Fillets with Japanese Spices

Southeast Asian Fish Steaks or Fillets with Papaya

Burmese Fish Packets

Sicilian Fish Stew to Accompany Couscous

Shrimp with Chinese Dipping Sauces

Shrimp with Japanese Miso Sauce

Shrimp with Caribbean Spicy Sauce

Gorgonzola Shrimp

Scallops with Sorrel Sauce

Scallops with Uncooked Tomato Sauce

Scallops with Sake and Ham

South Asian Mussels

Garlicky Clams

Squid Stuffed with Swiss Chard and Parmesan

Squid Rings

Fish and Shellfish

Fish

Steamed fish fit perfectly into today's dietary emphasis on natural tastes and light saucing. Cooks who love the delicate texture and pure flavor of properly cooked fish will quickly discover that the best way to ensure these qualities is through steaming. A fish doesn't need the complex vegetable and herb flavors imparted by poaching in a court bouillon, nor does its successful preparation depend on heavy spicing. These treatments mask what fish lovers most admire: clean, fresh taste.

Most fish are high in protein and low in fat and cholesterol. Fish has less sodium than beef has, and salt-water varieties, despite their habitat, carry no more sodium in their flesh than fresh-water fish. Sizable amounts of potassium, iron, and phosphorus are present in all fish.

This first section covers how to purchase fish, including which types are good for steaming, how to store it once it is home, basic steaming procedures, and serving tips. Following this are two sections, one on whole fish and one on steaks and fillets. Each includes basic instructions for preparation and an international array of recipes.

HOW TO PURCHASE AND STORE FISH

Of course, very fresh fish is preferable, but it is not always possible to find, especially if you are some distance from a source. If you are fortunate enough to live near a fishing area, research what types are indigenous to those waters and incorporate them into your menus. In many parts of the country, fish are frozen briefly for transport and they can be purchased in no other form. In this case, the care with which the fish are handled—if they are kept cool enough and are moved as quickly as possible—is critical.

The perishability of fish makes it important to locate a reputable supplier. A good market will always display its fish on crushed ice or live in tanks. Fish are generally available in three forms: whole, in steaks cut ½ to 1 inch thick, and in fillets, boneless pieces which are sometimes quite thin. Allow approximately 10 ounces per person if serving whole fish, and 6 to 8 ounces if serving steaks or fillets.

The first test of freshness is made with your nose. Any off smell, particularly an ammonia-based one, is an indication that the fish is not fresh. The eyes of whole fish should be clear and bright, the gills should be a light, reddish color (the darker the gills, the older the fish), the scales should be shiny and tight against the body, and the flesh should be firm to the touch. Fillets and steaks should look moist and freshly cut, and there should be no dryness at the edges.

If you must buy prepackaged fish, first look for a date on the package. It will tell you when the fish was packed, which is usually one day after the fish has arrived in the market. Avoid out-of-date packages and any that have standing water, a sure sign that the fish has been defrosted and has stood too long.

Delicate flat fish such as sole, flounder, and turbot can be steamed whole, but as a general rule the fillets are best quickly pan-fried. Fillets of halibut, also a flat fish, are the exception. If they are thick enough, at least a half inch, the flesh will firm up nicely when steamed.

Some cooks prefer not to steam oilier fish such as sablefish (also known as black cod) and bluefish. With steaming the oily quality is retained, whereas such high-heat methods as broiling or pan-frying "cook it out."

Since it would be impossible to mention every type of fish suitable for steaming, the list that follows is only a guideline. Sometimes the same fish goes under many names, so aliases are provided in parentheses. In general, firm white fish are the best for steaming; the pink-fleshed salmon is also highly recommended.

Bass: white sea bass, tilefish (Eastern sea bass and tile bass), striped bass

Carp

Catfish

Cod family: rockfish (Pacific snapper, red snapper, Pacific Ocean perch, rock cod), haddock, pollock, Pacific cod, scrod (Eastern name for small cod or haddock)

Croaker family: shortfin corvina, California whiting (gray sea trout)

Eastern lake trout

Grouper bass (baquetta, giant sea bass, black sea bass)

Halibut (Pacific halibut, northern halibut)

Lingcod

Mahi mahi (blue Pacific dolphin)

Monkfish (goosefish, bellyfish, angler fish, lotte)

Pacific barracuda

Pike

Pomfret (Pacific pompano)

Porgy: sheepshead and scup

Salmon: chinook or king, silver or coho, pink, sockeye, chum or keta, Lake whitefish

Shark (thresher, soupfin, mako, leopard, Pacific blue, bonito)

Striped mullet

Swordfish

Tuna (mackerel) family: bonito, Pacific mackerel (American, chub, or blue), Jack mackerel, tuna, albacore, blackfin tuna, bluefin tuna

Walleye pike

Yellowtail

Immediately following purchase, rinse fresh fish with cold water. Pat dry with paper toweling and store in a nonmetallic container (no aluminum foil), loosely covered, in the coldest part of the refrigerator. If the fish is wrapped tightly, it will not "breathe" properly and will spoil. The fish must be cooked within twenty-four hours.

When fully frozen fish fillets or steaks are all that is available, they may be steamed while they are still frozen (double the cooking time indicated). If you prefer to thaw the fish first, let it defrost in the refrigerator rather than at room temperature.

HOW TO STEAM FISH

Although some books recommend placing a whole fish, fillet, or steak on a rack over boiling water, I prefer steaming fish in a shallow dish, or in the case of whole fish, on a platter. This way all of the wonderful juices are saved and can be treated as a sauce.

You may find that you will be limited to steaming a whole fish of no more than 2 to 3 pounds because your steamer will not accommodate a larger one. A roasting pan or an electric frypan with an improvised rack can be pressed into service if its larger size is necessary to hold the fish. A fish poacher can also be used, but the fish will need to be set in a foil boat, or cradle, so the juices are not lost (see Equipment).

HOW TO TELL WHEN FISH IS DONE

Fish cooks relatively quickly and is easily ruined by overcooking. Recall how the fish looks before it is steamed: the flesh is translucent. When it is done, the flesh should have just turned opaque, or milky. With two forks, gently pull away the flesh at a center point of the fish and look for this opacity. Alternatively, cut a small slit in the center with a sharp knife and pull apart gently.

A general rule of thumb for steaming fish is to allow 9 to 10 minutes for each inch of thickness. Measure the thickest part of the fish (whole, fillet, or steak) when it is lying flat. If there are other ingredients in the dish, the cooking time may need to be increased slightly.

HOW TO SERVE STEAMED FISH

Steamed fish, whether whole, steaks, or fillets, can be served just with the juices that accumulate in the dish during the cooking. If the steamed fish has been only lightly seasoned, you may want to dress it with a sauce. Ideally, the sauce will also complement the other components of the meal. These accompaniments may include a vegetable, such as steamed Swiss chard, carrots, asparagus, or broccoli, and white or brown rice, polenta, or new potatoes. The Butter, Nut Butter, and Seed Butter sauces (especially sunflower and sesame seed), the Compound Butters, the Mayonnaises, the Pesto sauces and Hollandaise Sauce are all excellent with fish.

To add eye appeal to the presentation, garnish fish with such colorful touches as parsley, watercress, coriander, dill, or fennel sprigs; tomato, radish, or beet roses; lemon twists; carrot curls; green onion brushes; cucumber fans; avocado balls rubbed with fresh lemon juice; or halved cherry tomatoes. Let your imagination take over.

Whole Fish

BASIC INSTRUCTIONS
FOR READYING WHOLE FISH

Remove any scales or fins the fishmonger has missed, then check the fish's cavity. Be sure the gills have been closely trimmed and rinse out any blood or membrane with running cold water. Do not remove the tail and head. The cheeks, in fact, are the sweetest meat.

Some cooks, especially when preparing a Chinese-style steamed fish, score the fish so that it cooks more quickly and evenly, is easier to check for doneness, and because the seasonings permeate better. Beginning about 1 inch from the base of the head, cut diagonal slashes crosswise along the body of the fish, spacing them about 1 inch apart and stopping about 2 inches short of the tail. The slashes should go no deeper than within ½ inch of the backbone. Flip the fish over and repeat slashing pattern on the second side. The fish may also be steamed without scoring.

Specific fish are called for in the following recipes, but do not be limited to these suggestions. Let availability and individual taste choose the best fish for you.

Chinese Whole Sea Bass
with Brown Bean Sauce

Make this the dramatic centerpiece of a Cantonese feast that includes Chinese Pork and Tofu Balls, steamed white rice, and fresh mandarin oranges for dessert.

SERVES 4

1 whole sea bass or rock cod
   (2½ to 3 pounds)
1 tablespoon soy sauce
1 tablespoon Chinese rice wine
   or dry sherry
3 to 4 tablespoons brown bean
   sauce
3 slices ginger root, very finely
   slivered

3 large garlic cloves, very
   finely slivered
1 1-inch piece dried tangerine
   peel, soaked in warm water
   15 minutes to soften,
   drained, and finely slivered
2 teaspoons peanut oil
   Few drops Oriental sesame
   oil (optional)
   Fresh coriander sprigs

Follow Basic Instructions for Readying Whole Fish, then rub fish inside and out with soy sauce and wine. Place fish on a large platter and distribute brown bean sauce evenly over its surface. Strew ginger root, garlic, and tangerine peel over and drizzle with peanut oil and optional sesame oil.

Set platter on rack over boiling water, cover pot, and steam 15 minutes or until fish tests done. Remove fish from steamer and garnish with coriander sprigs.

Yucatecan Snapper with Orange Slices and Olives

The garnishes play an important role in the presentation of this flavorful whole fish. Take a few moments to arrange them attractively. Offer lightly steamed chayote and parsleyed new potatoes on the side.

SERVES 4

1 *whole red snapper (2½ to 3 pounds)*	¼ *teaspoon salt, or to taste*
½ *cup finely chopped onion*	¼ *teaspoon freshly ground black pepper, or to taste*
1 *tablespoon olive oil*	1 *unpeeled orange, sliced*
⅓ *cup chopped red or green bell pepper*	2 *hard-cooked eggs, chopped*
½ *cup small pimiento-stuffed olives*	6 *radishes, sliced*
1 *teaspoon ground coriander*	3 *green onions with tops, sliced*
2 *tablespoons fresh lemon juice*	1½ *cups finely shredded lettuce*

Follow Basic Instructions for Readying Whole Fish, placing fish on a large platter.

In a covered nonstick skillet cook onion in oil until soft. Add bell pepper and cook 3 minutes. Add olives, coriander, lemon juice, salt, and pepper. Stir well and remove from heat.

Distribute onion mixture evenly over fish and arrange orange slices on top. Set platter on rack over boiling water, cover pot, and steam 15 minutes, or until fish tests done.

Garnish fish and its sauce with eggs, radishes, and green onions. Make beds of shredded lettuce on individual serving plates. As fish is carved, transfer the portions onto the lettuce.

Iberian Pollock with Tomatoes

Cauliflower is a favorite vegetable on the Iberian peninsula. Steam 3 cups of florets separately, then arrange them on the platter around the fish just before serving. Tuck sprigs of watercress between the florets. Accompany with a salad of romaine lettuce, curly endive, and red onions dressed with fresh lemon juice and olive oil.

SERVES 4

1 *whole pollock (2½ to 3 pounds)*	2 *medium-size ripe tomatoes, sliced*
½ *teaspoon ground allspice*	2 *large garlic cloves, minced*
Salt and freshly ground black pepper to taste	¼ *cup minced fresh parsley*
1 *medium onion, sliced*	1 *tablespoon olive oil*

Follow Basic Instructions for Readying Whole Fish. Place fish on a platter and sprinkle with allspice, salt, and pepper. Top with onion and tomato slices. Strew garlic and parsley over and drizzle with olive oil.

Set platter on rack over boiling water, cover pot, and steam 15 minutes, or until fish tests done.

Stuffed Whole Fish

Add an extra-special touch to a beautiful fresh fish by filling it with a flavorful stuffing that will subtly season the fish as it steams. If desired, arrange 2 medium-size ripe tomatoes, cut in eighths, over the fish during the last 5 minutes of steaming.

The stuffings may be made ahead, but they should not be put into the fish until just before it is to be steamed.

SERVES 4

1 *striped bass (2½ to 3 pounds)*	*Vegetable, Mushroom, or Bulghur Stuffing (recipes follow)*
Soy sauce	

Follow Basic Instructions for Readying Whole Fish. Rub fish inside and out with soy sauce. Spoon stuffing of choice into cavity. Secure opening by closing with 3 or 4 tiny bamboo skewers. (If there seems to be no danger of the stuffing falling out of the cavity, you can omit this step.)

Place fish on a large platter. Set platter on rack over boiling water, cover pot, and steam 25 minutes, or until fish tests done.

Vegetable Stuffing for Whole Fish

MAKES APPROXIMATELY 1 ½ CUPS

½   cup finely chopped onion
¼   cup finely chopped carrot
*¼   cup finely chopped celery
      with some leaves*
*¼   cup finely chopped green
      or red bell pepper*
2   large garlic cloves, minced
*1½ teaspoons minced fresh
      oregano*
*1   teaspoon minced fresh
      basil*
2   tablespoons butter

¼   cup minced fresh parsley
1   cup fine fresh breadcrumbs
*⅓   cup lightly toasted chopped
      blanched almonds*
*1   tablespoon fresh lemon or
      lime juice*
*2   tablespoons dry white wine
      or vermouth
      Herb seasoning and freshly
      ground black pepper to
      taste*

In a large covered nonstick skillet, cook onion, carrot, celery, bell pepper, garlic, oregano, and basil in butter 5 minutes. Remove from heat and, with a fork, stir in parsley, breadcrumbs, almonds, lemon juice, and wine. Season with herb seasoning and pepper. Refrigerate until ready to stuff fish.

Mushroom Stuffing for Whole Fish

MAKES APPROXIMATELY 1 ½ CUPS

*¾   cup sliced mushrooms,
      steamed (see Mushroom
      entry in Vegetable
      Steaming Methods)*
1½ cups French bread croutons

*2   large garlic cloves, very
      finely minced*
*½   teaspoon crumbled dried
      oregano*

¼ cup minced green onions
with tops
2 tablespoons minced fresh
parsley
2 tablespoons minced
drained roasted pepper

2 teaspoons fresh lemon
juice, or to taste
Herb seasoning, cayenne
pepper, and freshly ground
white pepper to taste
Fish stock or bottled clam
juice, if needed

In a large mixing bowl, combine mushrooms and their steaming juices, croutons, garlic, oregano, green onions, parsley, roasted pepper, lemon juice, and seasonings. With a fork, stir to mix well. For a moister stuffing, add stock as desired. Taste and adjust seasonings. Refrigerate until ready to stuff fish.

Bulghur Stuffing for Whole Fish

MAKES APPROXIMATELY 1½ CUPS

1 small onion, very thinly
sliced
2 large garlic cloves, finely
minced
1 tablespoon peanut oil or
butter
1½ teaspoons curry powder

¼ cup golden raisins, soaked
20 minutes in 2
tablespoons Curaçao
3 tablespoons lightly toasted
pine nuts
1⅓ cups cooked bulghur (⅔
cup raw)
Salt and freshly ground
black pepper to taste

In a covered nonstick skillet, cook onion and garlic in oil 3 minutes. Stir in curry powder and cook, stirring, 2 minutes. Remove pan from heat and transfer mixture to a mixing bowl.

Drain raisins and reserve soaking liquid. Add raisins, pine nuts, bulghur, and salt and pepper to onion mixture and, with a fork, toss to mix well. Refrigerate until ready to stuff fish.

When the stuffed fish is ready to steam, pour the reserved liqueur over the top.

Fish Steaks and Fillets

A steak is a crosswise cut from a whole fish and is usually about 1 inch thick. A portion of the backbone is visible in the center of the steak and the skin is attached. Fillets are lengthwise pieces that have been cut away from the backbone. They should be boneless and without skin.

To bring out their fresh, natural flavor, marinate fish steaks and fillets in fresh lemon or lime juice for no more than 10 minutes, or the juice will begin to "cook" the flesh. Lift the fish from the marinade and pat dry with paper toweling. (This marination is not advised if citrus juice is used in the recipe.)

With the exception of Tarragon Salmon Steaks, specific fish varieties are not suggested in the following recipes. These preparations are so versatile that virtually any fish steak or fillet that you would normally steam can be used. Refer to the list in the general fish introduction for possible choices.

Fish steaks and fillets take well to numerous seasonings. The first recipe is an example of a simple seasoning mixture that will complement the delicate taste of any fish. Use it as a guideline for adapting your favorite flavorings to the basic steaming method.

Basic Fish Steaks or Fillets

For a quick-to-assemble meal, serve these herb-seasoned fish steaks with steamed sunchokes tossed in Herb Butter Sauce and broccoli florets with a squeeze of fresh lemon juice.

SERVES 4

4 *fish steaks or fillets (6 to 8 ounces each)*	2 *tablespoons minced shallot or green onion with tops*
2 *tablespoons dry white wine*	1 *tablespoon minced fresh chives, parsley, or chervil*
1/2 *teaspoon freshly ground white pepper*	1 *bay leaf, broken*

Arrange fish steaks on a platter. Pour wine over steaks and then sprinkle with pepper. Strew shallot, chives, and bay leaf over all.

Set platter on rack over boiling water, cover pot, and steam 8 to 10 minutes, or until fish tests done.

Tarragon Salmon Steaks

This simple treatment of salmon enhances its wonderful flavor. For accompaniments, steam new potatoes and asparagus and drizzle both with Hazelnut Butter Sauce.

SERVES 4

4   salmon steaks (6 to 8
    ounces each)
1   medium onion, sliced
1   tablespoon chopped fresh
    tarragon

¼   cup chopped fresh parsley
2   tablespoons fresh lime or
    lemon juice
    Herb seasoning and freshly
    ground white pepper to taste

Arrange salmon steaks on a platter. Strew with onion slices, tarragon, and parsley. Pour lime juice over and sprinkle with herb seasoning and pepper.

Set platter on rack over boiling water, cover pot, and steam 10 minutes, or until fish tests done.

Mediterranean Fish Steaks or Fillets with Smoked Ham

Fresh fettuccine with Parmesan cheese is all that is needed to make this unusual fish and ham combination a satisfying meal.

SERVES 6

6   fish steaks or fillets (6 to 8
    ounces each)
¼   cup fresh lemon or lime
    juice
½   teaspoon salt
½   teaspoon freshly ground
    black pepper
4   large garlic cloves, finely
    minced

1½ teaspoons crumbled dried
    basil
¾   cup slivered lean smoked
    ham
12 or more large pitted ripe
    olives, halved
2   medium-size ripe tomatoes,
    cut into eighths
1   tablespoon olive oil
    Minced fresh parsley

Arrange steaks on a platter. Pour lemon juice over and sprinkle with salt and pepper. Strew with garlic, basil, ham, and olives. Distribute tomatoes on top and drizzle with oil.

Set platter on rack over boiling water, cover pot, and steam 10 minutes, or until fish tests done. Sprinkle liberally with minced parsley.

Italian Anchovy Fish Steaks or Fillets

For an extra taste dimension, sprinkle sauced fish with some drained capers before steaming. Serve with artichokes and orzo (small rice-shaped pasta) with Brown Butter Sauce.

SERVES 2

- 2 *fish steaks or fillets (6 to 8 ounces each)*
- 1 *tablespoon olive oil*
- 1 *teaspoon anchovy paste*
- 1/4 *cup minced onion*
- 2 *tablespoons finely minced Italian parsley*
- 2 *tablespoons dry white wine, fish stock, and/or bottled clam juice*

Arrange fish steaks in a shallow dish. Thoroughly blend olive oil and anchovy paste, then stir in onion, parsley, and wine. Pour mixture over fish steaks.

Set dish on rack over boiling water, cover pot, and steam 10 minutes, or until fish tests done.

The following three recipes call for a number of Oriental seasonings, all of which can easily be found in supermarkets or shops that carry Asian foodstuffs. Any of the popular Asian vegetables, such as bok choy, snow peas, bean sprouts, or Napa cabbage, would go well with these dishes. Accompany with steamed rice.

Chinese Fish Steaks or Fillets with Three Sauces

SERVES 2

- 1 *tablespoon soy sauce*
- 1 *teaspoon hoisin sauce*
- 1 *teaspoon black bean sauce*
- 6 *drops Oriental sesame oil*

1 tablespoon finely minced
   garlic
1 teaspoon finely minced
   ginger root
2 fish steaks or fillets (6 to 8
   ounces each)

2 dried shiitake mushrooms,
   soaked in warm water 30
   minutes to soften, drained,
   stemmed, and cut into slivers
3 green onions with tops,
   slivered

Combine soy sauce, hoisin sauce, black bean sauce, sesame oil, garlic, and ginger root. Rub on both sides of fish steaks and place steaks in a shallow dish. Arrange mushrooms and green onions on top.

Set dish on a rack over boiling water, cover pot, and steam 10 minutes, or until fish tests done.

Miso Fish Steaks or Fillets

Either white or red miso may be used for this Japanese-inspired fish. Serve on a bed of shredded daikon and garnish with carrot curls.

SERVES 4

¼   cup miso
1½ teaspoons sugar
1½ teaspoons sake or dry
    white wine

4 fish steaks or fillets (6 to 8
   ounces each)

With the back of a wooden spoon press miso through a ¼-inch-mesh sieve into a small mixing bowl. Stir in sugar and sake and mix well. Place fish steaks on a platter and spread each steak with one-fourth of the miso mixture.

Set platter on rack over boiling water, cover pot, and steam 10 minutes, or until fish tests done.

Fish Steaks or Fillets with Japanese Spices

SERVES 4

4 fish steaks or fillets (6 to 8
   ounces each)
2 tablespoons sake

2 tablespoons soy sauce
2 tablespoons water
1 teaspoon sugar

| ¹/₂ | teaspoon minced ginger root | ¹/₂ | teaspoon shichimi, or to |
| ¹/₂ | teaspoon minced garlic | | taste |

Arrange fish steaks on a platter. Combine sake, soy sauce, water, sugar, ginger root, and garlic. Pour over fish and sprinkle shichimi over all.

Set platter on rack over boiling water, cover pot, and steam 10 minutes, or until fish tests done.

Southeast Asian Fish Steaks or Fillets with Papaya

The bright yellow-orange color of fresh papaya, wispy slivers of ginger root, and pink bits of dried shrimp make this tropical dish a spectacular sight. To accompany the fish, toss together bean sprouts and finely shredded carrot and cabbage; dress with white vinegar seasoned with a pinch each of sugar and chile powder. Pass a large bowl of white rice.

The papaya topping increases what would be the normal cooking time for these fish steaks.

SERVES 4

4	fish steaks, at least 1 inch thick (6 to 8 ounces each)	8	dried shrimp, soaked in warm water 15 minutes to soften, drained, and minced
1	medium-ripe papaya, peeled, seeded, and sliced crosswise ¹/₃-inch thick	1	small green hot chile pepper, finely minced
1¹/₂	tablespoons soy sauce	1	tablespoon fresh lemon juice
3	slices ginger root, cut into very thin strips	1¹/₂	teaspoons peanut oil
2	green onions with tops, minced	3	to 4 large garlic cloves, finely minced
¹/₂	to 1 teaspoon finely minced garlic		

Place fish steaks on a platter and arrange papaya slices on top. Pour soy sauce over and then strew with ginger root, onions, garlic, shrimp, and chile pepper. Drizzle with lemon juice.

Set platter on rack over boiling water, cover pot, and steam 15 minutes, or until fish tests done.

While fish is steaming, heat peanut oil in a small skillet. Add garlic and cook until it turns a deep golden color. Just before serving the fish, scatter the hot garlic mixture over the top.

Burmese Fish Packets

You will need to purchase bamboo or banana leaves to prepare this dish. Bamboo leaves, which are about 16 inches long and 3½ to 4 inches wide at the midpoint, are usually easier to locate. They are imported from Taiwan in 1-pound bundles and can be found in most markets that carry Southeast Asian and Chinese foodstuffs. Each package contains about 60 leaves. Banana leaves, because of their large size, are most often sold in sections. (Aluminum foil may be substituted for the leaves, but the flavor and texture of the fish will not be as good.)

To serve the fish packets, remove them from the steamer to individual serving plates, clip the twine, and open the packets up on the plates. The leaves make an attractive backdrop for the turmeric-colored seasoning mixture atop the white fish fillets. Accompany with glutinous rice and steamed long beans.

SERVES 6

12 bamboo leaves	¼ teaspoon Asian chili powder (see Note)
1 ounce bean thread noodles	
½ medium onion, cut into chunks	¼ teaspoon salt
4 large garlic cloves, chopped	¼ teaspoon freshly ground black pepper
2 large slices ginger root, chopped	1 teaspoon fish sauce
⅔ cup unsweetened dried (desiccated) coconut	2 teaspoons fresh lime or lemon juice
⅓ cup hot water	2 tablespoons sesame seeds, lightly toasted
¼ teaspoon ground turmeric	6 fish fillets (approximately 6 ounces each)

Place the bamboo leaves in a large shallow dish or pan and pour in hot water to cover; set aside. In a saucepan, soak bean threads in hot water to cover for 1 minute, or until flexible. Drain off water and cut bean threads with scissors into 2-inch lengths to measure ¾ cup. Return bean threads to saucepan and add water to cover by 1 inch. Bring to a boil, reduce heat, and simmer 2 minutes, or until noodles are transparent. Remove from heat, drain, and set aside.

In a blender or food processor fitted with metal blade combine onion, garlic, ginger root, and coconut and process until very finely minced and well blended. Add hot water and blend briefly to combine. Turn mixture into a mixing bowl and with a fork stir in turmeric, chili powder, salt, pepper, fish sauce, lemon juice, and sesame seeds. Mix in reserved bean thread noodles; taste and adjust seasonings. Set mixture aside.

Remove the bamboo leaves from the water and shake excess water off. Place the leaves rib side up on a flat work surface. You will need to use 2 leaves to make a packet wide enough to enclose the fish and topping. Place two leaves side by side, one with the stem end on the right, the other with the stem end on the left so they are pointing in opposite directions. The leaves should overlap by about 2 inches in the center.

Place a fish fillet in the center of each pair of leaves. If the fillet is very thin at one end, fold the end under to even out the thickness. Divide the coconut mixture evenly among the packets, spreading it over the fish fillets. Bring one end of the wrapper up and over to cover the fish. Fold in the wrapper sides and then bring the remaining uncovered wrapper end over the top to form a closed packet. Secure each packet with kitchen twine.

Arrange the packets directly on a rack over boiling water, cover pot, and steam 20 minutes.

Note: The most commonly available chili powder is a Mexican blend, but here the Asian-style powder, which does not have a strong cumin flavor, should be used. Asian chili powder can be found in Oriental markets. If unavailable, substitute any spice-shelf chili powder, such as Schilling's, or cayenne pepper.

Sicilian Fish Stew to Accompany Couscous

In Sicily this dish is called *cuscusu,* where it is the specialty of the port city of Trapani. Centuries ago, the Arabs brought their meat stews, called *couscous,* to this Mediterranean island, and the Sicilians quickly adapted the dish to locally available foods, developing a fish version.

You will need to refer to the directions on how to steam couscous (see Vegetables and Grains) to prepare this dish. Any firm fish steaks or fillets can be used for the stew. If possible, combine a slightly oily fish, such as tuna or mackerel, with a nonoily one, perhaps haddock, cod, turbot, or flounder. I prefer steaks, as they are thicker than fillets and not as likely to overcook.

Unlike Moroccan lamb stew, which is started in a Dutch oven and finished in the *couscousière,* this fish stew, which cooks quickly, can be prepared from beginning to end in the *couscousière* during the final steaming of the semolina. If you have improvised a *couscousière* by putting a colander inside a pot, or if you have any qualms about cooking in aluminum (see Steaming Techniques), you will need to prepare this dish in a separate saucepan.

Some Sicilian recipes call for flavoring the grains as they steam with spices, such as saffron, cinnamon, or nutmeg, or with minced garlic and onion. I prefer the couscous unseasoned so that it can act as a counterpoint to the richness of the fish mixture. Follow this Trapani specialty with a simple green salad.

SERVES 4

1 medium onion, minced	2 medium-size ripe tomatoes, chopped
3 large garlic cloves, minced	
3 tablespoons olive oil	1/2 teaspoon salt
2 pounds fish steaks or fillets	1/2 teaspoon freshly ground black pepper
6 fresh basil leaves, chopped, or 1 tablespoon chopped fresh oregano	6 cups fish stock, or equal parts bottled clam juice and water
2 tablespoons chopped fresh parsley	1 cup dry white wine

In the bottom pan of a *couscousière* sauté the onion and garlic in oil until the onion is soft. Arrange the fish steaks on top of the onion mixture and strew with basil and parsley. Distribute tomatoes over fish and sprinkle with salt and pepper. Pour in fish stock and wine, being careful not to disturb the layers.

Bring fish mixture to a boil and, following directions for couscous, complete the final steaming of the grains while the stew cooks.

Remove the couscous from the top pan and toss with the oil and butter as directed. To serve, transfer the couscous to a soup tureen or deep bowl and make a well in the center. Spoon a portion of the fish stew into the well and serve the remainder on the side. Alternatively, serve the grain and the fish stew in separate large bowls. Provide each diner with a shallow soup bowl.

Shellfish

Shellfish demands the same high standards of freshness as fish. Shop for shellfish at a reliable market and eat it as promptly as possible after purchase.

Shrimp, scallops, mussels, and clams lend themselves to steaming. One generally thinks of squid, a high-protein mollusk, as a candidate for sautéing or deep frying, but it steams surprisingly well.

Crabs and lobsters, which should always be purchased live, may be steamed. I prefer, however, to cook them by immersing them in boiling water, and in the case of lobsters, broiling them. To my taste, oysters should be eaten raw or broiled. If you wish to steam any of these, they can be placed over the steaming liquid on a plate or directly on a rack. The lobster and crab may be disjointed before steaming; the oysters can be easily opened once they are cooked.

Specific directions for readying shrimp, scallops, mussels, clams, and squid for steaming appear in the following pages. Included with each set of instructions are some marvelous recipes. For the shrimp I have concentrated on exotic dipping sauces. Delicate scallops are served three ways: with fresh tomatoes, tangy sorrel, or sake and ham. Each of the two recipes for mussels and clams has a distinctive blend of herbs and spices, one South Asian and one European. Finally, and best of all, there is stuffed squid that is so good it will disappear within moments of serving.

SHRIMP

Basic Instructions for Readying Shrimp: It is difficult to purchase truly fresh shrimp, for almost all shrimp are delivered to markets fast-frozen. Avoid buying the preshelled shrimp, for they lack flavor and their texture is often rubbery. Avoid, too, those sales advertising a low, low price per pound; once defrosted, you may find you have only 12 ounces or so of shrimp—and the market will not make up the difference. Make sure any shrimp you purchase are at least partially defrosted and that loose ice isn't weighed along with them.

One pound of shrimp (2½ to 3 inches long) contains approximately 28, which will serve 2 or 3 persons for a main course, or 5 or 6 persons as an appetizer course.

To Ready Shrimp for Steaming: Shrimp may be steamed in the shell, or they may be shelled and deveined and then steamed. Some cuisines, such as the Chinese, steam them in the shell because they believe it holds in the natural flavor. In this case, cut a slit along the rounded back of each unshelled shrimp with small sharp scissors and pull out and discard the vein. Rinse under cold water, place in a colander to drain, and pat dry with paper toweling. If shelling, pull off the shell with your fingers, being careful not to take the tail with the shell. With a small knife, slit the back and pull out the vein. Rinse, drain, and pat dry.

To Steam Shrimp: Use a steamer large enough so the shrimp can be steamed directly on the rack in a single layer. They may be steamed over beer, white wine, or water flavored with salt, bay leaves, fresh herbs, and/or fresh lemon or lime juice.

Depending on their size, shrimp will cook in 2 to 4 minutes. When they take on a pink color, they are ready; do not overcook them or they will toughen. To serve the shrimp cold, immediately plunge them in ice water to retard further cooking. Drain and refrigerate until serving time.

To Serve Steamed Shrimp: All the following dipping sauces are good with either shelled or unshelled shrimp. Each recipe is sufficient for serving with one pound of the shellfish. *Salsa Verde* (see *Bollito Misto*), *Nuoc Cham* (see Vietnamese Eggs with Crab), or any of the Mayonnaises are also appropriate accompaniments.

Mound the shrimp on an attractive serving plate and top with a colorful complementary garnish, such as parsley, watercress, or coriander sprigs, and lemon wedges. Provide each diner with a small portion of dipping sauce. If serving shrimp in the shell, set out lots of paper napkins and pass finger bowls at meal's end.

Chinese Dipping Sauces

Soy-Ginger Sauce

MAKES APPROXIMATELY ⅔ CUP

2 *tablespoons dark soy sauce*	3 *slices ginger root, finely*
3 *tablespoons light soy sauce*	*shredded*
2 *green onions, finely slivered*	¼ *cup peanut oil*

Combine all ingredients and let stand for 30 minutes before serving.

Soy-Chile Sauce

MAKES APPROXIMATELY ⅓ CUP

¼ *cup light soy sauce*	*rings halved; seeded, if*
1 *fresh hot green chile pepper,*	*desired*
sliced in thin rings, then	1 *tablespoon peanut oil*

In a small heatproof bowl combine soy sauce and chile pepper. In a small saucepan heat oil until smoking and pour into soy sauce and pepper mixture. Stir a few times before serving.

Garlic-Vinegar Sauce

MAKES APPROXIMATELY ¼ CUP

2　*large garlic cloves, finely minced*

¼　cup white rice vinegar

Combine garlic and vinegar and let stand 1 hour before serving.

Japanese Miso Sauce

MAKES APPROXIMATELY ¾ CUP

½　cup red or white miso
¼　cup distilled white vinegar

2　*tablespoons sugar*
¼　cup dashi, or as needed

With the back of a wooden spoon, press miso through a ¼-inch-mesh strainer into a small saucepan. Gradually stir in vinegar, sugar, and dashi until well mixed. Place pan over medium heat and, stirring constantly, heat until sugar dissolves and sauce is smooth. Add more dashi if a thinner sauce is desired. Serve at room temperature.

Caribbean Spicy Sauce

MAKES APPROXIMATELY 1 CUP

½　cup homemade or bottled chili sauce
½　cup homemade mayonnaise
3　*tablespoons finely grated onion*
2　*tablespoons fresh lime or lemon juice*

1　*tablespoon minced fresh parsley*
½　teaspoon Worcestershire sauce
¼　teaspoon salt
¼　teaspoon freshly ground black pepper
Hot pepper sauce

Combine all ingredients except hot pepper sauce and mix well. Taste and adjust seasonings. Add pepper sauce for desired heat.

Gorgonzola Shrimp

A perfect before- or after-theater dish. Serve over fluffy white or brown rice with a crisp spinach salad dressed with Herb Vinaigrette.

SERVES 4

1 pound shrimp	½ cup crumbled Gorgonzola
¼ cup dry white wine	cheese
1 tablespoon unsalted butter	Freshly ground black pepper
2 tablespoons finely minced	¼ cup minced fresh chives
shallots	

Following Basic Instructions for Shrimp, shell and devein shrimp. Bring the steaming liquid of choice almost to the boiling point.

In a skillet large enough to hold all the shrimp, combine the wine, butter, and shallots. Place over medium-high heat, cover, and bring to a boil. Lower heat and simmer for 2 minutes. Keep warm.

Steam the shrimp as directed and immediately add to the skillet containing the wine mixture. With 2 forks, quickly toss in the cheese. Immediately remove from the heat and spoon shrimp mixture over rice. Grind pepper over and top with chives.

SCALLOPS

Basic Instructions for Scallops: It is easy to sauté scallops in butter with shallots or other seasonings, but the sautéing process draws out juices, thus toughening the scallops and diluting the sauce. The solution to this dilemma is to steam the scallops. Have ready the sauce in which they will be briefly reheated, as well as the garnishes and accompaniments, and you will have mastered the perfectly cooked scallop.

One pound of sea scallops (an inch to an inch and a half in diameter) contains approximately 22, while a pound of bay scallops (about ½ inch in diameter) numbers about 50. I prefer sea scallops because of their size; the tiny scallops are easy to overcook and they don't have the same firm texture as the larger ones. The taste of the two, however, is similar and often the bay scallops are more reasonably priced. Use them in the following recipes if you wish, but be careful not to overcook.

In most parts of the country, scallops are only available frozen, so patronize a fish market that stores them properly.

To Ready Scallops for Steaming: If scallops are frozen, defrost them in the refrigerator. Marinate the thawed scallops no more than 10 minutes in fresh lemon or lime juice, drain, and pat dry with paper toweling.

To Steam Scallops: Steam scallops in a single layer directly on a rack over boiling liquid. (See Basic Instructions for Shrimp for steaming-liquid suggestions.) Scallops cook quickly, usually in 1 to 3 minutes depending upon their size. Watch carefully, for overcooking will toughen them and destroy their flavor. To test for doneness, cut a scallop in half. If it has turned almost completely opaque, it is time to remove the rest of the scallops from the steamer, for they will cook a little more in the sauce.

If planning to serve the scallops cold, steam them until they are completely opaque, then promptly immerse in ice water. Drain thoroughly and refrigerate. A few minutes before serving, toss scallops with slivered green onions (with tops), minced fresh parsley, slivered sun-dried tomatoes, chopped drained pimiento or roasted pepper, crisp garden peas or snow peas, thinly sliced raw mushrooms, and Lemon/Lime Vinaigrette.

Scallops with Sorrel Sauce

A mound of brown rice on a heated platter makes a perfect bed for this memorable scallop dish, masked with lemony Sorrel Sauce. Surround the rice with sliced cooked carrots sprinkled with minced fresh parsley. Tuck in lemon wedges at the edges.

SERVES 4

1 pound sea scallops

Sorrel Sauce (see Basic Savory Sauces)

Following Basic Instructions for Scallops, ready scallops for steaming. Make the Sorrel Sauce and keep warm. Steam the scallops as directed. Present scallops and sauce as suggested above.

Scallops with Uncooked Tomato Sauce

These tomato-sauced scallops can be the heart of a tasty pasta supper. Prepare fresh fettuccine at the same time you are steaming the scallops. Arrange the noodles on a heated serving platter, top with the scallops, and pour the tomato sauce over. Sprinkle generously with minced fresh Italian parsley.

At this point, a green salad and crusty French bread should already be on the table and your guests should be in their places.

SERVES 4

1 recipe Uncooked Tomato Sauce (see Basic Savory Sauces)	2 tablespoons dry white wine, or to taste
1 teaspoon tomato paste, or to taste	1 tablespoon butter
	1 pound sea scallops
	Minced fresh parsley

Following Basic Instructions for Scallops, ready scallops for steaming. In a large skillet, heat the tomato sauce and blend in tomato paste, wine, and butter. Adjust seasonings to taste and keep warm.

Steam the scallops and arrange in a heated shallow serving dish. Spoon the tomato sauce over the top and garnish with parsley. Alternatively, present scallops and sauce with fettuccine as suggested above.

Scallops with Sake and Ham

Ham and scallops have a natural affinity, and they are especially good with Japanese seasonings. For a meal that combines the flavors of East and West, serve a fresh mushroom and spinach salad and nutty brown rice tossed with lightly toasted sesame seeds.

SERVES 4

3 tablespoons sake	3 tablespoons minced green onion
2 to 3 slices ginger root, finely minced	
1 large garlic clove, minced	1 pound sea scallops
	½ cup shredded cooked ham

Following Basic Instructions for Scallops, ready scallops for steaming. Combine sake, ginger root, garlic, and onion. Place scallops in a shallow dish and strew ham over. Pour sake mixture evenly over scallops and ham, set dish on rack over boiling water, cover pot, and steam 5 minutes, or until scallops are just done. Serve directly from the dish, spooning juices over the scallops.

MUSSELS AND CLAMS

Basic Instructions for Mussels and Clams: Blue mussels from the East Coast and Europe are shipped all over the country. Those gathered on the West Coast, which are also blue, are considered by most gourmets as too large and too strong in flavor, but they are eaten in some areas. There are about 20 blue mussels in a pound; plan on about a pound per person for a main dish, half a pound for an appetizer serving. Large green mussels from New Zealand, with perhaps only 6 to 8 per pound, have recently become available in select fish markets. The good-sized meats have a flavor and texture similar to conventional mussels. They can be used in the following recipes, but steaming time may need to be increased slightly.

Only the small hard-shell clams, such as cherrystones and littlenecks, are suitable for steaming in the shell; they are available on both coasts. (Larger clams must be gutted before cooking.) Depending on their size and the weight of the shell, clams number from 9 to 15 per pound. Purchase about 1½ pounds per person for a main dish, half that or less for an appetizer.

To Ready Mussels and Clams for Steaming: The "beard," the black threads attached at the hinge of the mussel shell, must be removed and discarded. With the help of a screwdriver, twist and pull the beard off. Also discard any cracked mussels or those that are open and do not reclose when gently tapped. With a stiff-bristled brush, scrub the mussels under cold running water.

Transfer the mussels to a large vessel and add cold water to cover. Let stand for an hour or two; the mussels will eject the sand trapped in their shells. Some cooks recommend adding a handful of cornmeal to aid this cleansing process. Drain the mussels and rinse under running cold water.

Clams are readied for steaming in the same manner as mussels, but there is no beard to remove.

To Steam Mussels and Clams: If you have a clam steamer, simply put the mollusks in the basket and steam them over boiling liquid. In the absence of a specially designed steamer, place them on a low rack above the liquid. Steam for 7 to 8 minutes, or until the shells open. Discard any unopened shells.

The steaming liquid should be bottled clam broth, wine, and/or fish stock to which herbs and spices have been added. Serve the liquid with the shellfish as a dipping sauce. French bread is a must for sopping up the delicious broth.

South Asian Mussels

Serve guests white rice in shallow bowls. Let them spoon the flavorful steaming mixture over the rice with the mussels. Pass a platter of ripe mango slices.

SERVES 4

4   pounds mussels
1   cup minced onion
4   large garlic cloves, minced
3   slices ginger root, finely
    minced
1   tablespoon butter
1   tablespoon peanut oil

1   teaspoon dried red pepper
    flakes
1/2 teaspoon ground turmeric
1/2 teaspoon ground cumin
1/2 teaspoon salt
3   or 4 coriander sprigs
1   cup bottled clam juice

Following Basic Instructions for Mussels and Clams, ready mussels for steaming. In a clam or equivalent steamer, sauté onion, garlic, and ginger in butter and oil until onion softens. Add red pepper flakes, turmeric, cumin, and salt and cook, stirring, 2 minutes. Add coriander sprigs and clam juice and bring to a boil.

Add the mussels to the steamer and steam until they open. Serve at once.

Garlicky Clams

Serve the clams and steaming broth in deep bowls with forks and spoons. For extra flavor, accompany with minced garlic lightly browned in butter. Don't forget the French bread!

SERVES 2

2 1/2 to 3 pounds clams
  1/2 cup dry white wine or dry
      vermouth
  1/2 cup fish stock or bottled
      clam juice

2   tablespoons butter, cut up,
    at room temperature
6   large garlic cloves, lightly
    bruised and peeled
3   parsley sprigs

Following Basic Instructions for Mussels and Clams, ready clams for steaming. In a clam or equivalent steamer, combine wine, clam juice, butter, garlic, and parsley. Bring to a boil.

Add the clams to the steamer and steam until they open. Serve at once.

SQUID

Basic Instructions for Squid (Calamari): Squid is popular in the Orient and in the countries surrounding the Mediterranean, where it sometimes goes directly from the sea to the stove. It is almost impossible to find truly fresh squid in the United States, so feel very lucky if you do.

Select squid that are about 6 inches long. The cleaning procedure may sound difficult, but it becomes quite easy once you have done it a few times. And the reward of eating tender steamed squid is more than worth the trouble. One and one-half to 2 pounds will serve four persons.

To Ready Squid for Steaming: Rinse squid well in running cold water. Gently pull the head portion (the section that is topped by the tentacles) from the body; the innards and the ink sac will be attached to the base of it. Set this head portion aside on a cutting board. Pull the transparent cartilage from the body cavity and, with your index finger, remove and discard any loose "organs" and viscous material. Rinse the body well and set in a colander to drain.

With a sharp knife, cut a V shape between the eyes on the squid head to separate the tentacles from the rest of the head. Discard everything but the tentacles portion. (The black ink held in the ink sac is used in some recipes, but not in those given here.) If a small, round piece of cartilage is still attached to the base of the tentacles, remove and discard it. Rinse tentacles and place in colander to drain.

Unless the very thin, gray-pink skin has started to peel off the squid body, giving it a mottled and unattractive look, there is no need to remove it. It is what gives the steamed squid its beautiful purplish color.

To Steam Squid: See individual recipes for directions on arranging stuffed and cut-up squid in steamer and steaming times. Be careful not to overcook, as the squid will toughen.

Squid Stuffed with Swiss Chard and Parmesan

These tender, perfectly cooked stuffed squid are so delicious they don't need a sauce. They can be served hot or chilled, but it is unlikely that any will be left over. This scrumptious recipe is guaranteed to convert those who usually find squid to be a rubbery disappointment.

Even though there is Swiss chard in the stuffing, a side dish of this green adds just the right texture and color. Risotto made with fish stock and extra Parmesan completes this very special meal.

SERVES 4

12 6-inch squid
    (approximately 1½
    pounds)
⅓ cup finely minced onion
3 large garlic cloves, finely
    minced
2 tablespoons olive oil
1 cup finely chopped fresh
    Swiss chard or spinach
¾ cup fine fresh breadcrumbs

¼ cup freshly grated Parmesan
    cheese
3 tablespoons minced fresh
    Italian parsley
2 teaspoons fresh lemon juice,
    or to taste
    Herb seasoning and freshly
    ground black pepper to
    taste

Following Basic Instructions for Squid, ready the squid, then pat dry with paper toweling.

In a covered nonstick skillet, cook onion and garlic in olive oil for 3 minutes, or until onion is soft. Add Swiss chard and cook just until wilted. Remove from heat, cool slightly and, with a fork, toss in breadcrumbs, Parmesan cheese, parsley, lemon juice, and seasonings. Taste and adjust seasonings.

Using 2½ to 3 tablespoons for each, stuff squid bodies with bread mixture. Push stuffing down into the base of the body cavity; leave just enough room at the open end to pinch it closed and secure with a toothpick.

Arrange stuffed bodies (reserve tentacles) ½ inch apart on rack over boiling water, cover pot, and steam 2 minutes. Tuck tentacles around the bodies and steam an additional 2 minutes. Immediately remove squid from steamer to heated platter to prevent overcooking.

Squid Rings

Following Basic Instructions for Squid, ready the squid and then pat dry with paper toweling. Slice the bodies crosswise into ¾-inch-thick rings and leave the tentacles whole. Arrange the rings and tentacles in a single layer on a rack over boiling water, cover pot, and steam about 2 minutes. (Test by eating one ring.) Promptly remove from the steamer to prevent overcooking.

To serve squid hot, toss into Fresh Tomato Sauce; Oyster Sauce; Sorrel Sauce; or Lemon/Lime, Garlic/Shallot, or Anchovy Butter Sauce. Or serve with a side dish of one of the Pesto sauces or Salsa Verde (see *Bollito Misto*).

To serve squid cold, moisten with a little oil and then refrigerate. Several hours before planning to serve, toss with any of the Vinaigrettes. Just before serving, toss again with chopped ripe tomato, slivered black olives, and minced fresh herbs of your choice. Alternatively, dress with Oriental Dressing and garnish with coriander sprigs.

MEATS AND POULTRY

Meat-stuffed Whole
  Cabbage

Cabbage Rolls

Chinese Pork and Ham
  with Dried Mushrooms

Mexican Tamales

Bollito Misto

Veal Birds

Chinese One-Pot Rice
  Dishes

Classic Meatballs

Cornmeal with Ground
  Beef and Green
  Peppers

Beef Roll with Peppers,
  Olives, and Eggs

Rouladen (German Beef
  Rolls)

Korean Beef Ribs

Brisket of Corned Beef
  with Horseradish Sauce

Lamb Shanks in Red
  Wine

Mustard Lamb Shanks

Citrus Lamb Shanks with
  Mint

Lamb with Brown Lentils

Greek-style Lamb Blocks

Curried Lamb Ribs

Moroccan Lamb Stew to
  Accompany Couscous

Cumin Lamb Balls

Cantonese Pork with
  Duck Egg

Pork Chops with Sage

Pork Chops with Prunes

Sausage Dinner

Pork Spareribs in Hoisin
  Sauce

Pork Loin with Bourbon
  Sauce

Chinese Pork and Tofu
  Balls

Ham Loaf with Walnuts

Ham Hocks in Red Wine

Brandied Ham Steak

Osso Buco

Herbed Veal with Mushrooms

Calves' Liver with Onions

Mustard Rabbit

Rabbit Agrodolce

Rabbit Liver, Kidneys, and Heart with White Wine and Bay Leaves

Basic Herb Chicken

Mexican-style Chicken

South American-style Chicken

Italian-style Chicken

Hungarian-style Chicken

French-style Chicken

Swiss-style Chicken

Mideast-style Chicken

Moroccan-style Chicken

Japanese-style Chicken

Cantonese-style Chicken

Thai-style Chicken

Lemony Chicken

Oriental Whole Chicken

Chicken Livers Marsala

Cornish Hen with Cranberries

Crunchy Ground Turkey Loaf

Duckling Stock

Duckling with Port Wine Sauce

Whole Duckling with Cabbage-Chestnut Stuffing

Meats and Poultry

Meats

In a survey of household chefs, steaming would probably rank low on the list of ways to prepare meats. Sadly, this conventional wisdom eliminates a truly marvelous method of cooking what is usually the centerpiece of the meal.

When meats are roasted, the seasonings—fresh herbs, garlic, onion—dry out in the oven. With steaming, though, these same ingredients stay moist, so that their flavors continue to permeate the meat during cooking—a wonderful discovery! And when vegetables are steamed in the same dish, they absorb the essences of both the seasonings and the meat itself.

Contrary to what many people think, meats do not shrivel and toughen as they are steamed. In fact, they retain their natural juices better than when they are fried, roasted, or braised. And steamed meats sometimes cook even more quickly than braised or roasted ones. Eliminating the browning process necessary in most other methods saves an extra step and makes cleanup easier.

You need not give up using your favorite barbecue marinade when switching from the grill to the steamer. Marinate the meats as you would for barbecuing, but steam them instead. The only marinades that are not suitable are those made with yoghurt or other milk products, as they may curdle.

If you want to cook meat on the grill but would like to eliminate some of the fat that cannot be trimmed, steam the meat before you put it on the barbecue. Place it on a rack over boiling water, cover the pot, and steam for 5 to 10 minutes for sausages, 20 minutes for small cuts such as individual spareribs, 30 minutes for beef short ribs, and 40 minutes for a rack of pork ribs.

In general, the cheaper cuts of meat are better for steaming than the more expensive ones. In my experience, leg of lamb pieces tend to toughen, while shanks and stew meat steam beautifully. A steamer is no place for a filet mignon, but a brisket takes to it very well. The following recipes use a wide range of cuts. Not every cut of every meat appears, but from the examples provided you will be able to adapt your favorite cuts to these preparations.

Meat-stuffed Whole Cabbage

This spectacular one-dish meal, adapted from the traditional braised French *chou farci*, retains its classic flavors when steamed. It may be assembled in the morning and refrigerated until it is to be cooked for dinner. Serve with lots of French bread to dip into the juices.

SERVES 6

1 Savoy cabbage, approximately 2½ pounds Rich chicken, beef, or pork stock as needed	2 teaspoons cornstarch 2 teaspoons dry mustard ½ teaspoon salt
1 bay leaf	½ teaspoon freshly ground black pepper
1 pound very lean ground pork or pork sausage meat	6 turnips, lightly pared and halved if very large
1 pound ground veal	6 medium carrots, halved crosswise
¾ cup coarsely ground cooked ham	3 thyme sprigs
½ medium onion, finely diced	Minced fresh parsley
4 garlic cloves, minced	

Pull any wilted or discolored outer leaves from cabbage and discard; rinse head well. Pour enough stock into a large steamer (with rack in place) to reach just under top of rack; bring stock to a boil. Add bay leaf to stock and stand cabbage on rack. Cover steamer and steam 5 minutes, or until cabbage is limp.

Remove cabbage and set aside on cooling rack. If any of the outer leaves detach themselves from the head during the steaming, continue steaming those leaves until tender and reserve for soup (see Leftover Stuffed Cabbage Soup with this recipe).

Combine meats, onion, garlic, cornstarch, and seasonings. Place a teaspoon-size portion in a small dish. Set dish on rack over boiling stock, cover pot, and steam 5 minutes. Taste and adjust seasonings.

Starting at center of cabbage head and working outward, stuff 2 to 3 tablespoons of the meat mixture near the base of each row of leaves; do not stuff the final 3 or 4 leaves. If stuffing remains, add more between each row. Re-form cabbage into original shape by gently pressing the leaves with your hands. With kitchen twine, tie the head so that it will hold its shape as it cooks.

Place the cabbage head on a large square of doubled cheesecloth. Bring opposite corners of square up and around cabbage and tie corners in a knot at the top. Repeat with the other 2 corners.

Place cabbage directly on center of rack. Arrange whole turnips and carrots around cabbage. Top cabbage with thyme sprigs. Add more stock to steamer to return the liquid to its original level. Cover steamer and bring stock to a boil. Steam, adding more stock as needed, 20 to 25 minutes, or until cabbage center is tender when pierced with a cake tester or fork and vegetables are just cooked. (If turnips and carrots are young and cook faster than the cabbage, remove with tongs and keep warm until serving time.)

Lift cabbage from steamer; unwrap and remove cheesecloth. Place cabbage in center of a heated large, deep platter and surround with vegetables. Cut string and discard. Pour about 1 cup of the steaming juices over cabbage and vegetables and liberally sprinkle parsley over all. Cut cabbage into wedges and serve in warmed deep plates or large shallow soup bowls. If desired, pass remaining steaming juices.

Leftover Stuffed Cabbage Soup: Remove the meat from the cabbage and place the meat and cabbage in separate bowls. Add any leftover carrots and turnips and any reserved outer cabbage leaves to bowl with cabbage. Cover the bowls and refrigerate overnight. The next day, put all of the vegetables and steaming juices into a processor or blender and puree. Heat and thin with stock, milk, or half-and-half to soup consistency. Crumble any reserved meat into soup, season to taste, and reheat. Serve with French bread croutons.

Cabbage Rolls

Stuffed cabbage leaves are found around the world. Basic instructions for preparing the rolls are followed by three delicious filling recipes: the first is a classic beef mixture, the second a South African-inspired curried lamb, and the third, a Hungarian pork and caraway blend. Mashed potatoes or steamed new potatoes go well with any of the three.

For six servings, select a firm round red or white cabbage weighing 2½ to 3 pounds. Remove and discard any discolored leaves and cut out the core. Rinse cored cabbage and place on a rack over boiling water. Cover pot and steam 5 minutes, or until first outside leaf is limp and can be removed with tongs or lifted off with fingers. Place leaf flat, with rib side down, on work surface and continue removing leaves until you have 12.

Carefully cut out thickest part of rib along base of each leaf. Place about 2 to 2½ tablespoons filling on each stem end, roll one turn, tuck in sides, and continue to roll jelly-roll fashion. Place rolls seam side down on work surface or baking sheet.

Shred enough of the remaining cabbage head to measure approximately 2 cups; reserve rest of cabbage for another meal. Cover bottom of a shallow dish with a thin layer of shredded cabbage and sprinkle lightly with seasonings given with each filling recipe. Arrange cabbage rolls in a spoke pattern on the cabbage bed. Strew 1 to 2 garlic cloves, finely minced, over the dish and drizzle rolls with a little olive oil.

Place dish on rack over boiling water, cover pot, and steam 15 to 20 minutes, or until rolls are tender and shredded cabbage is cooked. Serve with suggested sauce.

Beef and Rice Filling for Cabbage Rolls

1 recipe *Classic Meatballs*	*Herb seasoning*
½ teaspoon *crumbled dried thyme*	*Basic Tomato Sauce (see Basic Savory Sauces)*
Freshly ground black pepper	

Prepare mixture for meatballs, but do not form into balls. Following directions for Cabbage Rolls, fill cabbage leaves, sprinkle cabbage bed with seasonings, arrange rolls on top, and add minced garlic and olive oil. Steam as directed. Pass Tomato Sauce separately.

South African Lamb Filling for Cabbage Rolls

The presence of a sizable East Indian population in South Africa has influenced the local cuisine—thus the use of curry powder in this filling.

1 *onion, minced*	1 *egg*
1 *tablespoon sunflower oil*	½ *teaspoon salt*
1 *teaspoon curry powder, or to taste*	½ *teaspoon freshly ground black pepper*
1 *pound lean ground lamb or beef*	¼ *teaspoon ground coriander*
1 *slice white bread, soaked in water, then squeezed dry*	*Additional salt and freshly ground black pepper*

> *Curry Sauce (see Basic*
> *Savory Sauces)*
> *Condiments: shredded*
> *coconut, chutney, cubed*
> *bananas and apples rubbed*

> *with lemon juice, lightly*
> *toasted chopped raw*
> *peanuts, slivered green*
> *onions*

In a covered nonstick skillet cook onion in oil until softened. Sprinkle with curry powder; cook and stir 2 minutes. Add lamb, bread, egg, salt, pepper, and coriander and mix well. Place a teaspoon-size portion in a shallow dish, set on rack over boiling water, cover pot, and steam 5 minutes. Taste and adjust seasonings.

Following directions for Cabbage Rolls, fill cabbage leaves, sprinkle cabbage bed lightly with salt and pepper, arrange rolls on top, and add minced garlic and olive oil. Steam as directed. Pass the Curry Sauce and serve with the condiments in small bowls.

Hungarian Pork Filling for Cabbage Rolls

1   *medium onion, minced*
1   *small green or red bell*
    pepper, seeded and diced
1   *large garlic clove, minced*
2   *tablespoons bacon drippings*
    or rendered pork fat
1   *teaspoon Hungarian paprika*
1/2   *teaspoon salt*

1/4   *teaspoon freshly ground*
    black pepper
2   *cups finely shredded cooked*
    pork roast
2   *tablespoons tomato puree*
1/2   *to 1 teaspoon caraway seeds*
    Additional salt and freshly
    ground black pepper
    Sour cream

In a covered nonstick skillet cook onion, bell pepper, and garlic in bacon drippings until onion is soft. Sprinkle with paprika, salt, and pepper. Cook and stir 2 minutes, then toss in pork, tomato puree, and caraway seeds. Stirring with a fork, cook 3 minutes to blend flavors. Taste and adjust seasonings.

Following directions for Cabbage Rolls, fill cabbage leaves, sprinkle cabbage bed lightly with salt and pepper, arrange rolls on top, and add minced garlic and olive oil. Steam as directed. Pass a bowl of sour cream.

Chinese Pork and Ham with Dried Mushrooms

Serve this simple ground pork and ham dish with steamed white rice and long beans with Hoisin Dressing.

SERVES 4

³/₄ pound very lean ground
   pork
²/₃ cup coarsely ground cooked
   ham
1 tablespoon cornstarch
¹/₄ cup finely minced water
   chestnuts
¹/₂ cup minced green onions
   with tops
¹/₄ teaspoon salt, or to taste
¹/₄ teaspoon freshly ground
   black pepper, or to taste

2 teaspoons soy sauce
1 tablespoon Chinese rice wine
   or dry vermouth
4 dried shiitake mushrooms,
   soaked 30 minutes in warm
   water to soften, drained,
   stemmed, and slivered
2 teaspoons peanut oil
4 to 6 drops Oriental sesame
   oil (optional)

Thoroughly mix together meats, cornstarch, water chestnuts, green onions, salt, pepper, soy sauce, and wine. Pat into a shallow dish that is 9 inches in diameter and 2 inches deep; the mixture should be about 1 inch high. Form a slight indentation in the center. Arrange mushroom slivers on top of meat mixture and drizzle oils over.

Place dish on rack over boiling water, cover pot, and steam 25 minutes. Spoon meat and juices directly from the dish.

Mexican Tamales

Make a large number of these versatile, traditionally steamed Mexican packets. Once they are cooked, they can be easily reheated two or three days later or frozen for future use. The preparation time is considerable, so set aside a full morning. Read completely through the recipe before beginning.

The fresh masa used for preparing the tamale "dough" is a corn-based mixture that must be purchased where Mexican foodstuffs are sold. Packaged in plastic bags, it is a stiff, thick preparation for which there is no substitute. Ask for fresh masa for tamales; the fresh masa used to make corn tortillas will not work properly. Masa harina, the dried, more readily available base for making the tamale dough, is not recommended because its quality is inconsistent.

Corn husks (*hojas*) for wrapping tamales are available in Mexican markets and some supermarkets. An 8-ounce package contains approximately 16 husks. Each husk can be divided into three or four wrappers, depending upon its width. You will need two of these packages to prepare the following recipes. Any leftover husks will keep indefinitely in a cool, dry place. Soak the husks in warm water to cover for 30 minutes and then gently pull apart. Rinse well and return to water until ready to fill.

The use of lard is customary in Mexico, where cooks usually render their own pork fat. There is no good substitute for the lard used in tamales, so I suggest you do not attempt to use one.

The following fillings may look similar at first glance, but they actually taste quite different. Make one or more of them, or create your own with any shredded cooked meats or chopped vegetables, including potatoes. Accompany the tamales with refried beans topped with melted cheese and shredded lettuce dressed with oil and vinegar flavored with ground cumin.

MAKES APPROXIMATELY 70 TAMALES

5 *pounds fresh masa*	1½ *cups pork stock*
1 *teaspoon salt*	¾ *pound (2½ cups) lard*
1 *teaspoon baking soda*	

Place masa in a large bowl. With hands, work in salt and baking soda. Gradually work in stock until thoroughly mixed. Melt lard and add half of it to the masa mixture. Cool briefly and then work lard in with hands until it is well blended with the masa. Add half of the remaining lard, work it in, and repeat until almost all of the lard has been incorporated.

To test amount of lard needed for proper consistency, take a small portion of the masa mixture in one hand and pat it onto the palm of the other hand, forming a small patty. Remove patty from palm and if no masa adheres to the skin, enough lard has been added.

The masa mixture will keep well-covered and refrigerated 2 or 3 days, or frozen several weeks. Defrost in the refrigerator overnight and bring to room temperature before using.

To Fill Corn Husks and Steam the Tamales: Work with one wide husk wrapper at a time or, if narrow, overlap two lengthwise. Remove husk from soaking water and dry with paper toweling. Place husk in palm of one hand with the narrow tip faced away from you. With your other hand, place 3 or 4 tablespoons of the masa mixture on the broad end. Pat masa into a circle 4 or 5 inches in diameter to cover broad end of the husk. Leave a ½-inch border uncovered on the bottom 3 sides.

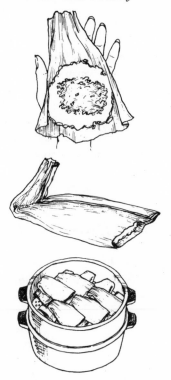

Place about 2 tablespoons of the filling in the center of the masa round and fold husk in half lengthwise so that side edges meet and the masa encloses the filling. To seal the packet, press side edges together and then fold these joined edges inward to form a ½-inch-wide lengthwise flap. Then fold the unfilled narrow end over to cover about ⅓ of the filled husk.

Place tamales folded side down on rack of steamer, arranging close together so that packets cannot come open. When steamer rack is completely covered, begin a second layer directly on top of the first, arranging the tamales close together crosswise to form a crosshatch pattern. A third layer may be added, but no more than that, or the layers will not cook evenly. To steam all of the tamales at one time, pack a second steamer tier in the same manner as the first, and reverse the tiers midway during steaming.

If you want to make all of the tamales but not steam them all at once, place those waiting to be steamed on a tray and cover with a lightly dampened tea towel to prevent them from drying out.

When ready to steam stacked tamales, cover the top layer with a double layer of soaked husks. Place rack over boiling water, cover steamer, and steam over rapidly boiling water 10 minutes. Reduce heat and continue steaming over gently boiling water 50 minutes. Check water level in steamer several times, adding more if needed to maintain original level.

Tamales are done when the masa is firm. To check for this, unwrap one of the tamales. They can be kept warm over warm water several hours if not eaten immediately.

Well wrapped, the steamed tamales may be refrigerated two or three days. To freeze, place on a baking sheet, freeze solid, wrap well, and store in freezer up to 1 month. To serve, remove freezer wrapping, place frozen tamales on rack over boiling water, and steam about 30 minutes.

Chicken Filling for Tamales

MAKES APPROXIMATELY 70 TAMALES

4   *large whole chicken breasts, split and skinned, or 16 large chicken thighs, skinned*
½   *cup fresh lemon juice*
    Herb seasoning
3   *cups finely chopped onion*
12 *to 14 large garlic cloves, minced*

3   *tablespoons lard, or as needed*
½   *cup juices from steaming chicken and/or chicken stock*
2   *cups Salsa Chile (recipe follows)*
    Salt and freshly ground black pepper to taste

Arrange chicken in shallow dishes and pour lemon juice over. Set dishes on racks over boiling water, cover pot, and steam 30 minutes, or until just cooked. Remove chicken from dishes, reserving juices, and let stand until cool enough to handle. With fingers, shred chicken into pieces about 1 inch long and ¼ inch wide.

In a large covered skillet cook onion and garlic in lard 5 minutes. Stir in shredded chicken, cover, and cook 5 minutes, stirring occasionally and adding lard if mixture appears dry. Add steaming juices and/or stock, stir to blend, and then mix in salsa. Season with salt and pepper and set aside to cool. Fill and steam tamales as directed.

Salsa Chile

Dried *pasilla* chiles are best for this traditional *salsa*. If you cannot find them, substitute dried mild New Mexican chiles (*chile de ristra*) or Anaheim or California varieties.

MAKES 2 CUPS

4 to 6 dried sweet red chile peppers (4 ounces)	*4 to 6 large garlic cloves, chopped*
1½ cups hot water	*2 to 3 teaspoons chopped fresh oregano*

Trim stem end of peppers and remove seeds and veins. Rinse peppers under cold running water. Place in a bowl and add hot water. Let stand 30 minutes.

Mince garlic and oregano in a blender or food processor. Drain peppers, reserving soaking water. Add peppers to blender with 1 cup of the soaking water and puree until smooth. Force through a medium-mesh sieve if a smoother consistency is desired. Thin with reserved soaking water to measure 2 cups.

If not using salsa immediately, jar, cover, and refrigerate up to 1 week or freeze up to 1 month.

Pork Filling for Tamales

MAKES APPROXIMATELY 70 TAMALES

3 cups minced onion	*5 cups shredded cooked pork*
12 to 14 large garlic cloves, minced	*½ cup rich pork stock*
2 cups minced green or red bell pepper	*2 cups Salsa Chile (see Chicken Filling for Tamales)*
3 tablespoons lard, or as needed	*Salt and freshly ground black pepper to taste*

In a large covered skillet cook onion, garlic, and bell pepper in lard 5 minutes. Stir in pork, cover, and cook 5 minutes, stirring occasionally and adding lard if mixture appears dry. Add stock, stir to blend, then mix in salsa. Season with salt and pepper and set aside to cool. Fill and steam tamales as directed.

Fresh Corn Filling for Tamales

If there is no corn on the cob in the market, commercially frozen corn may be used in place of fresh. A 10-ounce package measures approximately 2 cups.

MAKES APPROXIMATELY 70 TAMALES

3   cups minced onion
12   to 14 large garlic cloves, minced
3   tablespoons lard, or as needed
5   cups cooked corn kernels
½   teaspoon sugar
2   4-ounce cans diced mild green chiles

1   cup Salsa Chile (see Chicken Filling for Tamales)
     Salt and freshly ground black pepper to taste
5   cups shredded Monterey Jack cheese

In a large covered skillet cook onion and garlic in lard 5 minutes. Stir in corn kernels and sugar, cover, and cook 5 minutes. Add green chiles and salsa. Season with salt and pepper and set aside to cool. When filling, top the corn kernel mixture on each tamale with a tablespoon or so of the cheese. Steam as directed.

Bollito Misto (Italian Mixed Meats Dinner)

This elaborate northern Italian dish of mixed meats is customarily prepared as a boiled dinner, but it can also be successfully steamed. You will need a large two-tiered steamer and two large shallow bowls. You may substitute other meats, such as beef brisket, veal rump, or lean pork butt, for the ones given here.

The presentation of this dish is important. Some of the meats must be sliced and they all must be attractively arranged on the serving platter with the vegetables. As this takes considerable time, the steamed foods must be kept warm as you work. Leave the foods in the covered steamer with the heat off, or place them on a dish, cover them loosely with foil, and set in a low oven.

The mixed-meats boiled dinner is also a popular preparation in other regions and countries. In Alsace, *choucroute garnie* combines salt pork,

pork sausage, smoked baked ham, sauerkraut, and apple. The *hutspot met klapstuk* of the Netherlands is a mixture of smoked pork chops, beef round, lamb, leeks, cabbage, potatoes, and other vegetables. A Swiss specialty features smoked pork shoulder, pork sausage, new potatoes, and cabbage, served with a mustard sauce. These dishes can all be adapted to steaming in the same manner as the Italian one presented here.

SERVES 6

1	2-pound beef rump or bottom round roast		*Salt*	
2	carrots, cut into large chunks	1	7- to 8-ounce calf's tongue	
2	celery stalks, cut into large chunks	1	whole chicken breast, skinned and quartered	
½	cup chopped celery leaves	2	chicken thighs	
1	large onion, cut into eighths		Freshly ground white pepper	
12	black peppercorns, lightly crushed	2	leeks, white and 1 inch of green, cut into thick slices	
3	large bay leaves	4	4-ounce sweet or hot Italian sausages	
12	large parsley sprigs	12	small new red potatoes	
		½	cup minced fresh parsley	
			Salsa Verde (recipe follows)	

Place beef rump in the center of a large shallow dish. Strew half the carrots, celery, celery leaves, onion, and peppercorns over. Crumble 1 bay leaf over and top with 3 parsley sprigs. Set on rack over boiling water, cover pot, and steam 30 minutes.

While beef is cooking, place tongue in another large shallow dish and strew remaining carrots, celery, celery leaves, onion, and peppercorns over. Crumble 1 bay leaf over and top with 3 parsley sprigs. Place dish on second rack over boiling water and steam 1 hour.

Check dishes occasionally to see if juices are in danger of overflowing, in which case ladle out excess into a jar and reserve for soup stock. Watch the water level in the pot.

After the beef and tongue have steamed 1½ hours, it is time to add the chicken. Before doing this, reverse the tiers so that the beef is on the top. Sprinkle all surfaces of the chicken pieces with white pepper. Add the dark meat pieces to the dish with the tongue. Put the white meat pieces in with the beef. Crumble the remaining bay leaf over the chicken pieces and top with remaining parsley sprigs and the sliced leeks. Steam 20 minutes.

Add 2 sausages to each dish. Place the potatoes directly on the racks around the edges of the dishes. Steam 20 minutes, or until potatoes are cooked. Halfway through cooking, reverse the tiers.

Remove steamer from heat. Transfer the beef and tongue to a carving board and let stand 5 minutes. Skin the tongue and trim away gristle and fat. Thinly slice tongue and arrange on a large heated serving platter.

Thinly slice the beef and arrange next to the tongue. Surround meat with chicken pieces, sausages, and potatoes. Discard the parsley sprigs and spoon the vegetables from the dishes over all, moistening with some of the juices. Sprinkle with minced parsley and serve with Salsa Verde on the side.

Salsa Verde (Green Sauce)

MAKES ¾ CUP

3 to 4 large garlic cloves, chopped	1 hard-cooked egg yolk
½ cup chopped Italian parsley	1½ to 2 teaspoons anchovy paste
2 tablespoons drained capers	½ teaspoon crumbled dried basil
2 tablespoons fine fresh breadcrumbs	2 teaspoons fresh lemon juice
	½ cup olive oil

Finely mince garlic and parsley in a blender or food processor. Add all other ingredients except oil and blend until well mixed. With motor running, pour in oil in a slow, steady stream.

Serve salsa immediately, or cover and refrigerate no longer than 1 day. (If stored longer, the anchovy develops an off taste.) Bring to room temperature and stir well before using.

Veal Birds

A favorite dinner standby of American cooks, these customarily braised meat rolls can be assembled up to a day ahead. You will need high-quality veal scallops, each about 5 inches long and 3 to 4 inches wide. If they are *very* thin, they need not be pounded. Place any scallops that are more than 1/16 inch thick between two sheets of waxed paper and pound gently with a meat mallet until slices are evenly flattened.

Serve with freshly cooked pasta or steamed rice and a green vegetable such as Swiss chard.

SERVES 4 OR 5

14 ounces veal scallops   (approximately 12 slices)

¼ cup fresh lemon juice
½ pound lean ground beef
2 large garlic cloves, finely minced
¼ cup finely minced onion
2 tablespoons milk
2 tablespoons fine fresh breadcrumbs
2 tablespoons homemade or bottled chili sauce

⅓ cup minced fresh parsley
½ teaspoon salt
½ teaspoon herb seasoning
¼ teaspoon freshly ground black pepper
¾ cup freshly grated Parmesan or Romano cheese Mushroom Sauce (See Basic Savory Sauces)

Place veal scallops in a nonmetallic dish and pour 2 tablespoons of the lemon juice over. Let stand, turning occasionally, 1 hour.

In a mixing bowl, combine remaining lemon juice, beef, garlic, onion, milk, breadcrumbs, chili sauce, 3 tablespoons of the parsley, and seasonings. Place a teaspoon-size portion of the mixture in a shallow dish, set dish over boiling water, cover pot, and steam 5 minutes. Taste and adjust seasonings.

Remove veal scallops from dish and pat dry with paper toweling. Place them flat on work surface. Evenly spread a portion of the ground beef mixture over each slice to cover almost to the edges. Use all of the beef mixture, trying to divide it as evenly as possible among the veal scallops.

Sprinkle each covered veal slice with about 1 tablespoon cheese. Beginning at the narrow end, roll each slice into a tight cylinder. Place rolls seam side down directly on a rack over boiling water, cover pot, and steam 15 minutes.

Transfer veal rolls to a warmed platter or individual plates. Spoon Mushroom Sauce over the top and sprinkle with remaining parsley.

Chinese One-Pot Rice Dishes

To make these dishes, refer to the directions for White and Brown Rice. Prepare the rice up to the point where it is to be covered. Before topping with the lid, put any one of the following mixtures on top, spreading them evenly so that they have sufficient surface on which to cook. Cover the pot and proceed as directed. The rice must stand the full time indicated in the master recipe once the heat has been turned off.

If you are using an electric rice cooker, set a kitchen timer for 10 minutes once you have turned the cooker on. When the timer goes off, remove the lid of the cooker and quickly arrange ingredients on top of rice. Re-cover cooker and proceed as you would if steaming the rice plain.

It is important that the topping be assembled fully before lifting the lid of the rice cooker. If the top is left off too long, the cooking process will be interrupted to the point that the topping will not cook.

The following toppings are designed for cooking with 1 cup of raw rice. Each recipe will serve 2 persons.

Chicken Topping for Rice

1	cup slivered chicken meat	1	green onion with top,
1	tablespoon oyster sauce		slivered
1	teaspoon dry sherry	4	water chestnuts, minced
1	teaspoon soy sauce	1	large garlic clove, minced
		½	cup shelled green peas

Combine chicken, oyster sauce, sherry, and soy sauce and mix well. Following directions for Chinese One-Pot Rice Dishes, strew chicken mixture over rice. Sprinkle with all remaining ingredients, cover pot, and proceed as directed.

Ham Topping for Rice

1	cup slivered cooked ham		minutes to soften, drained,
3	dried shiitake mushrooms,		stemmed, and slivered
	soaked in warm water 30	6	tiny asparagus tips
			Soy Sauce

Following directions for Chinese One-Pot Rice Dishes, arrange ham, mushroom slivers, and asparagus tips over rice. Cover pot and proceed as directed. Pass the soy sauce.

Pork and Tofu Balls Topping for Rice

½	recipe Chinese Pork and	Oriental sesame oil
	Tofu Balls	

Following directions for Chinese One-Pot Rice Dishes, arrange spinach leaves over rice, and quickly drop pork mixture by teaspoonfuls on top of spinach. Drizzle with a little sesame oil, cover pot, and proceed as directed.

Vegetable Topping for Rice

½	cup slivered bamboo shoots	3	dried shiitake mushrooms,
¼	cup sliced water chestnuts		soaked in warm water 30

minutes to soften, drained,
stemmed, and slivered
½ cup very finely slivered long
beans

1 green onion with top,
slivered
8 slender carrot curls
Soy sauce

Following directions for Chinese One-Pot Rice Dishes, layer vegetables over rice in order given. Drizzle with a little soy sauce, cover pot, and steam as directed.

Classic Meatballs

Steaming results in meatballs with a softer, more delicate texture than ones that are baked or browned in a skillet. This finer consistency makes it more difficult to reheat the meatballs, however, because they are too fragile to take much handling, such as turning them in a sauce.

This basic recipe is designed to illustrate how any simple meatball preparation can be adapted to steaming. The mixture can also be steamed in a loaf shape; increase the cooking time to 40 minutes. Serve the meatballs with Basic Tomato Sauce, Sorrel Sauce, or Mornay Sauce, or with their own juices. Artichokes and steamed barley or Cornmeal Bread make good accompaniments.

SERVES 4 TO 6

½ pound lean ground beef
½ cup steamed white or brown
rice
2 green onions with tops,
minced
2 large garlic cloves, finely
minced
1 egg, lightly beaten
2 teaspoons soy sauce

1 teaspoon Worcestershire
sauce
¼ teaspoon herb seasoning
¼ teaspoon crumbled dried
thyme
¼ teaspoon freshly ground
black pepper
2 teaspoons tomato paste

Combine all ingredients and mix well. Place a teaspoon-size portion in a shallow dish, set on rack over boiling water, cover pot, and steam 5 minutes. Taste and adjust seasonings. Chill beef mixture until firm; this will help the meatballs hold together better.

Form mixture into 24 balls, each about the size of a walnut. Arrange the balls in 2 shallow dishes. Place dishes on racks over boiling water, cover pot, and steam 15 minutes, or until cooked through.

Cornmeal with Ground Beef and Green Peppers

This is an adaptation of a Caribbean cornmeal dish called *pastelles*. In the original, the cornmeal and meat filling are wrapped in banana leaves and steamed. During testing, I found the cornmeal took on a rather unpleasant texture when wrapped in the leaves, so I have dispensed with the leaves and instead layered the two mixtures in a shallow bowl. The result is a satisfying hearty dish that is bound to please.

Garnish the finished dish with sliced hard-cooked eggs and sliced pimiento-stuffed olives. Pass a bowl of raisins for diners to strew over their cornmeal and meat. Serve with a spinach salad dressed with Herb Vinaigrette and a sprinkling of lightly toasted chopped raw peanuts.

SERVES 4

1⅓	cups nondegerminated yellow cornmeal	2	tablespoons annatto oil (see Note)
¼	cup peanut or corn oil	½	teaspoon salt
¾	cup hot water	½	teaspoon freshly ground black pepper
2	medium-size ripe tomatoes, coarsely chopped	½	cup shredded cooked ham
1	medium onion, minced	3	tablespoons minced fresh coriander
4	large garlic cloves, finely minced	1	green bell pepper, cut into eighths
1	pound lean ground beef		Coriander sprigs

Measure cornmeal into a mixing bowl. Combine oil and water and pour over cornmeal. With a wooden spoon, stir until well mixed. Continue stirring 5 minutes, or until mixture has thickened slightly. Select a large shallow bowl for steaming the dish and spoon the cornmeal mixture into it; set aside.

In a large skillet cook tomato, onion, garlic, and beef, stirring with a fork to break up the meat, until meat is no longer pink. Add annatto oil, salt, pepper, and ham. Stir well and cook 2 or 3 minutes longer. Remove from heat, stir in minced coriander, and let cool slightly.

Spoon meat mixture over cornmeal in dish. Set dish on rack over boiling water, cover pot, and steam 20 minutes. Arrange bell peppers in spoke fashion on top of meat mixture, re-cover pot, and steam another 10 minutes. Garnish as suggested above and tuck coriander sprigs around the edge of the dish.

Note: Annatto (or *achiote*) seeds are small, hard red seeds from a tropical tree. They lend a delicate flavor and bright orange color to Caribbean and South American dishes, and can be purchased in Latin American groceries. To make the oil, combine 1 tablespoon seeds and 2 tablespoons peanut or corn oil in a saucepan. Heat until very hot, reduce heat, cover, and simmer 2 minutes. Remove from heat and strain; discard seeds.

Beef Roll with Pepper, Olives, and Eggs

This interesting way of treating ground beef is the pride and joy of one of my Mexican friends. It is reminiscent of Argentinian *matambre*, which is a braised flank steak roll. You may not be able to fit all of the pepper strips, eggs, and olives onto the meat circle, but have these quantities ready just in case.

Serve this stunning beef roll, a pinwheel of colorful ingredients, hot or at room temperature. Offer sour cream or Uncooked Tomato Sauce on the side. Accompany with corn on the cob and a romaine salad dressed with Garlic Vinaigrette.

SERVES 4 TO 6

1 pound lean ground beef	1/2 large green bell pepper
3/4 teaspoon crumbled dried oregano	2 hard-cooked eggs
3/4 teaspoon salt	3 large pitted ripe olives
1/2 teaspoon freshly ground black pepper	5 large pimiento-stuffed olives
2 large garlic cloves, finely minced	6 whole cloves
2 to 3 teaspoons Salsa Chile (see Tamales) or bottled catsup	Avocado slices rubbed with fresh lemon juice Coriander sprigs

Thoroughly combine the meat, oregano, salt, pepper, garlic, and salsa. Place a teaspoon-size portion in a shallow dish, set on rack over boiling water, cover pot, and steam 5 minutes. Taste and adjust seasonings. Refrigerate meat mixture 30 minutes.

Cut the green pepper into strips approximately ¾ inch wide and 3 inches long; set aside. Halve the eggs lengthwise and remove yolks. Set yolks aside and cut each egg white half into 6 lengthwise strips; set aside. Cut the ripe olives into quarters lengthwise; set aside. Halve the pimiento-stuffed olives lengthwise; set aside.

Place a tea towel (at least 14 inches wide) on work surface. Mound the meat mixture in the center of the towel and, with fingers, pat the meat into a circle 11 inches in diameter. On the side of the circle nearest you, 1 inch in from the edge, place 2 or 3 of the pepper strips in a horizontal row, or as many as needed to reach to the outer edges of the circle. Lifting the towel to facilitate the rolling process, roll the uncovered edge of the meat circle over the pepper strips to encase them completely. Place a row of egg white strips horizontally (again, they must reach to the outer edges) along the rolled edge and roll the meat over the strips, again encasing the filling. Continuing to roll the meat in this manner, make and encase a row of black olives, then yolks (slice them as you work; they will be at the midpoint of the circle), pimiento-stuffed olives, a second row of pepper strips, and finally another row of egg whites.

Gently pat the roll so that it is firm and compact. Carefully transfer the meat roll to a second work surface. Fold the tea towel in half and place the meat roll 3 inches in from one of the narrow sides. Cover the meat roll with the uncovered 3-inch edge and then roll the meat roll up into the towel as if the towel were wrapping paper and the meat roll a cardboard cylinder.

Clasp one end of the towel with your fist and tie it securely with the end of a 2-foot length of kitchen twine. Make 2 to 3 loops along the roll with the twine to reach the untied end. Clasp this end and tie securely. The roll will look like an old-fashioned rolling pin or a large sausage.

Place the roll on a rack in a large steamer, roasting pan, or fish poacher above boiling water. Add the cloves to the water. Cover pot and steam 2 hours, adding water as needed to keep original level.

Remove steamer from heat and let roll stand 10 minutes, or until just cool enough to remove twine. Cut away and discard twine and very carefully unroll the meat roll from the towel. Slice the roll and arrange on a warmed serving platter. Garnish with coriander sprigs and avocado slices.

Rouladen (German Beef Rolls)

Of German origin, *rouladen* are beef slices wrapped around fillings and braised in stock or red wine. The rolls steam well, however, and are easily prepared ahead for the evening meal. Serve with crisp hash browned potatoes and kohlrabi. The Caper Mustard Sauce must be added with a light hand.

SERVES 4 TO 6

1   2-pound beef top round, no
    more than ½ inch thick
    Herb seasoning and freshly
    ground black pepper to taste
½   cup very finely minced
    carrot
½   cup very finely minced
    onion
½   cup very finely minced
    bacon (approximately 3
    slices)

¼   cup very finely minced
    mushrooms, or
    ⅛ ounce dried cèpes,
    softened in warm water,
    drained, and finely minced
2   tablespoons minced fresh
    parsley
¼   cup dry red wine
    Caper Mustard Sauce (recipe
    follows)

Trim off any fat from the beef round and cut into 6 equal rectangles. Pound each portion with a meat mallet until it is about ⅛ inch thick. Sprinkle each slice with herb seasoning and pepper. Divide the carrot, onion, bacon, mushrooms, and parsley among the slices, spreading out evenly. Roll each slice into a tight cylinder and tie with kitchen twine so cylinders will keep their shape.

Arrange beef rolls in a large shallow dish and pour wine over. Turning rolls occasionally, let stand 2 hours. If making ahead, cover and refrigerate overnight; bring to room temperature before steaming.

Place dish on rack over boiling water, cover pot, and steam 40 minutes while you prepare the Caper Mustard Sauce. Serve directly from the dish and pass a bowl of the sauce.

Caper Mustard Sauce

MAKES APPROXIMATELY ½ CUP

1¼ cups rich beef stock (if using canned, use beef broth rather than consommé, which is too salty)

1 teaspoon cornstarch, dissolved in 1 tablespoon cold water

1 tablespoon German-style prepared mustard, or to taste

1 teaspoon drained capers, or to taste

2 teaspoons minced fresh parsley

Bring stock to a boil in a small saucepan. Lower heat slightly and cook at a gentle boil until stock is reduced to ½ cup; this will take 15 to 20 minutes. Stir in cornstarch mixture and cook, stirring constantly, until sauce is slightly thickened and appears translucent.

Stir in mustard and capers and reheat. Stir in parsley and transfer to sauceboat.

Korean Beef Ribs

The Koreans are great barbecuers. Their favorite seasonings—garlic, sesame, soy sauce, ginger—for grilled beef successfully make the move to the steamer. To my mind, in fact, these seasonings permeate steamed meats even better than grilled ones. If you miss the rich color of barbecued meat, slip steamed ribs under a broiler or onto the grill for a few minutes before serving.

Baby beef back ribs may be used in this recipe, but generally speaking, despite their meaty appearance, they have a great deal of bone and waste. Instead use large beef short ribs weighing about 10 ounces each. They are usually available already scored at 3- to 4-inch intervals for easily separating into pieces. If they have not been scored, ask your butcher to cut them.

Serve the ribs with steamed white rice, mung bean sprouts lightly dressed with Oriental sesame oil, and kim chee.

SERVES 2

3 large garlic cloves, minced	1 teaspoon sugar
3 green onions with tops, slivered	1 tablespoon minced ginger root
3 tablespoons soy sauce	1/4 teaspoon freshly ground black pepper, or to taste
1/2 teaspoon Oriental sesame oil, or to taste	1 1/2 to 2 pounds meaty beef short ribs, each rib cut into
2 teaspoons lightly toasted sesame seeds	3 or 4 pieces
2 teaspoons cider vinegar	

In a shallow dish thoroughly combine all ingredients except ribs. Add ribs, turn to coat all sides, and marinate 3 or 4 hours, turning often.

Place dish on rack over boiling water, cover pot, and steam 45 minutes, or until ribs are very tender.

Brisket of Corned Beef with Horseradish Sauce

To prepare a larger brisket than the one called for in this recipe, increase the marinade ingredients proportionately and lengthen the steaming time to 2½ to 3 hours, or until the meat is tender.

If you do not have a shallow dish large enough for the brisket, place it directly on the rack. I find the corned beef has a somewhat better texture, however, when it is steamed in a dish.

To steam a traditional New England boiled dinner, place unpeeled whole beets, thick-skinned potatoes, peeled and halved, and cabbage wedges directly on the rack around the brisket. See individual listings in Vegetable Steaming Methods for cooking times.

Corned beef is especially good with Boston Brown Bread. Cap off the meal with Cranberry Pudding for a "fully steamed" repast.

SERVES 4 TO 6

1 2¾- to 3-pound corned beef brisket	1 lime, sliced
	1 bay leaf, crumbled

4 whole cloves
3 cardamom seeds or allspice
   berries, lightly crushed
4 black peppercorns, lightly
   crushed

1 teaspoon dry mustard, or as
   needed
   Parsley sprigs
   Prepared mustard
   Horseradish Sauce (recipe
   follows)

Place corned beef in a glass or ceramic dish and pour in water just to cover. Top brisket with lime slices and strew bay leaf, cloves, cardamom seeds, and peppercorns over. Cover with plastic wrap and refrigerate 24 to 36 hours, turning the brisket over several times.

When ready to steam, remove brisket from dish and pat dry with paper toweling. Rub brisket with dry mustard to coat lightly and evenly. Place brisket in a shallow dish, set dish on rack over boiling water, cover pot, and steam 2 hours, or until tender. Check for doneness by piercing with a fork or slicing off a small end portion.

Check water in steamer every 30 minutes, adding more as needed. If juices accumulate in the dish to the point of overflowing, ladle excess into a saucepan and reserve for serving with beef.

When brisket is done, remove to a large platter and let stand 10 minutes. Pour the juices from the shallow dish into the saucepan with any you have already removed, and heat to serving temperature. Slice the brisket and arrange on a warmed platter. Moisten the meat with some of the heated juices. Pour the remaining juices into a small bowl to be passed at table. Garnish the platter with parsley sprigs. Serve with prepared mustard and/or Horseradish Sauce.

Horseradish Sauce

MAKES APPROXIMATELY ½ CUP

1/3 cup sour cream
2 tablespoons prepared
   horseradish, or to taste
1 teaspoon fresh lemon juice,
   or to taste

1 teaspoon Dijon-style
   mustard, or to taste
   Salt and freshly ground
   white pepper to taste
   Minced fresh chives or
   parsley

Mix together all ingredients except chives, blending well. Transfer to a small bowl and sprinkle with chives.

Lamb Shanks

Lamb shanks, thought of as a very long-cooking meat, steam surprisingly fast. Have the butcher crack them and then, to make them easier to handle, separate each shank into 2 or 3 pieces. The shanks can also be boned, which will shorten the steaming time by 20 minutes or so. (Be sure to save the bones and scraps for soup stock.) When properly cooked, the meat from the bone-in shanks should be so tender as to almost fall off the bone.

The following recipes are prepared in a shallow dish, but a Yunnan pot will work just as well; the shanks will cook a little more quickly.

Lamb Shanks in Red Wine

Toss freshly cooked orzo (rice-shaped pasta) with Brown Butter Sauce for an accompaniment to this delectable lamb dish. Follow with Belgian endive dressed with Lemon/Lime Vinaigrette and sprinkled with lightly toasted chopped walnuts.

SERVES 2

2 *large lamb shanks (at least 1 pound each), cracked*	3 *large garlic cloves, slivered*
½ *cup full-bodied red wine, such as Zinfandel*	3 *or 4 rosemary sprigs* *Herb seasoning and freshly ground black pepper to taste*
2 *tablespoons olive oil*	*Minced fresh parsley*
1 *medium onion, sliced*	

Separate each cracked lamb shank into 2 or 3 pieces. Place shanks in a large shallow dish. Pour wine and oil over and top with onion, garlic, and rosemary. Let stand, turning occasionally, 2 hours.

Sprinkle shanks with herb seasoning and pepper, set dish on rack over boiling water, cover pot, and steam 1½ hours, or until meat is tender. Garnish with minced parsley.

Mustard Lamb Shanks

Cook up a pot of Great Northern beans lightly seasoned with garlic and onion. Arrange lamb shanks on individual serving plates and top with the mustardy steaming juices. Spoon a mound of the beans alongside. Sprinkle plates liberally with minced fresh chives.

SERVES 2

<table>
<tr><td>¼</td><td>cup French's Bold N' Spicy mustard</td><td>2</td><td>large lamb shanks (at least 1 pound each), cracked</td></tr>
<tr><td>2½</td><td>to 3 tablespoons prepared horseradish</td><td>1</td><td>cup finely chopped onion</td></tr>
<tr><td>¼</td><td>cup rich lamb or beef stock</td><td>1</td><td>tablespoon butter</td></tr>
</table>

Combine mustard, horseradish, and stock. Separate the lamb shanks into 2 or 3 pieces. Place shanks in a large shallow dish and pour mustard mixture over. Let stand 30 minutes, turning occasionally.

In a covered skillet, cook onion in butter until just starting to turn golden. Spoon onion over shanks and set dish on rack over boiling water. Cover pot and steam 1½ hours, or until meat is tender.

Citrus Lamb Shanks with Mint

Arrange these subtly flavored lamb shanks on a bed of saffron rice. Surround with strips of steamed eggplant in a spoke pattern and spoon some of the steaming juices over all. Garnish with minced fresh mint and serve with homemade fig or other fruit chutney.

SERVES 2

<table>
<tr><td>2</td><td>large lamb shanks (at least 1 pound each), cracked</td><td>½</td><td>teaspoon ground coriander</td></tr>
<tr><td>½</td><td>teaspoon salt</td><td>2</td><td>medium oranges, sliced</td></tr>
<tr><td>¼</td><td>teaspoon freshly ground black pepper</td><td>1</td><td>lemon, sliced</td></tr>
<tr><td></td><td></td><td>1</td><td>sweet red onion, sliced</td></tr>
<tr><td></td><td></td><td>3</td><td>or 4 mint sprigs</td></tr>
</table>

Separate the lamb shanks into 2 or 3 pieces. Sprinkle the shanks with salt, pepper, and coriander and place them in a large shallow dish. Arrange orange, lemon, and onion slices over shanks and top with mint sprigs.

Set dish on rack over boiling water, cover pot, and steam 1½ hours, or until meat is tender. Discard orange, lemon, onion, and mint before serving.

Lamb with Brown Lentils

The lentils retain their identity when steamed in this stewlike dish, but they do not absorb as much flavor as when they have been simmered on top of the stove. Although lentils cook best in the closed environment of a Yunnan pot, you may use a shallow dish.

Serve with French bread and spinach salad dressed with Herb Vinaigrette.

SERVES 4

3½ pounds bone-in lamb shoulder stew meat	3 rosemary sprigs
⅓ cup fresh lime or lemon juice	2 tablespoons olive oil
1 teaspoon ground cumin	½ cup full-bodied red wine, such as Zinfandel
½ teaspoon freshly ground black pepper	1 cup brown lentils
5 large garlic cloves, slivered	3 medium carrots, cut into ½-inch slices
	Minced fresh parsley

Rinse lamb pieces and pat dry with paper toweling. Place in a large Yunnan pot (at least 2-quart capacity) and pour lime juice over. Sprinkle with cumin and pepper. Top with garlic and rosemary and drizzle oil over. Pour in wine and let stand 2 hours, turning pieces occasionally.

Place lentils in a small saucepan with a lid, pour boiling water over, cover saucepan, and let stand 1½ to 2 hours. Drain lentils and add to lamb, stirring so lentils are evenly distributed.

Set Yunnan pot on saucepan over boiling water, cover, and steam 1½ hours. Strew carrot slices over, re-cover pot, and steam 30 minutes, or until lamb is tender. Garnish with minced parsley.

Greek-style Lamb Blocks

Lamb blocks, cut from the shoulder, are neglected by most cooks. They tend to be quite bony and sometimes have considerable fat. Nonetheless, blocks are one of the most flavorful of all the lamb cuts and are very reasonably priced. To remove as much fat as possible, steam the blocks several hours or a day ahead.

Serve with freshly cooked egg noodles or steamed barley and artichokes with Greek Lemon Sauce.

SERVES 2 OR 3

2 *lamb blocks, approximately 1 pound 2 ounces each*	3 *large fresh oregano sprigs*
3 *tablespoons fresh lemon juice*	4 *large garlic cloves, slivered*
	Salt and freshly ground black pepper to taste
1 *tablespoon olive oil*	*Minced fresh parsley*

Rinse lamb blocks, pat dry with paper toweling, and place in a large shallow dish. Pour lemon juice and oil over and arrange sprigs on top. Strew garlic over all. Let stand 2 to 3 hours, turning meat several times.

Sprinkle lamb with salt and pepper. Place dish on rack over boiling water, cover pot, and steam 2 hours, or until lamb is very tender. Remove lamb blocks from dish with tongs and set aside to cool. Pour juices from dish into a saucepan and set aside.

When lamb blocks are cool enough to handle, remove meat from bones and trim off all visible fat. Add the bones and trimmings to the saucepan with the juices. Transfer meat to a bowl, cover, and refrigerate.

Cover saucepan containing juices and trimmings, place over high heat, and bring to a boil. Lower heat and simmer 1 hour. Strain juices, then cool, cover, and refrigerate.

When the fat has congealed on the strained juices, lift it off with a spoon and discard. Place lamb meat in a saucepan or nonstick skillet. Add enough of the defatted juices to moisten. (Reserve remaining juices for making gravies, sauces, or stocks.) Reheat meat to serving temperature; taste and adjust seasonings. Transfer meat to a heated serving dish and sprinkle with parsley.

Curried Lamb Ribs

Yoghurt and Indian spices give this modestly priced lamb cut an expensive taste. Millet is a natural accompaniment; spoon some of the curry sauce over the grain. Serve with a dish of steamed cauliflower and carrots and pass a bowl of your favorite chutney.

SERVES 4

3 *racks of meaty lamb ribs (approximately 4 pounds)*	*Salt and freshly ground black pepper*

1	medium onion, finely chopped	1	tablespoon curry powder, or to taste
4	large garlic cloves, minced	1/2	cup lamb or other stock
1 1/2	teaspoons very finely minced ginger root	1/2	cup plain yoghurt
1	tablespoon olive oil	2	teaspoons fresh lemon or lime juice, or to taste
1	tablespoon butter		

Make sure your butcher has cracked the lamb ribs. Cut them into pieces with 2 or 3 ribs to each piece. Sprinkle both sides of each piece with salt and pepper and place them directly on a rack over boiling water; do not make more than 3 layers. Cover pot and steam 40 minutes.

In a covered nonstick skillet cook onion, garlic, and ginger root in oil and butter 5 minutes. Sprinkle with curry powder and cook, stirring, 2 minutes. Stir in stock, yoghurt, and lemon juice. Cook and stir until mixture is blended. Taste and adjust seasonings.

Transfer lamb ribs to Yunnan pot and pour curry mixture over. Set Yunnan pot on saucepan over boiling water, cover, and steam 1 hour and 20 minutes, or until lamb is very tender.

Moroccan Lamb Stew to Accompany Couscous

Though many cookery books recommend cooking the stew that is to accompany couscous in the lower pot of the *couscousière*, I find that it is easier to cook it almost completely in a Dutch oven and then transfer it to the *couscousière* for the final steaming of the couscous. This is because *couscousières* are most commonly available in lightweight aluminum, which I do not like for browning and stewing. If you have improvised a steamer for the couscous, the stew must be cooked completely in a separate pot.

Serve lamb stew and couscous with thinly sliced peeled oranges and sweet onions dressed with fresh lemon juice and olive oil. Pass a bowl of Mediterranean-style black olives. Let guests help themselves to the very hot Harissa Sauce.

SERVES 4

2	pounds boneless lamb stew, trimmed of fat and cut into 1-inch cubes	1	large onion, cut into eighths
		3	large garlic cloves, minced

½   teaspoon ground turmeric
½   teaspoon ground ginger
½   teaspoon salt
*½   teaspoon freshly ground
     black pepper*
2   tablespoons olive oil
2   tablespoons butter
2   cups chicken stock
1   4-inch cinnamon stick
*2   medium-size ripe tomatoes,
     coarsely chopped*
*2   tablespoons chopped fresh
     parsley*

*2   tablespoons chopped fresh
     mint*
*1½ cups cooked garbanzo
     beans*
*2   small carrots, cut into
     1-inch chunks*
*½   pound pumpkin, peeled
     and cut into 1-inch chunks*
*2   medium-size zucchini, cut
     into 1-inch chunks
     Harissa Sauce (recipe
     follows)*

In a large Dutch oven sauté lamb, onion, garlic, and seasonings in oil and butter, stirring with a fork, until lamb is evenly browned. Add chicken stock, cinnamon stick, tomatoes, parsley, and mint. Cover, bring to a gentle boil, lower heat, and cook 20 minutes, stirring occasionally.

Add garbanzo beans, carrots, and pumpkin to pot and continue cooking 20 minutes. Transfer to *couscousière* and add zucchini. Bring stew back to boil and, following directions for Couscous, complete the final steaming of the grains.

Remove couscous from top pan and toss with the oil and butter as directed. Mound couscous on a large heated platter. With the back of a large spoon make a depression in the center of the mound and spoon the vegetables from the stew into the hollow. Arrange the meat around the edge of the couscous mound to completely encircle it. Serve with Harissa Sauce.

Harissa Sauce

MAKES ⅔ CUP

4   teaspoons cayenne pepper
1½ teaspoons ground cumin
2   large garlic cloves, minced

¼   teaspoon salt
⅔   cup olive oil

In a blender container or in a mortar with a pestle, grind together the pepper, cumin, garlic, and salt until mixture forms a well-blended paste. Transfer to a small saucepan and add olive oil. Place over medium heat and cook, stirring constantly, for 5 minutes. Remove from the heat, pour into a bowl, and let cool. Stir a few times before serving.

To store, cover and refrigerate for up to 1 week. Bring to room temperature before serving.

Cumin Lamb Balls

If your whole-grain bread includes millet as one of the grains, these lamb balls will have a slight crunch to them. They may be steamed directly on a rack, or they may be divided between two large shallow dishes. In the latter case, the juices that accumulate can serve as a sauce, or the meatballs, steamed by either method, may be served on a bed of brown rice with Basic Tomato or Sorrel Sauce spooned over them. Steamed greens dressed with lemon juice complete the meal.

SERVES 4 TO 6

½ cup fresh whole-grain breadcrumbs	1 medium onion, finely minced
3 tablespoons low-fat milk	½ teaspoon salt, or to taste
1 egg	½ teaspoon freshly ground black pepper, or to taste
3 tablespoons homemade or bottled chili sauce	½ teaspoon ground cumin, or to taste
3 large garlic cloves, finely minced	1 pound lean ground lamb

In a large mixing bowl soak crumbs in milk until very soft, about 5 minutes. Stir in all remaining ingredients except lamb and mix well. With fingers, work lamb into breadcrumb mixture.

Place a teaspoonful-size portion of the meat mixture in a small shallow bowl, set over boiling water, cover, and steam 5 minutes. Taste and adjust seasonings.

Chill meat mixture 30 minutes or until firm enough to handle. Form into 4 dozen balls approximately 1 inch in diameter. Arrange balls in 2 large shallow dishes and set on racks over boiling water, or arrange balls directly on racks over boiling water. Cover pot and steam 12 minutes, or until meatballs are just cooked through.

Cantonese Pork with Duck Egg

This simple minced pork preparation is a favorite of the Cantonese. Salted duck egg yolks can be found in Chinese markets. They usually come packaged in plastic and look very much like vibrantly colored dried apricots.

Bok choy drizzled with oyster sauce and a bowl of steamed white rice complement this homestyle dish.

SERVES 4

12	ounces coarsely minced lean pork butt	1	salted duck egg yolk, diced
1/2	teaspoon salt	12	thin slices ginger root
1	egg white	1	tablespoon peanut oil, heated to smoking point
1	tablespoon cornstarch		Fresh coriander sprigs

Combine pork, salt, egg white, and cornstarch. Pat into a shallow dish to 1/4 inch thickness. Top with salted duck egg and ginger root.

Set dish on rack over boiling water, cover pot, and steam 7 to 8 minutes. Pour peanut oil over and garnish with coriander sprigs.

Pork Chops with Sage

Aromatic fresh sage leaves infuse pork with a pungent flavor. Purchase either boneless or bone-in chops no more than 1 inch thick. Allow 1 large chop or 2 small chops per serving.

The steaming time will depend upon the thickness of the chops and how tightly they fit in the dish. The directions call for a shallow dish, but if you have a Yunnan pot, it also works very well.

Remember, pork toughens if overcooked, so watch carefully. To test for doneness, cut into one of the chops. There should be only the tiniest tinge of pinkness.

Serve with scalloped potatoes and green beans with Mustard Sauce.

SERVES 4

4	large pork chops	1/3	to 1/2 cup rich pork or chicken stock
	Herb seasoning and freshly ground black pepper to taste	2	cups finely shredded red cabbage
2	large garlic cloves, slivered		
8	fresh sage leaves		

Sprinkle pork chops with herb seasoning and pepper and arrange in a large shallow dish. Strew garlic and sage leaves over and pour in stock. Place dish on rack over boiling water, cover pot, and steam 35 minutes.

Arrange cabbage evenly on top of chops, re-cover pot, and steam another 10 minutes, or until meat is tender and cabbage is just cooked.

Pork Chops with Prunes

This German-inspired dish is complemented by fluffy mashed potatoes and Brussels sprouts with Hazelnut Butter Sauce.

SERVES 4

12 *pitted dried prunes*	4 *oregano sprigs*
2 *tablespoons orange liqueur*	4 *parsley sprigs*
4 *large boneless pork chops*	*Herb seasoning and freshly*
2 *tablespoons dry white wine*	*ground black pepper to*
or dry vermouth	*taste*
3 *garlic cloves, slivered*	*Thin orange slices*
1 *medium onion, sliced*	*Sour cream*

In a small bowl soak prunes in liqueur 1 hour. Arrange pork chops in a Yunnan pot. Pour wine over, then strew chops with garlic and onion. Top with oregano and parsley sprigs. Sprinkle with herb seasoning and pepper and let stand 30 minutes.

Arrange liqueur-soaked prunes around chops and pour any liqueur remaining in bowl over the chops. Set Yunnan pot on a saucepan over boiling water, cover, and steam 30 minutes, or until meat is tender. Garnish with orange slices and pass a bowl of sour cream.

Sausage Dinner

Central Europe is home to many types of sausages—the mild pork and veal bratwurst, garlic-scented pork and beef knackwurst, smoked mixed-meat kielbasa. These varieties steam well and taste especially good when prepared on a bed of sauerkraut with or without grated tart apple (4 parts sauerkraut to 1 part apple).

Arrange rinsed and well-drained sauerkraut in a Yunnan pot. Add a splash of red wine to the sauerkraut. Set pot on a saucepan over boiling water, cover, and steam 1 hour. Place the sausages on top of the sauerkraut, re-cover Yunnan pot, and continue to steam another 10 to 15 minutes. The sausages are cooked when they have swelled and the casings have begun to pull away from the meat. Serve with steamed new potatoes and Mustard Sauce or Caper Mustard Sauce, or with prepared mustard.

For a different flavor, steam the sausages directly on a rack over boiling beer for 10 to 15 minutes, depending on the size of the sausage. Accompany with hard rolls, prepared mustard, and cornichons.

Pork Spareribs in Hoisin Sauce

Pork spareribs coated with richly colored, slightly sweet hoisin sauce taste best and are more healthful when some of their fat has been leached out by presteaming.

Steamed white rice and crisp snow peas will complete the meal.

SERVES 2

1 pound pork spareribs, cut into individual ribs	2 green onions, slivered
2 tablespoons hoisin sauce	1 tablespoon lightly toasted sesame seeds
1 tablespoon dry sherry	

Place ribs directly on rack over boiling water, cover pot, and steam 10 minutes. Blend the hoisin sauce and sherry in a shallow dish large enough to hold the ribs. Add the partially steamed ribs and turn to coat evenly with the sauce.

Place the dish on a rack over boiling water, cover pot, and steam 30 to 40 minutes. Garnish with green onions and sesame seeds.

Pork Loin with Bourbon Sauce

For a one-steamer meal, arrange unpeeled yams or new potatoes alongside the dish holding the pork loin and then tuck in broccoli spears (see individual listings in Vegetable Steaming Methods for timing). Prepare the Bourbon Sauce while the pork steams.

SERVES 4 TO 6

1 *center-cut pork loin roast (4½ to 5 pounds)*	*Herb seasoning, salt, and freshly ground black pepper to taste*
6 *large garlic cloves, slivered*	1 *medium onion, sliced*
6 *oregano sprigs*	*Watercress sprigs*
⅓ *cup bourbon*	*Bourbon Sauce (recipe follows)*

Have your butcher cut chops almost all the way through the roast (some roasts are sold already cut). Trim off as much visible fat as possible and place roast in a shallow dish. Tuck some of garlic slivers and oregano sprigs between the cuts. Strew remaining garlic and oregano over top of roast and in dish. Pour bourbon over and let stand, turning occasionally, 3 hours.

Pour off bourbon and juices and discard. The garlic and oregano should remain on the meat. Season roast with herb seasoning, salt, and pepper. Place onion slices on top and around roast. Set dish on rack over boiling water, cover pot, and steam 1½ hours. Check frequently and ladle the juices that threaten to overflow the shallow dish into a jar or bowl; reserve for soup stock.

Remove pork loin to a cutting board and let stand 10 minutes before carving. Strain juices in dish into jar with already reserved juices; set onion slices aside on a warmed platter. Slice and arrange loin on the platter and surround with the onion slices. Garnish with watercress and serve with Bourbon Sauce on the side.

Bourbon Sauce

MAKES APPROXIMATELY 1 CUP

3 *tablespoons minced onion*	2 *thyme sprigs*
2 *tablespoons minced carrot*	2 *Italian parsley sprigs*
2 *tablespoons minced celery*	½ *bay leaf, crumbled*
2 *large garlic cloves, minced*	2 *teaspoons Dijon-style mustard, or to taste*
1 *tablespoon butter*	1 *tablespoon bourbon, or to taste*
½ *cup dry vermouth*	*Additional stock, if needed*
1½ *cups pork or beef stock*	
1 *tablespoon unbleached flour, dissolved in 3 tablespoons cold water*	

In a covered nonstick skillet cook onion, carrot, celery, and garlic in butter until onion is soft. Stir in vermouth and cook over medium-high heat, stirring occasionally, until vermouth has almost evaporated. Add stock and flour-water mixture and stir well. Add thyme, parsley, and bay leaf. Cook, stirring often, 30 minutes. If sauce thickens too much, add a little stock to thin to proper sauce consistency.

Strain sauce into a saucepan and stir in mustard and bourbon. Reheat to serving temperature, adding stock as needed.

Chinese Pork and Tofu Balls

These light-colored spheres look appetizing against the deep green of the spinach leaves, so serve the tofu balls and their spinach bed directly from the steaming dishes. A dipping sauce of soy and chile oil adds just the right spark to these soft-textured balls. Provide each diner with a bowl of white rice, and be sure everyone is served some of the spinach.

SERVES 4 TO 6

1 egg	2 teaspoons soy sauce
2/3 cup soft tofu, drained	2 teaspoons cornstarch
1/2 pound lean ground pork	1/2 teaspoon salt
1 to 2 large garlic cloves, very finely minced	1/4 teaspoon freshly ground black pepper
1/2 to 1 teaspoon very finely minced ginger root	Spinach leaves, tough stems removed

Beat egg lightly in a mixing bowl. Add all remaining ingredients except spinach. Mix well and place a teaspoon-size portion in a shallow dish. Set dish on rack over boiling water, cover pot, and steam 5 minutes. Taste and adjust seasonings.

Line 2 large shallow dishes with spinach leaves, overlapping the leaves but making only one layer. With a fork or spoon, drop walnut-size portions of the pork mixture, no less than 1/2 inch apart, onto the bed of spinach. (The mixture is too delicate to form into compact balls.)

Place dish on rack over boiling water, cover pot, and steam 10 to 15 minutes, or until pork is just cooked through.

Ham Loaf with Walnuts

Walnuts add just the right "crunch" to this fine-textured meat loaf. If you haven't a cooked potato left over from last night's dinner, substitute about 1 cup steamed white or brown rice.

Hot Cornmeal Bread and steamed sliced mushrooms and shelled peas dressed with Lemon/Lime Butter Sauce make good accompaniments. If desired, spoon a ribbon of Mornay Sauce over each serving of meat.

SERVES 4 TO 6

2   eggs
4   teaspoons prepared mustard
    with horseradish
1   tablespoon grated onion
1   steamed thick-skinned
    potato, chilled, peeled, and
    grated to measure
    approximately 1 cup
1/3   cup cooked shredded
    zucchini, very well drained
    (optional)

1/4   cup minced fresh parsley
1/4   cup milk
1/4   cup fine dry breadcrumbs
2   tablespoons homemade or
    bottled chili sauce
1/2   cup finely chopped walnuts
1/4   teaspoon freshly ground
    black pepper, or to taste
3   cups ground cooked ham

Beat eggs lightly in a large mixing bowl. Add remaining ingredients except ham, mixing well with wooden spoon. Add ham and with fork stir just until blended. Form into a loaf shape and place in the center of a shallow dish. Wrap steamer lid in a tea towel. Set dish on rack over boiling water, cover pot, and steam 45 minutes.

Ham Hocks in Red Wine

Though many think of ham hocks afloat in a pot of simmering white beans, they are also delicious steamed alone and then served with side dishes of Swiss chard with a squeeze of fresh lemon juice and a pilaf of lentils and white rice.

SERVES 2

1 ham hock (approximately 1 pound 2 ounces)	⅛ teaspoon ground cloves
⅓ cup full-bodied red wine, such as Zinfandel	⅛ teaspoon ground allspice
	Minced fresh parsley

Place ham hock in a shallow dish and pour wine over. Sprinkle with cloves and allspice and set dish on rack over boiling water. Cover pot and steam 1 hour. Turn ham hock over, re-cover pot, and steam 1 hour, or until meat is so tender that it begins to fall away from the bone.

To serve, pull the meat from the bone and arrange on individual serving plates. Drizzle some of the accumulated juices over the meat and the lentil-rice pilaf. Sprinkle parsley over all.

Brandied Ham Steak

When you yearn for a slice of ham but don't want to purchase a large amount, try steaming a ham steak just big enough for 1 or 2 servings. With yams steamed right in the dish with the ham, and broccoli or cauliflower florets tucked around the dish directly on the rack, you have a complete one-steamer meal with almost no preparation.

The juices that accumulate in the steaming dish are a light, delicious sauce for the meat and vegetables. Accompany with freshly baked butter-milk biscuits.

SERVES 2

1 10-ounce ham steak (approximately ¾ inch thick)	1 to 2 teaspoons brown sugar
3 tablespoons brandy	1 8- to 9-ounce yam, peeled and cut into 1-inch chunks
1½ teaspoons Dijon-style mustard	1 large broccoli stalk or ¼ head of cauliflower, divided into florets
⅛ teaspoon ground cloves	

Place ham steak in a large shallow dish and pour brandy over. Spread top of ham with mustard and sprinkle with cloves and brown sugar. Let stand 30 minutes.

Arrange yam chunks around ham in dish. Set dish on rack over boiling water, cover pot, and steam 25 minutes. Tuck broccoli directly on rack around the dish and steam an additional 5 to 10 minutes.

Osso Buco (Veal Shanks with Anchovy)

If the Milanese were to steam rather than braise this well-known dish, they would discover a more delicate and equally delicious feast. A shallow dish or dishes can be used instead of the Yunnan pot.

Serve shanks with risotto and chicory dressed with olive oil and fresh lemon juice.

SERVES 2

2 large veal shanks, approximately 1 pound 3 ounces each	2 medium-size ripe tomatoes, coarsely chopped
⅓ cup fresh lemon juice	3 thyme sprigs
1 medium carrot, finely chopped	3 parsley sprigs
	1 bay leaf, broken
1 celery stalk, finely chopped	2 to 3 teaspoons anchovy paste
1 medium onion, finely chopped	3 tablespoons minced fresh parsley
2 large garlic cloves, minced	1 teaspoon freshly grated lemon peel
⅓ cup dry white wine	Parsley sprigs
Herb seasoning and freshly ground black pepper to taste	

Have butcher saw each veal shank into 3 pieces. Rinse, pat dry with paper toweling, and place in a nonmetallic dish. Pour ¼ cup of the lemon juice over, cover, and refrigerate 4 hours or overnight, turning occasionally.

Arrange chopped vegetables and garlic on bottom of a large Yunnan pot. Pour in wine. Remove veal shanks from marinade, pat dry with paper toweling, and sprinkle with herb seasoning and pepper.

Place meat on top of vegetables in Yunnan pot and tuck tomatoes around the shanks. Top with thyme and parsley sprigs and strew bay leaf pieces over. Place Yunnan pot on a sauce pan over boiling water, cover, and steam 2 hours, or until meat is very tender. The meat should be starting to fall away from the bones.

Combine remaining lemon juice with anchovy paste, minced parsley, and lemon peel. With tongs, remove meat to a warmed plate and quickly stir anchovy paste mixture into juices in pot. Return shanks to pot and turn to coat with sauce. Garnish with parsley sprigs and bring to the table in the Yunnan pot.

Herbed Veal with Mushrooms

This is a simplified version of *blanquette de veau,* the braised veal shoulder in cream sauce of provincial France. The French, like the Italians, season their veal with fresh lemon juice to bring out the subtle flavor. The yolk and heavy cream enrichment are optional, for the juices formed during steaming are flavorful on their own.

Serve with sliced ripe tomatoes and French bread.

SERVES 2

1 *pound boneless veal stew meat (shoulder or breast)*

2 *tablespoons fresh lemon juice*

2 *to 3 garlic cloves, finely minced*

2 *whole cloves*

2 *whole allspice berries, lightly crushed*
  Salt and freshly ground white pepper to taste

1 *small yellow onion, cut into fourths*

1 *small carrot, cut into chunks*

1 *small celery stalk with some leaves, halved*

3 *parsley sprigs*

2 *thyme sprigs*

1 *bay leaf*

6 *small white boiling onions*

1/2 *cup sliced fresh mushrooms*

1/2 *cup shelled peas*

1 *teaspoon Dijon-style mustard, or to taste*

1 *teaspoon freshly grated lemon peel*

3 *tablespoons minced fresh parsley*

1 *egg yolk (optional)*

1/4 *cup heavy cream (optional)*

Trim any fat and membrane from veal and cut the trimmed meat into 1½- to 2-inch pieces. Place the meat in a shallow dish and pour lemon juice over. Strew the garlic, cloves, and allspice over. Let stand 1 hour, stirring occasionally.

Sprinkle the meat with salt and pepper and add onion and carrot to the dish. Place celery, parsley and thyme sprigs, and bay leaf on top of meat and vegetables. Place dish on rack over boiling water, cover pot, and steam 1 hour.

With tongs, remove and discard the yellow onion, carrot, celery, parsley and thyme sprigs, and bay leaf. Add the small white onions to the dish, re-cover, and steam 20 minutes. Add the mushrooms, re-cover, and steam 5 minutes. Add the peas and steam a final 5 minutes.

Remove the dish from the steamer and, if you do not wish to enrich the juices, stir in mustard with a fork. Garnish the veal and vegetables with lemon peel and minced parsley.

If you wish to enrich the juices, do not stir the mustard directly into the dish but, in a small mixing bowl, beat together the egg yolk, cream, and mustard until smooth and set aside. With a slotted spoon, transfer the meat and vegetables to a warmed platter, lightly cover with foil, and place in a low oven. Pour the juices from the dish into a saucepan and bring just to a boil. Whisk a little of the hot juices into the egg yolk mixture, then whisk the mixture into saucepan with remaining juices. Cook, stirring constantly, until lightly thickened. Spoon sauce over veal and vegetables and garnish with lemon peel and minced parsley.

Calves' Liver with Onions

Surprisingly enough, calves' liver, normally sautéed in butter and oil, is tender and moist when steamed, and the texture is firm but delicate.

Serve with crisp bacon slices, mashed potatoes, and asparagus dressed with Lemon/Lime Butter Sauce.

SERVES 4

4 *thin slices calves' liver (approximately 4 ounces each)*	2 *tablespoons dry sherry or vermouth*
2 *medium onions, thinly sliced*	1 *tablespoon soy sauce*
2 *large garlic cloves, minced*	*Minced fresh parsley*

Arrange liver slices in a large shallow dish. Strew onions and garlic on top of the liver and pour sherry and soy sauce over all. Let stand 30 minutes. Place dish on rack over boiling water, cover pot, and steam 10 minutes, or until liver is just cooked through; it should still be slightly pink. Sprinkle with parsley and serve immediately.

Rabbit

The flavor and texture of rabbit are often said to be similar to those of chicken, though I find rabbit has its own distinctive qualities. Rabbit requires longer cooking than chicken, and the seasonings must be added with a light hand so as not to mask its subtle natural flavor.

Although rabbit is expensive in most areas, there is less bone, fat, and waste than on a chicken, and a three-pound rabbit will serve four generously. A covered vessel provides the best heat, but the rabbit may be steamed in two large shallow dishes instead of a Yunnan pot.

The liver, heart, and kidneys are usually included when you purchase a dressed rabbit. The liver is considered by many—and *is*—a delicacy, especially when it is steamed. The kidneys and heart are equally good. Unfortunately, to my knowledge they are never sold separately. A recipe suggestion for these variety meats follows the rabbit recipes.

Mustard Rabbit

Serve this French-seasoned rabbit with a platter of asparagus spears drizzled with Almond Butter Sauce. Spinach or Parsley Dumplings (steamed separately) and a garnish of halved cherry tomatoes and minced fresh parsley or chives will complete this special meal.

SERVES 4

1 *fryer rabbit (3 to 3½ pounds), cut into serving pieces*	2 *tablespoons Dijon-style mustard, or to taste*
3 *tablespoons fresh lemon juice*	⅓ *cup brandy*
½ *teaspoon salt*	2 *large shallots, finely minced*
½ *teaspoon freshly ground white pepper*	2 *tablespoons drained green peppercorns (optional)*
	¼ *cup heavy cream (optional)*

Rinse rabbit in cold water and pat dry with paper toweling. Remove and discard any visible fat and place meat in a nonmetallic container. Pour lemon juice over and let stand 2 hours.

Remove rabbit from marinade and arrange in Yunnan pot. Sprinkle with salt and pepper and spread each piece with a thin coating of mustard. Pour in brandy and strew shallots over all. Set Yunnan pot on saucepan over boiling water, cover, and steam 1 hour. Turn rabbit pieces over and continue steaming another 20 minutes, or until rabbit is tender.

Scatter peppercorns over rabbit, if desired, and then pour in optional cream. Steam 5 minutes, or until heated through. Serve from the Yunnan pot.

Rabbit Agrodolce

The Sicilians prepare a sweet and sour rabbit dish from which this recipe has been adapted. Lemon-sprinkled zucchini and a mound of fluffy couscous, a Trapani specialty traditionally served only with fish, will round out this southern Italian meal.

SERVES 4

1	fryer rabbit (3 to 3½ pounds), cut into serving pieces	1	bay leaf, broken
3	tablespoons fresh lemon juice	4	black peppercorns, lightly crushed
1	cup Marsala		Salt
1	medium onion, sliced	2½	tablespoons sugar
4	parsley sprigs	1	tablespoon water
2	rosemary sprigs	⅓	cup red wine vinegar, or to taste
2	thyme sprigs		Minced fresh parsley

Rinse rabbit pieces in cold water and pat dry with paper toweling. Remove and discard any visible fat and place pieces in a nonmetallic container. Pour lemon juice over and let stand 2 hours.

Bring Marsala, onion, herb sprigs, bay leaf, and peppercorns to a boil in a medium saucepan. Lower heat and simmer 3 minutes. Remove rabbit pieces from marinade and arrange in Yunnan pot. Pour Marsala mixture over and sprinkle rabbit lightly with salt. Set Yunnan pot on saucepan over boiling water, cover, and steam 1 hour. Turn rabbit pieces over and continue to steam another 20 minutes, or until rabbit is tender.

In a small saucepan combine sugar and water. Without stirring, cook over medium-high heat until sugar starts to turn a golden color. Stir in vinegar and continue to heat and stir until mixture is smooth.

Discard herb sprigs and bay leaf from Yunnan pot and ladle about ½ cup of the juices in the pot into the vinegar mixture. Stir well and pour over rabbit pieces. Sprinkle minced parsley over all and serve directly from the Yunnan pot.

Rabbit Liver, Kidneys, and Heart with White Wine and Bay Leaves

Steam these delicious morsels from the rabbit you have steamed for another meal to serve 2 as a light luncheon dish over risotto, with a green salad on the side, or offer them as an accompaniment to the rabbit itself.

Place the liver and kidneys in a small shallow dish. Pour 2 tablespoons dry white wine over them and top with 1 or 2 crumbled bay leaves. Sprinkle with salt and pepper and cover with 4 or 5 slices of onion. Set dish on rack over boiling water, cover pot, and steam 5 minutes. Tuck the heart into the dish, cover pot, and steam 15 minutes.

Serve the variety meats from the dish with a sprinkling of minced fresh parsley. Spoon some of the juices over the risotto.

Poultry

Poultry takes well to steaming. The meat firms up beautifully without drying out and the vitamins and natural flavors are retained. This cooking method is particularly good if you intend to use the poultry meat for making salads, as the flesh is tender, holds its color well, and has a pleasantly silky texture.

Put whole birds or serving pieces directly on the steamer rack, in a shallow dish, or, in the case of pieces, in a Yunnan pot. Putting the poultry in a vessel is preferable, because the cooking juices are not lost in the steaming liquid. If you skin the meat and remove any visible fat, the fat content of the juices is negligible.

Steamed poultry retains its natural pale color when cooked. Colorful sauces, garnishes, and accompaniments can counteract this. You can also choose not to skin the pieces and brown them briefly before steaming. Whole steamed chickens can be placed under the broiler for a few minutes before serving, though they will not brown evenly.

Any stuffed fowl can be steamed instead of roasted, and the cooking time will be much the same. Remember: to avoid the possibility of introducing dangerous bacteria, don't stuff the bird until you are ready to steam.

Featured in this chapter are a whole range of poultry preparations. Chicken parts are seasoned with herbs and spices from around the world; there are two recipes for whole chickens, Marsala-laced chicken livers, and a Cornish hen dish with colorful cranberries. Pistachios give crunch to an unusual turkey loaf, and duck appears two ways: whole, stuffed with chestnuts and cabbage, and quartered and served with Port wine sauce.

CHICKEN PARTS IN A VARIETY OF STYLES

To Prepare Chicken for Steaming: Cut the chicken into serving parts and remove skin and fat. Reserve skin, fat, wing tips, back, and any other scraps for soup stock. If the chicken is not completely fresh, or has been frozen, place the parts in a nonmetallic container, pour ¼ cup fresh lemon juice over, cover, and marinate several hours or overnight in the refrigerator.

To Steam Chicken: Drain chicken parts, pat dry with paper toweling, and arrange in a large Yunnan pot or a shallow dish (use two dishes if chicken is too crowded in one). Add one of the seasoning combinations from the following recipes and marinate as directed.

As the chicken cooks it will release juices. If you wish to have a large quantity of liquid in the finished dish, add ¼ to ½ cup chicken stock to the vessel with the other ingredients.

White meat cooks faster than dark meat, so if you are using two vessels, put the white meat on the upper tier of the steamer. If you are not using two vessels, remove white meat from marinade and return to dish after dark meat has steamed 10 minutes.

Set dish on a rack over boiling water in steamer, or set Yunnan pot directly over a saucepan of boiling water (see Equipment). Cover pot or Yunnan pot and steam 35 to 45 minutes, or until juices of thigh run clear when pierced with the tines of a fork. Keep in mind that the more crowded the chicken pieces, the longer they will take to cook.

As the chicken and other ingredients release juices in the dish or Yunnan pot, the level of liquid in the vessel will rise. If it is rising dangerously high, use a ladle to remove enough to stave off any overflow. The removed portion can be saved for serving with the chicken or for adding to soup stock.

To Serve Chicken: Serve the chicken directly from the Yunnan pot or dish at table, spooning juices over each portion. Accompany as suggested in each recipe.

TURKEY PARTS

Turkey breasts, whole or halved, are available in a range of weights, from barely larger than a chicken breast to as heavy as 4 pounds. Thighs and legs, which are also good for steaming, vary just as widely.

Turkey parts are steamed in the same manner as chicken parts, but cooking time must be increased to as long as 2 hours for the larger pieces. The Basic Herb, Italian, Japanese, and Cantonese recipes included under Chicken Parts in a Variety of Styles would be equally good made with turkey. The quantities of the other ingredients will need to be adjusted according to the size of the turkey pieces. The seasonings called for in Cornish Hen with Cranberries will also complement turkey.

Basic Herb Chicken

This preparation is simple and versatile. Add vegetables at intervals for a complete meal in one pot. See Vegetable Steaming Methods for timing; increase the recommended times slightly.

Consider color and texture when choosing the vegetables. For example, peeled yam chunks and broccoli florets make a colorful combination with contrasting textures. Equally attractive are carrot chunks and small white onions, with shelled green peas strewn over the last few minutes.

SERVES 3 OR 4

1 3-to 4-pound chicken, cut into serving parts	Herb seasoning and/or salt to taste
1/4 cup dry white wine	Freshly ground white pepper to taste
3 to 4 large garlic cloves, minced	2 green onions with tops
1 to 2 tablespoons minced fresh tarragon, basil, oregano, or herb of choice	4 parsley sprigs

Place chicken parts in vessel. Pour wine over and sprinkle with garlic, tarragon, herb seasoning, and pepper. Place green onions and 2 of the parsley sprigs on top of the chicken and steam as directed. Discard green onions and parsley and garnish with remaining parsley sprigs.

Mexican-style Chicken

Garnish this chicken with chopped ripe tomatoes and fresh coriander sprigs. Serve with rice, zucchini, and warmed corn tortillas.

SERVES 3 OR 4

1/2 cup minced onion	1 teaspoon crumbled dried oregano
2 to 3 large garlic cloves, minced	1/2 teaspoon ground cumin

1 3- to 4-pound chicken, cut into serving parts	2 tablespoons chopped fresh coriander
½ cup canned diced Anaheim or California green chiles	Freshly ground black pepper and salt to taste

Combine onion, garlic, oregano, and cumin. Toss with chicken parts and let stand 30 minutes, turning occasionally. Place chicken and marinade in vessel, strew chiles and chopped coriander over, and sprinkle with pepper and salt. Steam as directed.

South American-style Chicken

The tomatoes and peas serve as the vegetable, so a side dish of steamed white rice and a garnish of avocado slices rubbed with fresh lemon juice make this a complete meal.

Canned tomatoes are called for in this recipe because the vast majority of store-bought fresh tomatoes lack sufficient flavor. If you have garden-fresh tomatoes, use them instead.

SERVES 3 OR 4

½ cup chopped onion	1 16-ounce can whole plum tomatoes, well-drained
2 to 3 large garlic cloves, minced	Freshly ground black pepper and salt to taste
1 teaspoon chili powder	1 cup shelled peas
3 tablespoons fresh lime juice	
1 3- to 4-pound chicken, cut into serving parts	

Combine onion, garlic, chili powder, and lime juice. Toss with chicken parts and let stand 2 hours, turning occasionally. Place chicken and marinade in vessel and tuck tomatoes between pieces. Sprinkle with pepper and salt. Steam as directed. Five minutes before chicken is done, add peas.

Italian-style Chicken

A sprinkling of minced fresh Italian parsley will add color to this tasty chicken with olives. Serve with pasta bows moistened with the chicken juices, and Italian green beans with lightly toasted pine nuts.

SERVES 3 OR 4

3   tablespoons fresh lemon
     juice
3   tablespoons dry vermouth
1   tablespoon olive oil
2   to 3 teaspoons chopped
     fresh rosemary

2   large garlic cloves, minced
1   3- to 4-pound chicken, cut
     into serving parts
     Freshly ground black pepper
     and herb seasoning to taste
18 pitted ripe olives

Combine lemon juice, vermouth, oil, rosemary, and garlic. Toss with chicken parts and let stand 2 hours, turning occasionally. Place chicken and marinade in vessel and sprinkle with pepper and herb seasoning. Steam as directed. Add olives during the last 10 minutes of cooking.

Variation: Substitute chopped fresh basil for the rosemary and add 2 tablespoons drained capers to marinade. Omit olives and add 2 ounces prosciutto, cut into strips, during the last 10 minutes of steaming.

Hungarian-style Chicken

Pass a bowl of sour cream for diners to spoon over the chicken. Offer freshly cooked egg noodles tossed with Caraway Seed Butter Sauce and asparagus dressed with lemon juice.

SERVES 3 OR 4

2   cups chopped onions
1   tablespoon Hungarian
     paprika
1   tablespoon butter
2   medium-size ripe tomatoes,
     chopped

1   3- to 4-pound chicken, cut
     into serving parts
     Freshly ground black pepper
     and salt to taste
1   large green bell pepper, cut
     into eighths lengthwise

In a covered nonstick skillet cook onions and 2 teaspoons of the paprika in butter, stirring occasionally, 5 minutes. Remove from heat, stir in tomatoes, and spoon into vessel to be used for steaming. Sprinkle chicken parts with black pepper, salt, and remaining 1 teaspoon paprika. Place chicken pieces on tomato-onion mixture and steam as directed. Ten minutes before chicken is done, tuck bell pepper pieces in between the chicken parts.

French-style Chicken

Shallots and Brie make this chicken indescribably good. Parsley new potatoes and French-cut green beans dressed with Lemon/Lime Butter Sauce make it even better. Garnish the chicken with very finely shredded romaine lettuce.

SERVES 3 OR 4

3　*tablespoons fresh lemon
　juice*
2　*tablespoons minced shallots*
2　*large garlic cloves, minced*
1　*3- to 4-pound chicken, cut
　into serving parts*

*Freshly ground white pepper
to taste*
¾　*cup diced Brie cheese with
　rind*
¼　*cup minced fresh chives or
　green onion tops*

Combine lemon juice, shallots, and garlic. Toss with chicken parts and marinate 2 hours, turning occasionally. Place chicken and marinade in vessel, sprinkle with pepper, and strew cheese over. Sprinkle with chives and steam as directed.

Swiss-style Chicken

The famous Swiss crispy-fried shredded potatoes, *rösti*, or the Swabian specialty *spaetzle*, made by forcing egg noodle dough through a large-holed "sieve" into boiling water, would be perfect with this subtly flavored chicken.

SERVES 3 OR 4

¼　*cup dry white wine*
3　*tablespoons Dijon-style
　mustard*
1　*3- to 4-pound chicken, cut
　into serving parts*
3　*tablespoons chopped fresh
　tarragon*

½　*cup chopped green onions
　with tops*
　*Freshly ground white
　pepper and salt to taste*
1½　*cups sliced fresh
　mushrooms*
1½　*cups chopped spinach or
　Swiss chard*

Combine wine and mustard. Toss with chicken parts and let stand 30 minutes. Place chicken and marinade in vessel and sprinkle with tarragon, green onions, and pepper and salt. Steam as directed. For the last 10 minutes of cooking, strew mushrooms over the chicken; in the last 5 minutes, add spinach.

Mideast-style Chicken

Bulghur pilaf and cold eggplant strips dressed with fresh lemon juice go well with this fruity, rich chicken dish.

SERVES 3 OR 4

2 large Granny Smith or other tart apples, pared, cored, and coarsely grated	1 large onion, chopped
	3 tablespoons chopped fresh coriander
1 3- to 4-pound chicken, cut into serving parts	1/4 cup golden raisins
1 teaspoon ground cinnamon	8 dried apricot halves
1/2 teaspoon ground cardamom	8 pitted prunes
Freshly ground black pepper and salt to taste	1/2 cup fresh orange juice
	1 to 2 tablespoons mild honey

Arrange grated apple evenly on bottom of vessel. Sprinkle chicken parts with cinnamon, cardamom, and pepper and salt. Place chicken on top of apples and strew onion and chopped coriander over. Tuck raisins, apricots, and prunes between pieces. Pour orange juice over and drizzle with honey. Steam as directed.

Morroccan-style Chicken

Saffron, cumin, and ginger combine to give this North African-inspired chicken its exotic taste. Accompany with a side dish of couscous and a salad of thinly sliced radishes and oranges drizzled with a sweet-sour dressing of lemon juice and sugar. Pass a bowl of lightly slivered blanched almonds for guests to sprinkle on their chicken servings.

SERVES 3 OR 4

> Pinch of saffron threads
> 3   tablespoons fresh lemon
>   juice
> 1   tablespoon peanut oil
> ½   teaspoon ground ginger
> ¼   teaspoon ground cumin

> ¼   teaspoon freshly ground
>   black pepper
> 1   cup chopped onions
> 1   3- to 4-pound chicken, cut
>   into serving parts
> ¾   cup minced fresh parsley

Stir saffron into lemon juice and let stand 10 minutes. Combine lemon mixture with oil, ginger, cumin, pepper, and onions. Toss with chicken parts and let stand 2 hours, turning occasionally. Place chicken and marinade in vessel and strew parsley over. Steam as directed.

Japanese-style Chicken

Garnish this delicate chicken and shiitake mushroom dish with carrot curls. Let guests help themselves to lightly toasted sesame seeds for sprinkling over the chicken. Provide bowls of rice and small side dishes of *tsukemono*, pickled vegetables sold in jars and plastic packages in Japanese markets.

SERVES 3 OR 4

> ¼   cup sake or dry sherry
> 2   tablespoons soy sauce
> 4   large garlic cloves, slivered
> 4   large slices ginger root,
>   slivered
> 1   3- to 4-pound chicken, cut
>   into serving parts

> 2   teaspoons peanut oil
> 4   dried shiitake mushrooms,
>   soaked in warm water 30
>   minutes to soften, drained,
>   stemmed, and slivered
> 4   green onions with tops,
>   slivered

In a large nonmetallic dish combine sake, soy sauce, garlic, and ginger and toss with chicken parts. Drizzle oil over, cover, and refrigerate several hours, turning occasionally. Place chicken and marinade in vessel and strew mushrooms and onions over. Steam as directed.

Cantonese-style Chicken

Don't be alarmed by the number of ginger root slices called for in this dish; they infuse the chicken with a wonderful pungent flavor. Coriander sprigs make a colorful garnish. Serve with stir-fried snow peas and water chestnuts and fluffy long-grain rice.

SERVES 3 OR 4

3   tablespoons Chinese rice
    wine or dry sherry
2   tablespoons light soy sauce
1   3- to 4-pound chicken, cut
    into serving parts
4   large garlic cloves, minced

20 slices ginger root
3   green onions with tops,
    slivered
½   to 1 teaspoon Oriental
    sesame oil

In a large nonmetallic dish combine wine and soy sauce. Toss with chicken parts and strew garlic and ginger root over. Let stand 2 hours, turning occasionally. Place chicken and marinade in vessel, strew onions over, and sprinkle with sesame oil. Steam as directed.

Thai-style Chicken

The fish sauce, hot chile peppers, and lemon grass are typical of Thai cooking. Try to locate the slender red hot chiles that are favored by the Thais. If they are impossible to find, any red, green, or yellow chile pepper will do.

Steamed rice and spinach stir-fried with chopped garlic and fish sauce are typical accompaniments. Garnish with fresh coriander sprigs and pass a large bowl of toasted chopped peanuts, a popular Thai condiment, to strew over the chicken.

SERVES 3 OR 4

3   tablespoons dry sherry
2   tablespoons minced shallots
2   large garlic cloves, minced
1   tablespoon fish sauce

1   tablespoon chopped fresh
    basil
½   teaspoon granulated sugar
1   fresh hot chile pepper,
    minced

1 3- to 4-pound chicken, cut into serving parts Freshly ground black pepper to taste	1 stalk lemon grass or 2 teaspooons freshly grated lemon peel

Combine sherry, shallots, garlic, fish sauce, basil, sugar, and chile pepper. Toss with chicken parts and let stand 30 minutes, turning occasionally. Place chicken and marinade in vessel and sprinkle with pepper. Cut lemon grass into 2-inch pieces and lightly bruise with back of fork. Tuck pieces around chicken. Alternatively, strew lemon peel over chicken. Steam as directed.

Lemony Chicken

This tasty whole chicken needs no additional sauce, for the juices are imbued with the flavors of the fresh herbs and the lemon juice. Steamed barley and asparagus add texture and color. Spoon the juices over all.

SERVES 3 OR 4

1 3- to 4-pound chicken	$^1\!/_2$ teaspoon herb seasoning
5 large garlic cloves	$^1\!/_4$ teaspoon freshly ground black pepper
2 teaspoons minced fresh oregano	1 lemon, sliced
2 teaspoons minced fresh parsley	2 oregano sprigs
$^1\!/_2$ teaspoon minced fresh rosemary	4 parsley sprigs
$^1\!/_2$ teaspoon paprika	3 to 4 tablespoons fresh lemon juice

Rinse chicken and place upside down on rack to drain. Pat dry inside and out with paper toweling. In a mortar with pestle, mash 3 of the garlic cloves with the minced oregano, minced parsley, and rosemary. Stir in paprika, herb seasoning, and pepper. Rub outside of chicken with mixture. Bruise the remaining 2 garlic cloves and place in the cavity of the chicken along with half the lemon slices and the oregano and parsley sprigs.

Place chicken in a shallow dish, arrange remaining lemon slices on top of chicken, set dish on rack over boiling water, cover pot, and steam 1 hour, or until juices run clear when thigh is pierced with a fork. Remove dish from steamer, pour lemon juice over chicken, and let stand 10 minutes before carving into serving portions.

Oriental Whole Chicken

Sprinkle lightly toasted sesame seeds over the carved chicken for texture and flavor. Accompany with stir-fried long beans and steamed rice.

SERVES 3 OR 4

1 3- to 4-pound chicken	4 green onions with tops
1 teaspoon salt	3 tablespoons Chinese plum
1 teaspoon coarsely ground	sauce or hoisin sauce
black pepper	1 tablespoon Chinese rice wine
6 large garlic cloves, bruised	or dry sherry
6 slices ginger root	

Rinse chicken and place upside down on rack to drain. Pat dry inside and out with paper toweling. Combine salt, pepper, garlic, ginger root, and onions. Place in chicken cavity. Combine plum sauce and wine and rub over outside of chicken.

Place chicken in a shallow dish, set dish on rack over boiling water, cover pot, and steam 1 hour, or until juices of thigh run clear when pierced with a fork. Remove dish from steamer and let chicken stand for 10 minutes before carving.

Chicken Livers Marsala

An easy luncheon or supper dish accompanied by pasta or rice and a green salad dressed with Herb Vinaigrette. Sprinkle the steamed livers with lots of minced fresh parsley and serve directly from the dish. Sliced chicken hearts can also be cooked in this manner; reduce cooking time by half.

SERVES 2

4 pairs chicken livers	Salt and freshly ground
(approximately 5 ounces)	black pepper to taste
2 tablespoons Marsala	1/2 cup slivered cooked ham
1/4 teaspoon ground sage	1/2 cup sliced mushrooms

Separate chicken livers, trim off any fat, and cut each liver in half. Place in a shallow dish and pour Marsala over. Sprinkle with sage, salt, and pepper. Set dish on rack over boiling water, cover pot, and steam 15 minutes. Tuck ham slivers around livers and strew mushroom slices over the top. Continue steaming 10 minutes, or until livers are barely cooked through and mushrooms are tender.

Cornish Hen with Cranberries

The Cornish hen, first introduced to this country by Victor Borge over 20 years ago, is a small domesticated bird with a gentle flavor and texture, perfect for an elegant at-home dinner for two. The cranberries, available fresh in late autumn and frozen year-round, add a gorgeous color to the hen.

For a complete steamed meal, tuck whole yams and broccoli florets directly on the rack to steam alongside the Cornish hen as it cooks (see Vegetable Steaming Methods).

SERVES 2

1	*large Cornish hen (approximately 1 pound 6 ounces)*	2	*tablespoons dry sherry*
			Herb seasoning and freshly ground white pepper to
2	*lime or lemon slices*		*taste*
¾	*cup fresh or thawed frozen cranberries*	1½	*to 2 tablespoons honey*
		4	*thin unpeeled orange slices*

Rinse hen and place upside down on rack to drain. Pat dry inside and out with paper toweling. Put lime slices in cavity and place bird in a shallow dish.

Surround hen with cranberries and pour sherry over all. Sprinkle bird with herb seasoning and pepper and drizzle honey over the cranberries. Tuck orange slices into cranberry bed. Set dish on rack over boiling water, cover pot, and steam 45 to 50 minutes, or until thigh pulls easily away from body of bird. Remove dish from steamer and let hen stand 5 minutes before splitting to serve.

Crunchy Ground Turkey Loaf

The pistachios give a slight crunch to this soft-textured loaf. Steaming keeps it moist and less firmly packed than a conventional baked meat loaf. With this recipe as a guide, try steaming your favorite meat loaf.

Hash-browned potatoes and green beans are a good combination to serve with this turkey loaf, which is so moist it needs no sauce except the steaming juices. With luck, there will be leftovers for sandwiches.

SERVES 6

1 pound raw ground turkey meat
3/4 cup steamed brown or white rice
1 egg, lightly beaten
3 tablespoons homemade or bottled chili sauce
1/3 cup chopped unsalted pistachios
1/4 cup fine dry breadcrumbs

1/4 cup finely minced onion
2 to 3 large garlic cloves, finely minced
1/3 cup minced fresh parsley
1 teaspoon ground sage
1/4 teaspoon herb seasoning
1/4 teaspoon salt
1/4 teaspoon freshly ground black pepper

Combine all ingredients and mix well. Place a teaspoon-size portion in a small shallow dish, set on rack over boiling water, cover pot, and steam 5 minutes. Taste and adjust seasonings.

Form turkey mixture into a loaf shape about 4 inches high. Place loaf on a shallow dish. Set dish on rack over boiling water, cover pot, and steam 45 minutes.

Duckling

This fowl makes a particularly elegant meal for a special occasion. Both of the following recipes call for duckling stock, so purchase the duckling a day ahead and prepare the stock in advance. You will need a bird with its giblets, weighing between 4½ and 5 pounds, to serve 3 or 4 persons.

Unwrap the duckling and remove the giblets from the cavity. Rinse the bird under cold running water, drain, and pat dry with paper toweling. With poultry shears, snip off the tip and second joint of each wing. Place giblets and wing sections aside.

If the duckling is to be left whole for stuffing, remove any visible fat and any loose skin that will not be needed for securing the cavities closed.

If the duckling is to be quartered, remove all loose skin, visible fat, and the tail. Place all of these scraps aside with the giblets and wing sections. Cover and refrigerate the duckling.

Prepare the stock with the giblets and trimmings according to the following method and use as directed in the duckling recipes.

Duckling Stock

MAKES APPROXIMATELY 3 CUPS

1   celery stalk with leaves, coarsely chopped
1   small carrot, coarsely chopped
½   medium onion, chopped
2   tablespoons rendered duck or chicken fat or butter
     Reserved duckling giblets, wing sections, and scraps

1   bay leaf
3   parsley sprigs
2   thyme sprigs
4   or 5 fresh sage leaves
6   black peppercorns, lightly crushed
3   cups water or chicken stock

In a saucepan brown the celery, carrot, and onion in duck fat. Add all remaining ingredients, cover, bring to a slow boil, reduce heat, and cook gently 2 hours; at intervals, check the giblets and remove them as they are cooked. Cook, cover, and refrigerate. Use the giblets as directed in the stuffing for the whole duckling, or reserve for another use.

Strain stock, then jar, cool, cover, and refrigerate. Skim off congealed fat before using. Use any leftover stock as you would chicken stock.

Duckling with Port Wine Sauce

Browning the duckling before steaming releases much of the trapped fat, thereby cutting down on cholesterol and calories. Turnip puree seasoned with ground thyme and wild rice make excellent accompaniments to this spectacular dish.

SERVES 3 OR 4

1   readied duckling (see duckling introduction)

Salt and freshly ground black pepper
Watercress sprigs

Sauce

³/₄ cup Port
³/₄ cup Duckling Stock (see
       preceding recipe)
2   teaspoons butter
1   bay leaf
2   large garlic cloves, finely
    minced

2   tablespoons minced onion
¹/₂ teaspoon minced fresh
       thyme
¹/₄ cup Crème Fraîche (see
       Basic Savory Sauces)
    Salt and freshly ground
    black pepper to taste

Quarter duckling and sprinkle all surfaces with salt and pepper. Heat a large iron skillet until very hot. Place duck quarters, not touching, in skillet and brown well on all sides; the heat must remain very high so that the pieces brown quickly. Remove the skillet from the heat and transfer duck pieces skin side up directly onto a rack over boiling water. (Do not wash skillet.) Cover pot and steam 45 minutes.

While duck is steaming, prepare the sauce. Place unwashed skillet over medium heat and add Port and stock. Bring to a boil, scraping up any browned bits. Add butter, bay leaf, garlic, onion, and thyme, lower heat slightly, and simmer to reduce volume by half. Stir in Crème Fraîche and reheat to a simmer. Add salt and pepper and discard bay leaf. If preparing sauce ahead, set aside until serving time, then reheat gently. If necessary, thin with a little wine or stock.

Place duck pieces on a warmed platter and spoon some of the sauce over each piece. Garnish platter with watercress sprigs and serve remaining sauce on the side.

Whole Duckling with
Cabbage-Chestnut Stuffing

The interesting combination of cabbage and chestnut makes this duckling stuffing unique. Dried chestnuts give it a delightfully smoky flavor that is absent when you use fresh. While the bird steams, prepare the aromatic green peppercorn sauce, which is spooned over the duck meat at the table.

The stuffing is the vegetable course; add creamy mashed potatoes and a simple green salad dressed with fresh lemon juice and olive oil to complete the menu.

SERVES 3 OR 4

½ cup minced onion
2   to 3 large garlic cloves,
    minced
    Reserved cooked giblets,
    minced
2   teaspoons butter
5   or 6 large cabbage leaves,
    steamed until limp
½ tart apple
¼ pound dried chestnuts,
    cooked and chopped (see
    Note)

½ cup fresh breadcrumbs
¼ teaspoon ground sage
    Salt and freshly ground
    black pepper to taste
1   readied duckling (see
    duckling introduction)
    Soy sauce (optional)
    Shallot and Green
    Peppercorn Sauce (recipe
    follows)

To prepare the stuffing, cook onion, garlic, and giblets in butter in a covered skillet until onion is soft. Finely shred the limp cabbage leaves to measure approximately 2 cups. Chop the apple to measure approximately 1 cup.

In a mixing bowl combine the onion mixture with cabbage, apple, chestnuts, breadcrumbs, sage, salt, and pepper. If not using immediately, cover and refrigerate.

Just before steaming, remove the duckling from the refrigerator and place on a cutting board. With a sharp-tined fork, prick the entire skin surface of the bird; this permits the fat to drain off during steaming. Stuff cabbage mixture into the neck and tail cavities of the duckling. Truss openings closed with poultry pins.

Place the duckling, breast side up, directly on a rack over boiling water. Sprinkle with salt and freshly ground black pepper, cover pot, and steam 1 hour and 45 minutes. Remove bird to warmed serving platter and, if desired, rub with a little soy sauce to add color. Cover and let stand 15 minutes. Spoon stuffing out onto center of a warmed platter. Cut duckling into quarters and arrange around stuffing. Pass a bowl of Green Peppercorn Sauce for the duckling meat.

If the paleness of the duck distresses you, reduce steaming time to 1 hour and 15 minutes. Transfer bird to a rack set in a roasting pan and roast uncovered in a preheated 400° F oven 30 minutes, or until golden brown. Remove from oven, transfer to a warmed platter, cover, and let stand 15 minutes before carving.

Note: Dried chestnuts can be found in Chinese markets and in shops that stock imported French and Italian foods. To cook, rinse chestnuts well in cold water, place in a saucepan, cover with duckling or chicken stock, cover pan, and bring to a boil. Reduce heat and simmer, adding more stock if needed, 45 minutes, or until chestnuts are tender but not too soft. Drain chestnuts, reserving stock for another use.

Shallot and Green Peppercorn Sauce

This sauce can also be used on chicken dishes, in which case substitute chicken stock for the duckling stock.

MAKES APPROXIMATELY 1 CUP

¼ cup dry vermouth	1½ cups Duckling Stock (see
1 tablespoon brandy	recipe)
2 teaspoons minced shallots	½ to ⅔ cup heavy cream or
1 tablespoon drained green	Crème Fraîche (see Basic
peppercorns	Savory Sauces)

In a saucepan or skillet bring vermouth, brandy, shallots, and peppercorns to a slow boil. Stirring occasionally, let boil gently until mixture is reduced by half. Add stock, bring back to gentle boil, and cook, stirring often, 30 minutes, or until slightly thickened. Blend in cream and cook and stir 10 minutes.

If sauce has been made ahead and is too thick when reheated, thin with stock or cream.

BASIC SAVORY SAUCES

Béchamel Sauce

Mornay Sauce

Curry Sauce

Sorrel Sauce

Oyster Sauce

Mushroom Sauce

Basic Tomato Sauce

Uncooked Tomato Sauce

Butter Sauces

Nut Butter Sauces

Seed Butters

Compound Butters

Pesto

Watercress Pesto

Greek Lemon Sauce

Mustard Sauce

Crème Fraîche

Mayonnaise

Sour Cream Mayonnaise

"Healthful" Hollandaise Sauce

Vinaigrette

Oriental Dressing

Tahini Dressing

Avocado Tahini Dressing

Peanut Sauce

No-Oil Dressings

See Index for sauces used in other recipes

Basic Savory Sauces

Many steamed dishes are enhanced by a sauce, whether it be a simple seasoned butter lightly coating a green vegetable, a fresh tomato sauce spooned over chicken breasts, a lemony sesame-seed blend masking fish fillets, or a thyme-scented curry sauce streaked over eggplant fingers.

In this chapter you will find a wide array of basic sauces, all of which are incorporated into a dish or used as a topping. This includes cream-based sauces such as Béchamel and Mornay, tomato sauces, melted butter and compound butter combinations, mayonnaises, and vinaigrettes. More unusual creations also appear, such as a tangy Sorrel Sauce, a peppery Peanut Sauce, and a full-bodied Oyster Sauce. All of these sauces are called for throughout the book.

At the end of the chapter there are four no-oil salad dressings for those who are closely watching the fats in their diets. They can be used to dress steamed vegetables, but are best on raw vegetable salads that are served with low-calorie steamed dishes.

In most cases I use salted butter when preparing sauces, but if you are watching salt intake carefully or prefer unsalted butter, feel free to substitute it. Margarine can't match the flavor of butter, especially when browned, but it can also be used. Look for polyunsaturated margarine with no preservatives.

Some of you may have hoped to see less cream in this chapter. I have attempted wherever possible to use half-and-half cream and stock in place of heavy cream, and at this point the proportion of cream is greatly reduced from the amounts found in classic preparations. I have discovered, however, that cream cannot be eliminated completely if good flavor is to be maintained. A few dairy substitutes appear in Terms and Ingredients; experiment with them in the sauce recipes that call for cream.

192

The way to enjoy sauced steamed foods and maintain a clear conscience about eating properly for your health is to be moderate in your serving portions. Don't bathe the food; a light coating is all that is necessary. A rich sauce should be treated almost as a seasoning; use it sparingly so it does not overpower the dish.

Béchamel Sauce (Cream or White Sauce)

To lighten this sauce I have used half stock and half milk or half-and-half cream. Vary the seasonings with ground cumin, freshly grated nutmeg, ground thyme, finely minced fresh herbs, Worcestershire sauce, or, for a spicy touch, hot pepper sauce. Use any stock that will complement the dish you are serving: chicken stock for a chicken dish, fish stock for a fish dish, and so on.

For a low-fat cream sauce, dissolve 1½ teaspoons of arrowroot in 1 cup of nonfat milk and place over medium heat. Cook, stirring, until smooth and thickened. Add ½ teaspoon chicken stock base, Marmite, or other bouillon flavoring, and season as for béchamel sauce. The calories are decreased with this method, but the good flavor is as well.

Cream sauce can be covered and refrigerated up to 2 days or frozen up to 1 month. To reheat, warm slowly, stirring constantly and adding additional stock or cream to thin to sauce consistency.

MAKES 1 CUP

2 tablespoons butter	½ cup rich stock, or as needed
2 tablespoons unbleached flour	Freshly ground white pepper and herb seasoning to taste
½ cup half-and-half cream or milk	

In a nonstick skillet or saucepan melt butter until bubbly. Sprinkle with flour and cook, stirring, 2 to 3 minutes to form a roux. Remove from heat and gradually stir in half-and-half and stock. Return to medium-low heat and cook, stirring, until sauce is smooth and thickened. Cook 5 to 7 more minutes, stirring occasionally and adding stock to desired consistency. Add seasonings and adjust to taste.

Variations:

Add 2 to 3 teaspoons finely minced onion or green onion to the butter when melting, cover, and cook until onion is softened. Then add flour and proceed as above.

Heat half-and-half and stock 5 to 6 minutes with 1 small onion, 1 whole clove, 1 parsley sprig, 1 garlic clove, bruised, and ½ bay leaf before adding to butter-flour roux.

Substitute ¼ cup dry white wine for ¼ cup of the stock.

Mornay Sauce (Cheese Sauce)

This isn't a classic Mornay because the cream sauce base is made with stock. It has the same wonderful qualities, though, so I have used the traditional name. It may be stored in the same manner as Béchamel Sauce.

MAKES 1 CUP

1   recipe Béchamel Sauce (see
    preceding recipe)
2   tablespoons freshly grated
    Parmesan cheese

2   tablespoons freshly shredded
    Gruyère cheese

Heat Béchamel Sauce gently and gradually stir in cheeses. Cook, stirring constantly, until cheeses are melted; do not allow to boil.

Variation: Substitute ⅓ cup grated cheddar or Monterey Jack cheese for the Parmesan and Gruyère.

Curry Sauce

If you like a spicier blend, increase the curry powder in this easy-to-make all-purpose sauce. It goes well with chicken, lamb, eggplant, mixed-vegetable dishes, or brown or white rice. Storage directions are the same as for Béchamel Sauce.

MAKES 1¼ CUPS

3   tablespoons finely minced
     onion
1½   teaspoons butter
1   teaspoon curry powder, or
     to taste

1   small bay leaf
1   thyme sprig
1   recipe Béchamel Sauce
¼   cup rich stock, or as
     needed

In a covered nonstick skillet cook onion in butter until soft. Sprinkle with curry powder and cook, stirring, 2 to 3 minutes. Add bay leaf, thyme, Béchamel Sauce, and stock and blend well. Cook, stirring often, over medium heat 10 to 15 minutes, adding more stock if sauce thickens too much. Strain through a sieve and reheat just before serving.

Sorrel Sauce

This tart sauce is especially good with scallops, but it may be used for any simply cooked fish or on cauliflower. It should be stored no longer than 2 days in the refrigerator—and do not freeze, as the flavor suffers.

MAKES APPROXIMATELY 1 CUP

6   ounces sorrel
2   tablespoons minced shallots
3   tablespoons dry vermouth or
     white rice vinegar
1   tablespoon butter
½   cup half-and-half cream,
     or as needed

¼   cup Crème Fraîche or heavy
     cream
2   teaspoons fresh lemon juice,
     or to taste
     Salt and freshly ground
     white pepper to taste
     Chicken stock, as needed

Remove stems and any tough ribs from sorrel and finely chop to measure approximately 1¼ cups firmly packed. Set aside.

In a covered nonstick skillet cook shallots in vermouth 3 minutes. Uncover and cook until almost all moisture has evaporated. Add butter, heat to melt, and then add reserved sorrel. Cover and cook 2 minutes, or until sorrel darkens. Stir in cream and Crème Fraîche and mix well. Add lemon juice, salt, and pepper. If a thinner sauce is desired, thin with a little more half-and-half or chicken stock.

Oyster Sauce

Particularly good over steamed monkfish fillet, this sauce can also be mixed with scallops or shrimp. A garnish of minced fresh chives or parsley adds flavor and color.

MAKES APPROXIMATELY 1 CUP

¼   cup dry vermouth
⅓   cup minced shallots

2   *tablespoons butter*
2   *shucked oysters (about 1½*
      ounces each), very finely
      chopped
½   *cup half-and-half cream, or*
      as needed

½   *cup fish stock or bottled*
      clam juice, or as needed
      Freshly ground white pepper
      to taste
      Fresh lemon juice to taste

In a skillet or saucepan cook vermouth and shallots until almost all the vermouth has boiled away. Add butter; when hot, add oysters and any juices. Cook, stirring, 5 minutes. Add half-and-half and fish stock; cook and stir until heated through. Season with pepper and lemon juice.

If not using immediately, cool, cover, and refrigerate up to 1 day. Gently reheat before serving.

Mushroom Sauce

Meat loaf, chicken, veal shanks, vegetables such as broccoli or cauliflower, or timbales would all be enhanced by the addition of this shallot-seasoned fresh mushroom sauce.

MAKES APPROXIMATELY 2 CUPS

¼   *cup minced shallots*
3   *tablespoons butter and/or*
      rendered chicken fat
12   *ounces fresh mushrooms,*
      sliced
¼   *teaspoon ground oregano*
¼   *teaspoon salt*

¼   *teaspoon freshly ground*
      white pepper
⅓   *cup dry vermouth*
⅓   *cup Crème Fraîche*
2   *tablespoons minced fresh*
      chives or garlic chives

In a large nonstick skillet cook shallots in butter 2 to 3 minutes, or until they start to soften. Add mushrooms and cook, stirring, 5 minutes, sprinkling with seasonings as they cook.

Raise heat slightly and stir in vermouth. Let boil gently, stirring occasionally, 3 to 4 minutes. Stir in Crème Fraîche and cook until slightly reduced and thickened. Adjust seasonings and stir in chives.

If not using immediately, cool, cover, and refrigerate up to 2 days.

Basic Tomato Sauce

MAKES APPROXIMATELY 2 CUPS

½   medium onion, diced
4   large garlic cloves, minced
1   small red or green bell
*   pepper, minced*
2   tablespoons olive oil
1   pound ripe tomatoes, peeled
*   and chopped*
2   teaspoons chopped fresh
*   basil*
2   teaspoons chopped fresh
*   oregano*

2   tablespoons chopped fresh
*   Italian parsley*
1   bay leaf
½   teaspoon freshly ground
*   black pepper*
1   tablespoon fresh lemon or
*   lime juice*
1   teaspoon anchovy paste, or
*   to taste*

In a large covered skillet cook onion, garlic, and bell pepper in oil 5 minutes. Add tomatoes, herbs, and black pepper. Stirring occasionally, cook uncovered 15 minutes. Stir in lemon juice and anchovy paste.

If not using immediately, cool, cover, and refrigerate up to 2 days or freeze up to 1 month.

Uncooked Tomato Sauce

This relishlike sauce is delicious with cold or hot meats, such as beef brisket, tongue, meat loaf, or pork loin.

MAKES APPROXIMATELY 2 CUPS

4   large ripe tomatoes
¼   cup minced onion
2   large garlic cloves, minced
2   tablespoons minced green
*   or red bell pepper*
*   (optional)*

1½ tablespoons olive oil
1   teaspoon minced fresh
*   basil or oregano*
*   Pinch granulated sugar*
*   Salt and freshly ground*
*   black pepper to taste*

Combine all ingredients in a mixing bowl. Let stand at room temperature 2 hours.

To store, cover and refrigerate up to 1 day.

Butter Sauces

A steamed vegetable is turned into a special dish with the addition of one of these butter sauces. When preparing any of them, allow 1 to 2 teaspoons of finished sauce per serving.

Brown Butter Sauce: Melt butter in a saucepan, then cook over medium heat, being careful not to burn, until butter is a rich brown color.

Lemon/Lime Butter Sauce: Melt butter in a saucepan and add ½ teaspoon fresh lemon or lime juice for each tablespoon butter. Alternatively, boil 2 tablespoons fresh lemon or lime juice until reduced to 2 teaspoons. Bit by bit, whisk in 4 tablespoons butter until well incorporated and sauce is slightly fluffy. This method gives a slightly creamy look to the butter.

Garlic/Shallot Butter Sauce: In a saucepan combine 1 teaspoon very finely minced garlic or 2 teaspoons finely minced shallots with 2 tablespoons white wine vinegar; boil until reduced to 2 teaspoons. Bit by bit, whisk in 3 to 4 tablespoons butter until well incorporated and sauce is slightly fluffy.

Herb Butter Sauce: In a saucepan melt 2 tablespoons butter until foamy. Add 1 to 2 teaspoons mixed minced fresh herbs such as basil, parsley, oregano, watercress, thyme, rosemary, tarragon, burnet, chives, chervil. Season with fresh lemon or lime juice to taste.

Anchovy Butter Sauce: Into 3 tablespoons melted butter or Garlic Butter Sauce stir ¼ to ½ teaspoon anchovy paste or 1 to 2 anchovy fillets, mashed. Add 1 to 2 teaspoons minced fresh parsley and fresh lemon or lime juice to taste.

Nut Butter Sauces

Allow 1 to 2 teaspoons butter and 1 to 2 teaspoons chopped, sliced, or slivered nuts per serving. (If chopping, do not use blender or processor; nuts will be unevenly chopped and may become oily.) Add lightly toasted nuts to Brown Butter Sauce, or brown untoasted nuts in butter as it melts.

Suggested nuts: chopped walnuts, hazelnuts, pecans, or peanuts; whole or coarsely chopped pine nuts; sliced, chopped, or blanched and slivered almonds; cooked and finely minced chestnuts.

Seed Butter Sauces

Allow 1 to 2 teaspoons butter and ½ to 1 teaspoon seeds per serving. Proceed as for nut butters.

Suggested seeds: caraway seeds; poppy seeds; lightly toasted sesame, pumpkin, or sunflower seeds.

Compound Butters

These butters are especially good with fish, but are also delicious on vegetables. Serve prepared butter immediately, or form into a log shape, wrap well in waxed paper, and store in the refrigerator up to 1 week or in the freezer up to 2 weeks. Cut into slices, let come to room temperature, and place on hot steamed foods. Allow 1 to 2 teaspoons butter mixture per serving.

Onion Butter: In covered skillet cook 3 tablespoons finely minced onion in 1½ teaspoons butter until onion has softened. Cool and add ⅛ teaspoon paprika. Stir into 4 to 5 tablespoons softened butter and beat until creamy.

Garlic Butter: Beat 1 to 2 garlic cloves, very finely minced, into 4 to 5 tablespoons softened butter. Add ⅛ teaspoon powdered thyme or oregano. Beat until creamy.

Anchovy Butter: Beat 4 to 5 tablespoons butter until creamy. Stir in 2½ teaspoons anchovy paste, or to taste, and 1 teaspoon grated onion. If desired, add fresh lemon juice and/or minced fresh parsley to taste.

Herb Butter: Blanch for 30 seconds 3 to 4 tablespoons mixed minced fresh herbs such as parsley, basil, watercress, oregano, thyme, rosemary, tarragon. Drain thoroughly and, if desired, combine with 1 tablespoon well-drained cooked chopped spinach or Swiss chard. Stir herbs into 4 to 5 tablespoons softened butter or Garlic Butter and mix well with fork to prevent bruising herbs . Add fresh lemon or lime juice and freshly ground white pepper to taste.

Tomato Butter: Finely chop 1 medium-size ripe tomato. Place in sieve and drain well, pushing all moisture out with back of wooden spoon. Stir tomato pulp into 4 to 5 tablespoons softened butter along with 1 tablespoon finely minced fresh parsley and/or chives.

Lemon/Lime Butter: Beat into 4 to 5 tablespoons softened butter 2 teaspoons fresh lemon or lime juice and ¼ teaspoon freshly grated lemon or lime peel.

Nut Butter: Beat into Lemon/Lime Butter (preceding recipe) 2 teaspoons finely chopped almonds, walnuts, or pecans or cooked and finely chopped chestnuts. Season with ground thyme or oregano to taste.

Green Peppercorn Butter: Beat into 4 to 5 tablespoons softened butter 2 tablespoons minced fresh parsley, 2 to 3 teaspoons drained green pep-

percorns, 1 teaspoon fresh lemon juice, and Dijon-style mustard, Worcestershire sauce, and freshly ground white pepper to taste.

Pesto

Pesto has become extremely popular as a sauce for pasta, but it has many
other uses. This garlicky version adds spark to steamed vegetables, such
as potatoes and spaghetti squash, and looks beautiful alongside a steamed
white fish fillet.

MAKES APPROXIMATELY 1 1/4 CUPS

- 3 to 4 large garlic cloves, chopped
- 1/2 teaspoon salt
- 1/3 cup pine nuts
- 2 1/2 cups firmly packed fresh basil leaves
- 1/2 cup freshly grated Parmesan cheese
- 1/4 cup freshly grated Romano or pecorino cheese
- 3 to 4 tablespoons fresh Italian parsley leaves
- 3/4 to 1 cup olive oil
- 1 to 2 teaspoons fresh lemon or lime juice

In a blender or food processor fitted with metal blade, whirl garlic
cloves and salt until very finely minced. Add pine nuts and whirl briefly.
Add basil, cheeses, and parsley; whirl briefly. With motor running, add
olive oil in a slow, steady stream. Add lemon juice and blend just until
well mixed.

If not using immediately, transfer to a jar, cover with a film of olive oil,
cover jar tightly, and refrigerate up to 1 week. If freezing (up to 1 month),
omit cheeses and blend in when defrosted. Bring to room temperature
and stir well before serving.

Variations:

Beat a few tablespoons of softened butter into finished sauce.
Season sauce with freshly grated nutmeg to taste.
Substitute coarsely chopped walnuts for the pine nuts.

Watercress Pesto

When fresh basil is out of season, try this unique watercress-based pesto. Without the Parmesan and pine nuts, the watercress mixture can be added in small amounts to Mayonnaise to produce a variation of Herb Mayonnaise.

MAKES APPROXIMATELY ⅔ CUP

1½ cups firmly packed
watercress leaves
½ cup chopped fresh parsley
leaves
2 large garlic cloves, cut up
1 teaspoon crumbled dried
basil

¼ to ⅓ cup olive oil
½ cup freshly grated
Parmesan cheese
2 tablespoons pine nuts or
walnuts, finely chopped

In a blender or food processor with metal blade in place, whirl watercress, parsley, garlic, and basil until finely minced. With motor running, add oil in a slow, steady stream and continue to blend until mixture is well combined. Transfer to a mixing bowl and stir in cheese and pine nuts.

If not using immediately, cover and refrigerate up to 4 days. If freezing (up to 1 month), omit cheese and pine nuts and blend in when defrosted. Bring to room temperature and stir well before serving.

Greek Lemon Sauce

Good with artichokes, asparagus, and almost any other green vegetable.

MAKES APPROXIMATELY 1¼ CUPS

1 tablespoon cornstarch
2 tablespoons cold water
1 cup chicken stock

2 egg yolks
⅓ cup fresh lemon juice, or to
taste

Dissolve cornstarch in water. Heat stock to boiling and stir in cornstarch mixture. Lower heat slightly and, stirring constantly, cook until stock is thickened, smooth, and translucent.

Beat egg yolks in a mixing bowl with a wooden spoon until thick and lemon-colored. Beating constantly, pour in hot stock mixture in a slow, steady stream. Beat until smooth and stir in lemon juice. Serve immediately.

Should there be any sauce left over, refrigerate in a covered jar up to 2 days. To reheat, set jar, uncovered, in a saucepan with water halfway up sides of jar. Stirring often, heat water until sauce is warmed. The consistency and flavor will not be as good as it was originally.

Mustard Sauce

Use this tangy sauce in place of prepared mustard with beef brisket, tongue, or sausages, or serve on tender-crisp green beans.

MAKES APPROXIMATELY ⅔ CUP

4 *teaspoons finely minced shallots*	4 *tablespoons cold butter, cut into bits*
½ *cup fresh lemon juice*	*Freshly ground white*
½ *cup half-and-half cream*	*pepper to taste*
2½ *teaspoons Dijon-style mustard, or to taste*	

In a small saucepan combine shallots, lemon juice, and half-and-half cream. Bring to boil, lower heat slightly, and cook until reduced by half, stirring occasionally. Stir in mustard and, bit by bit, whisk in butter. Remove from heat and season with pepper.

If not using immediately, cool, jar, cover, and refrigerate up to 2 days. Bring to room temperature and stir well before serving.

Crème Fraîche

The rich, tangy flavor of true French crème fraîche, a thick, smooth cultured cream used in sauces and as a topping, is impossible to duplicate precisely in the home kitchen. Your efforts, however, will result in a very satisfactory product. One of the beauties of crème fraîche is that it can be heated in a sauce or with other foods without curdling the way sour cream does. A small dollop of plain crème fraîche on almost any vegetable or steamed fruit gives an elegant touch.

Cream with a butterfat content of 40 percent is preferred. The heavy cream usually found in the supermarket is lower in butterfat, but it can be used. Three methods work well, so try them all to see which produces the flavor that appeals to you.

1) Combine 2 tablespoons buttermilk and 1 cup heavy cream. Let stand uncovered at room temperature for 14 to 16 hours. If not using immediately, cover and refrigerate up to 1 week.

2) Combine 1 tablespoon buttermilk and 1 cup heavy cream and let stand uncovered at room temperature for 24 hours. If not using immediately, cover and refrigerate up to 1 week.

3) Combine equal parts sour cream and heavy cream. Let stand overnight and stir well. If not using immediately, cover and refrigerate up to 2 weeks.

Mayonnaise

Mayonnaise made with egg yolks by the hand method results in a more flavorful, lighter-bodied sauce than this machine-made version. But this blender mayonnaise has less fat and cholesterol, because it is made with a whole egg instead of 2 egg yolks, and a much longer life, up to 3 weeks in a covered jar in the refrigerator.

I prefer the flavor of olive and safflower oils, so I have suggested them here. The latter is polyunsaturated, another good reason for using it. The larger measurement of oil will make a heavier, firmer mayonnaise.

MAKES APPROXIMATELY 1¼ CUPS

1 egg	*Pinch of paprika*
1½ to 2 teaspoons cider, wine, white rice, or other vinegar of choice	*Pinch of cayenne pepper (optional)*
⅛ teaspoon salt	1 to 1¼ cups olive or safflower oil
⅛ teaspoon freshly ground white pepper	

Break egg into a blender or bowl of food processor fitted with steel blade. Add vinegar, salt, pepper, paprika, and cayenne pepper. Blend to mix well; with motor running, add olive oil in a slow, steady stream. Adjust seasonings.

Variations:

Lemon/Lime Mayonnaise: Substitute fresh lemon or lime juice for vinegar.

Mustard Mayonnaise: To finished Mayonnaise or Lemon/Lime Mayonnaise add prepared mustard (such as Dijon) to taste.

Ginger Mayonnaise: To Mayonnaise, Lemon/Lime Mayonnaise, or Mustard Mayonnaise add 1 to 1½ teaspoons freshly grated ginger root.

Garlic Mayonnaise: Finely mince 3 to 4 garlic cloves in blender or processor before adding egg yolk. Proceed as directed.

Curry Mayonnaise: To Mayonnaise or Lemon/Lime Mayonnaise add ½ teaspoon curry powder, or to taste.

Herb Mayonnaise: With the egg yolk blend 1 to 2 teaspoons minced fresh herbs of choice.

Sour Cream Mayonnaise

The addition of sour cream makes this mayonnaise a bit lighter in flavor than commercial mayonnaise, and the herbs give it a lovely color.

MAKES APPROXIMATELY 2 CUPS

1 large garlic clove	¼ cup sour cream
2 small green onions with 3 inches of green tops	2 to 3 teaspoons minced fresh dill
2 parsley sprigs, tough stems removed	1 to 2 teaspoons fresh lemon or lime juice
½ cup Mayonnaise (see preceding recipe)	Salt and freshly ground white pepper to taste

In a blender or food processor fitted with metal blade, whirl garlic, green onions, and parsley until finely minced. Add all remaining ingredients, blending *just* until smooth; do not overmix. Adjust seasonings to taste and store as for Mayonnaise.

Variations:

Add 1 teaspoon anchovy paste when blending.

Stir into finished sauce 1 to 2 teaspoons drained capers or green peppercorns, chopped.

Add hot pepper sauce to taste when adjusting seasonings.

"Healthful" Hollandaise Sauce

This recipe is not for those who want to prepare a classic hollandaise sauce. To save the cook time, the butter is not clarified, and the traditional egg yolks have been replaced by whole eggs to cut down on cholesterol. To reduce the cholesterol even further by increasing the volume of the sauce, beat in 2 to 3 tablespoons plain yoghurt at the finish.

Despite these changes, the flavor and consistency of this hollandaise match those of the classic, and it holds longer without separating. The sauce can be refrigerated up to 2 days and then gently rewarmed in a double boiler or heavy nonstick saucepan.

Spark up this foolproof sauce with cayenne pepper, chili powder, or grated orange peel.

MAKES APPROXIMATELY 1 CUP

2   *whole eggs*
2   *tablespoons fresh lemon*
    juice

¾   *cup cold butter, cut into*
    small bits

In the top pan of a double boiler off the heat, beat together eggs and lemon juice with a wire whisk until well blended and slightly fluffy. Place pan over simmering water and continue beating until thickened, about 5 to 6 minutes. Beating constantly, add butter bit by bit. When all of the butter is incorporated, remove the double boiler from the heat.

If not using immediately, stir occasionally until serving. The sauce will hold at least 30 minutes.

Vinaigrette

Almost any minced fresh herb or herb combination or finely minced foods such as hard-cooked eggs, sun-dried tomato, bell pepper or roasted pepper, celery, or pimiento-stuffed olives can be added to this basic vinaigrette. Substitute safflower, walnut, or other oil for the olive oil, and cider, tarragon, or other vinegar for the wine vinegar.

MAKES 1 CUP

¹/₄ to ¹/₂ teaspoon salt	*¹/₄ cup white or red wine*
¹/₄ teaspoon freshly ground	*vinegar*
white or black pepper	*²/₃ cup olive oil*

Combine salt and pepper in a small wooden bowl. Add vinegar and stir to dissolve salt. Add oil in a slow, steady stream, whisking until well blended and slightly thickened.

Transfer to a jar, cover, and refrigerate up to 1 week. Bring to room temperature before serving.

Variations:

Lemon/Lime Vinaigrette: Substitute fresh lemon or lime juice for the vinegar.

Mustard Vinaigrette: With salt and pepper mix 1 teaspoon Dijon-style mustard or ¹/₂ teaspoon dry mustard, or to taste.

Herb Vinaigrette: With vinegar mixture combine 1 tablespoon minced fresh herbs of choice or 1¹/₂ teaspoons dried herbs, and 1 to 2 tablespoons finely chopped and well-drained cooked spinach or sorrel.

Anchovy Vinaigrette: Blend ¹/₂ to 1 teaspoon anchovy paste or mashed anchovy fillets into vinegar mixture.

Shallot Vinaigrette: Add 1 to 2 teaspoons finely minced shallots to vinegar mixture.

Blue Cheese Vinaigrette: Add 2 to 3 tablespoons crumbled blue cheese to Vinaigrette or Lemon/Lime Vinaigrette.

Oriental Dressing

MAKES APPROXIMATELY 1 CUP

¹/₂ cup white rice vinegar	*1 teaspoon finely minced*
3 tablespoons light soy sauce	*garlic*
3 tablespoons corn or peanut	*¹/₂ teaspoon granulated sugar*
oil	*2 tablespoons finely minced*
	green onion tops

Combine all ingredients thoroughly. If not using immediately, jar, cover, and refrigerate up to 3 days.

Variation: Add ½ teaspoon dry mustard, 1 tablespoon toasted sesame seeds, chile oil to taste, or 1 teaspoon finely minced ginger root.

Tahini Dressing

Tahini is a paste made from ground sesame seeds. It is most commonly sold in 16-ounce jars and can be found in Mideast specialty shops, natural and health-food stores, and in some supermarkets. Stir the paste well before using, as it tends to separate. Once opened, store in the refrigerator.

Serve this full-flavored dressing as a topping or dip for vegetables, or as an accompaniment to fish fillets.

MAKES APPROXIMATELY 1 CUP

3 large garlic cloves, minced	½ cup tahini
2 tablespoons minced fresh parsley	½ cup fresh lemon or lime juice
2 tablespoons minced fresh coriander (optional)	1 tablespoon olive oil, or as needed
¼ teaspoon salt	1 tablespoon cold water, or as needed
¼ teaspoon freshly ground white pepper	3 to 4 drops Tabasco

In a blender or food processor fitted with metal blade, whirl the garlic, parsley, coriander, salt, and pepper until garlic is very finely minced. Add tahini, lemon juice, oil, water, and Tabasco sauce; whirl until mixture is well blended and smooth. Taste and adjust seasonings, adding more oil and/or water to thin dressing to desired consistency.

If not using immediately, cover and refrigerate up to 1 week. Bring to room temperature and stir well before serving.

Avocado Tahini Dressing

The addition of avocado gives Tahini Dressing a smooth, silky quality.

MAKES APPROXIMATELY 1⅔ CUPS

*1 large ripe avocado, mashed
     with 1 tablespoon fresh
     lemon or lime juice*

*1 recipe Tahini Dressing (see
     preceding recipe)
     Ground cumin to taste*

Combine all ingredients, beating until smooth. If a very smooth consistency is preferred, whirl in a blender or food processor. Adjust seasonings.

If not using immediately, cover and refrigerate up to 2 days. Bring to room temperature and stir well before serving.

Peanut Sauce

I have adapted this favorite Southeast Asian sauce to the Western kitchen. If desired, add 2 tablespoons of catsup to give it a mellower flavor and slightly thinner consistency.

This rich sauce will give an exotic touch to vegetables, meats, and egg dishes.

MAKES APPROXIMATELY 1⅓ CUPS

*1 medium onion, minced
2 large garlic cloves, minced
1 tablespoon peanut oil
1 cup coconut milk (see
     Note)
1 cup crunchy peanut butter*

*½ teaspoon firmly packed
     brown sugar
1 teaspoon soy sauce
¼ teaspoon salt
1½ tablespoons fresh lemon
     juice
¼ teaspoon cayenne pepper*

In a covered nonstick skillet cook onion and garlic in oil until soft. Uncover and add coconut milk. Cook and stir 2 minutes, lower heat to medium low, and gradually stir in peanut butter. Add all remaining ingredients and blend until sauce is smooth. Taste and adjust seasonings.

If not using sauce immediately, cover and refrigerate up to 1 week. Bring to room temperature and stir well before using.

Note: For information on coconut milk, see Thai Sticky Rice with Mangoes in the Desserts chapter.

No-Oil Dressings

These four salad dressings are perfect for the cautious eater, as they contain no oil and are made with healthful ingredients. Serve them with steamed vegetables or use on tossed salads.

Hoisin Dressing

MAKES APPROXIMATELY ⅔ CUP

⅓ cup hoisin sauce
⅓ cup fresh lemon juice
1 small garlic clove, very
    finely minced

1 small slice ginger root, very
    finely minced

In a small mixing bowl, beat hoisin sauce with a wooden spoon until smooth. Gradually beat in lemon juice, then stir in garlic and ginger root. If not using immediately, jar, cover, and refrigerate up to 1 week.

Tofu Dressing

MAKES APPROXIMATELY ⅔ CUP

1 small garlic clove, finely
    minced
1 small slice ginger root,
    finely minced
2 tablespoons minced fresh
    parsley
2 tablespoons minced fresh
    coriander
1½ tablespoons minced fresh
    chives

6 ounces firm or soft tofu
½ tablespoon soy sauce or
    red or white miso, or to
    taste
3 tablespoons fresh lemon
    juice, or to taste
    Cayenne pepper to taste
    Freshly ground white
    pepper to taste

In a blender or food processor fitted with metal blade, whirl the garlic and ginger root until very finely minced. Add parsley, coriander, and chives. Whirl briefly, then add tofu, soy sauce, and lemon juice. Whirl until smooth and transfer to a mixing bowl. Season with cayenne and white pepper. Taste and adjust seasonings.

If not using immediately, cover and refrigerate up to 2 days. Stir well before serving.

Buttermilk-Herb Dressing

This low-calorie, low-fat creamy buttermilk dressing and the cottage cheese one that follows are taken from *The American Heart Association Cookbook*, a valuable guide for those concerned with keeping cholesterol in check.

The buttermilk dressing is very thin. You may wish to add mayonnaise or yoghurt for a thicker consistency.

MAKES APPROXIMATELY 1 CUP

1 cup buttermilk	1/8 teaspoon dried dillweed
1 tablespoon prepared mustard	2 teaspoons finely chopped parsley
1 teaspoon minced onion	Freshly ground black pepper

Combine all ingredients in a jar, cover tightly, and shake to blend. Chill overnight or for several hours. Shake well before serving.

Store in the refrigerator tightly covered for up to 1 week.

Creamy Cottage Cheese Dressing

MAKES 1½ CUPS

1 cup low-fat cottage cheese	1/3 cup buttermilk

In a blender or food processor mix cheese and buttermilk on medium speed until smooth and creamy. More buttermilk may be added for a thinner consistency.

Variations:

Blue Cheese: Add 1 tablespoon blue cheese and freshly ground white pepper to taste.

Creamy French: Add 1 teaspoon paprika with dry mustard, Worcestershire sauce, and onion and garlic powders to taste. Thin with tomato juice to the desired consistency.

Green Goddess: Add 3 anchovy fillets, 1 teaspoon chopped green onion, 1 tablespoon chopped fresh parsley, and crumbled dried tarragon to taste.

Italian: Add crumbled dried oregano, garlic powder, and onion flakes to taste.

Horseradish: Add 1 to 2 tablespoons grated horseradish. (Excellent with cold roast beef.)

Thousand Island: Add 2 tablespoons bottled pickle relish or chili sauce, and dry mustard to taste.

Dill: Add ½ to 1 teaspoon dried dillweed or 1 tablespoon chopped fresh dill.

DESSERTS AND DESSERT SAUCES

Pumpkin Pudding

Persimmon Pudding

Cranberry Pudding

Christmas Plum Pudding

Mock Plum Pudding

Amaretto Chocolate Pudding

Chocolate Brandy Pudding

Cocoa-topped Egg Custard

Mexican Banana Flan

Chinese Lemon Sponge Cake

Sweet Couscous

Chinese Buns with Sweet Bean Paste

Thai Sticky Rice with Mangoes

Fresh Fruit Desserts

Yuletide Hard Sauce

Thin Chocolate Sauce

Creamy Chocolate Sauce

Bourbon Dessert Sauce

Foamy Rum Sauce

Custard Sauce

Lemon Sauce

Persimmon Sauce

Raspberry Sauce

Desserts and
Dessert Sauces

Those who appreciate the traditional steamed puddings of the winter season will find several inviting ones in this chapter. There is a long-cooking Christmas Plum Pudding, perfect for holiday gifts, and a mock version that is ready in less than half the time of the classic. Pumpkin, persimmon, and cranberry are featured in three other festive creations.

The two plum puddings must be prepared several days ahead and then steamed to reheat before serving. During this storage period, the flavors of the puddings will mellow. The reheating is also important because these puddings need further cooking. The other dried fruit puddings may also be reheated, but they are best when served directly from the steamer.

Two chocolate puddings are included, each wonderfully silky and not too sweet. One is spiked with brandy, the other with almond-scented amaretto. Unlike the fruit puddings, neither can be reheated. A whole-egg flan from Mexico is enhanced by the addition of ripe bananas, while couscous is gently tossed with pistachios and apricots.

Succulent mango slices nestle alongside coconut-flavored sticky rice in a favorite Thai sweet. From China there is a pair of delicacies: steamed buns filled with a sweet paste of red beans, and a light, lemony sponge cake.

Egg custard, which is commonly baked, successfully moves to the steamer, thereby economizing on fuel. Fruits usually simmered in liquid retain their natural flavor and texture better when steamed than when poached.

213

At the end of the chapter is a selection of marvelous sauces for when you want to dress up a dessert. Don't be restricted to the suggestions that appear with the recipes. These are versatile toppings; use your imagination to match complementary flavors, colors, and textures.

Basic Instructions for Steaming Puddings

Steamed puddings, unlike many steamed dishes, are cooked partially immersed in water rather than above it. This immersion insures that these dense mixtures receive the direct, intense heat they need to cook fully and evenly.

These instructions cover the preparation of the basin and the basic steaming directions for the following pudding recipes. There are other recipes in this book, such as savory mousses and timbales, that require the same procedure, and they are referred to this section.

First select the proper basin for the pudding mixture. Each recipe states the necessary cup capacity. If you don't know the capacity of a particular basin, measure it by adding water 1 cup at a time. Dry thoroughly before buttering or the butter will not adhere.

Next, select a pot in which to steam the pudding. It should be large enough to hold the basin with room to spare and have a tightly fitting lid. Place a low rack or folded towel or dishcloth on the center of the pot bottom. To determine the correct amount of steaming water, place the empty pudding basin in the pot and add water to come ⅔ to ¾ up the sides of the basin. Remove the basin and cover the pot.

Now butter the basin well with lecithin butter. If desired, lightly dust the buttered interior with fine dry breadcrumbs. To do this, put 2 to 3 tablespoons breadcrumbs into the basin and then tip and shake it to move the crumbs over the entire surface. The crumbs will readily adhere to the lecithin butter. Tap out the excess crumbs. The basin is now ready to be filled; set it aside.

Take a sheet of waxed paper large enough to fit over the top of the basin with an inch or two of overhang, and spread it lightly with lecithin butter. Cut a piece of foil about 3 inches greater in diameter than the basin top and fashion a lid (see Improvised Lids). Set these covers aside.

Prepare the pudding mixture as directed in the individual recipes. About 10 minutes before you have finished assembling and mixing the ingredients, heat the water in the covered steamer almost to boiling. When it reaches this point, turn the heat to low until you are ready to place the pudding in the pot.

Spoon the pudding mixture into the prepared basin, being careful not to disturb the coating. Place the buttered waxed paper over the filled basin, buttered side down, and press the overhang against the basin's sides. Place the foil lid over the waxed-paper cover, crimp the edges, then secure in place with kitchen twine or a rubber band.

If the steamer is just a little larger in diameter than the basin, which makes it difficult to lower the basin into the pot and to remove it, make a sling. Spread a tea towel large enough to encompass the basin on a work surface and place the filled and covered basin in the center of the towel. Bring the opposite ends of the towel up to meet at the top of the basin, tie them in a knot, and repeat with the other towel ends. Shove the handle of a long-handled wooden spoon under the knot and use this "pole" to raise and lower the basin into the pot.

Place the basin on the platform on the pot bottom, cover the pot, and bring the water to a full boil. Lower the heat until the water is boiling gently and steam the amount of time indicated in each recipe. The water must be kept at approximately the original level throughout the steaming; check the pot every 20 or 30 minutes and add boiling water as needed. Do not disturb the cover on the pudding basin before the specified cooking time has elapsed.

When reheating an already-steamed pudding, follow the same procedure for covering the basin (the waxed-paper cover is not necessary), readying the steamer and steaming in gently boiling water. Reheating times are given in the plum pudding recipes. Though I do not recommend reheating the other dried fruit puddings, they can be reheated. It will take 45 minutes to 1 hour.

Some of these puddings may look formidable because of their long ingredients lists. Don't be discouraged, for if you plan ahead and assemble everything you need before you begin mixing, the actual preparation time will not be very long. Make the long-cooking puddings when you are spending the whole day at home.

Pumpkin Pudding

SERVES 8 TO 10

3 eggs, lightly beaten	*¹/₄ cup firmly packed dark*
¹/₄ cup golden syrup	*brown sugar*
1¹/₄ cups of pumpkin puree	*3 tablespoons butter, melted*
¹/₄ cup grated peeled Granny	*and cooled*
Smith or other tart apple	

1   cup finely chopped
    walnuts, lightly toasted
1   cup coarsely chopped
    prunes (cut with scissors)
1   teaspoon pure vanilla
    extract
2   teaspoons freshly grated
    ginger root
2   cups sifted unbleached
    flour

1½   teaspoons baking soda
¾   teaspoon salt
1½   teaspoons ground
     cinnamon
½   teaspoon freshly grated
     nutmeg
½   teaspoon ground allspice
¼   teaspoon ground cloves
     Custard Sauce

Using a 1½-quart basin, follow Basic Instructions for Steaming Puddings.

In a large bowl combine eggs, syrup, pumpkin, apple, brown sugar, butter, walnuts, prunes, vanilla, and ginger root. Mix well. Combine all dry ingredients in a sifter and sift into pumpkin mixture. Stir just until dry ingredients are moistened.

Spoon batter into prepared basin, cover as directed, and steam 2 hours. Remove to cooling rack and let stand 15 minutes. Uncover and invert onto serving platter. Serve warm with Custard Sauce on the side.

Persimmon Pudding

SERVES 6 TO 8

¾   cup coarsely chopped dried
    apricots (cut with scissors)
½   cup golden raisins
½   cup chopped pecans
2   teaspoons freshly grated
    orange peel
2   teaspoons fresh lemon juice
¼   cup brandy
1   egg
½   cup butter, melted and
    cooled
1   cup firmly packed dark
    brown sugar
¼   cup milk

1   cup persimmon pulp (from
    2 medium-size very ripe
    persimmons) combined with
    2 teaspoons baking soda
1   teaspoon pure vanilla
    extract
1   cup unbleached flour
¼   teaspoon salt
1   teaspoon ground cinnamon
¼   teaspoon ground ginger
¼   teaspoon freshly grated
    nutmeg
¼   teaspoon ground cloves
    Raspberry Sauce

Combine apricots, raisins, pecans, orange peel, lemon juice, and brandy in a medium bowl. Let stand, stirring occasionally, 2 to 3 hours.

Using a 2-quart basin, follow Basic Instructions for Steaming Puddings.

Lightly beat egg in a large bowl. Mix in butter, sugar, milk, persimmon mixture, and vanilla. Stir in apricot mixture.

Combine all dry ingredients in a sifter and sift into bowl with persimmon mixture; mix well.

Spoon mixture into prepared basin, cover as directed, and steam 2 hours. Remove to cooling rack and let stand 15 minutes. Uncover and invert onto a serving platter.

Serve warm with Raspberry Sauce on the side.

Cranberry Pudding

SERVES 6 TO 8

1 egg	1/4 teaspoon ground ginger
1/3 cup firmly packed dark brown sugar	1/4 teaspoon freshly grated nutmeg
1/2 cup granulated sugar	1/4 teaspoon cream of tartar
4 tablespoons butter, melted and cooled	1/4 teaspoon salt
1 tablespoon freshly grated orange peel	2 tablespoons fine dry breadcrumbs
2 tablespoons orange or cranberry liqueur	1 1/2 cups coarsely chopped cranberries
1/2 cup unbleached flour	1/2 cup chopped pecans, walnuts, or almonds
1/4 cup whole wheat flour	Persimmon Sauce
1/2 teaspoon ground cinnamon	

Using a 3-cup basin, follow Basic Instructions for Steaming Puddings.

Beat together egg and sugars in a large mixing bowl until fluffy. Stir in butter, orange peel, and liqueur.

Combine flours, spices, cream of tartar, and salt in a sifter and sift into a mixing bowl; toss in breadcrumbs to mix well. Add flour mixture to sugar mixture and stir just until dry ingredients are moistened. Fold in cranberries and nuts.

Spoon into prepared basin, cover as directed, and steam 2 hours. Remove to cooling rack and let stand 15 minutes. Uncover and invert pudding onto a serving platter.

Serve warm with Persimmon Sauce on the side.

Christmas Plum Pudding

This traditional Christmas pudding is ideal to make several weeks ahead and give as holiday gifts. Steam in four 2-cup basins. Provide the recipients with directions on how to reheat and explain that the puddings are best if kept at least 1 week before eating, or may be stored for as long as 3 weeks. (Storage and reheating directions are included in the recipe method.) They should also douse the puddings with a tablespoon or so of brandy every other day to make them even more delicious.

The pudding is prepared over a 2-day period, so plan accordingly. Dried prunes, apricots, and/or peaches may be substituted for the dates. The fruit cake mix, a combination of diced preserved fruits, is easy to find at holiday time. Look for it in the produce section of your supermarket. Suet, which makes this a true plum pudding and for which there is no substitute, can be purchased in pieces or coarsely ground in the meat department of most supermarkets.

SERVES 16 TO 20

1¼ cups dark raisins
1 cup golden raisins
½ cup dried currants
½ cup coarsely chopped dates (cut with scissors)
½ cup fruit cake mix
1 small whole orange (unpeeled), finely chopped (¾ cup)
½ lemon (unpeeled), finely chopped (½ cup)
1 cup slivered blanched almonds, coarsely chopped
⅓ cup grated carrot or peeled Granny Smith or other tart apple
⅓ cup dark rum
1 cup firmly packed brown sugar

1¼ cups fine fresh breadcrumbs
1¼ cups coarsely ground or finely minced suet (approximately 5½ ounces)
2 eggs, lightly beaten
¼ cup milk
⅔ cup unbleached flour
1½ teaspoons ground cinnamon
½ teaspoon ground cardamom
½ teaspoon ground cloves
½ teaspoon freshly grated nutmeg
½ teaspoon ground allspice
½ teaspoon salt
Yuletide Hard Sauce

In a large mixing bowl combine raisins, currants, dates, fruit cake mix, orange, lemon, almonds, carrot, and rum. Let stand several hours, stirring occasionally. Stir in sugar, breadcrumbs, suet, eggs, and milk. In a sifter combine flour, spices, and salt and sift into fruit mixture. Lifting and turning with 2 wooden spoons, mix until well blended. Cover bowl and refrigerate overnight.

Using a 2-quart basin, follow Basic Instructions for Steaming Puddings.

Spoon pudding mixture into prepared basin, cover as directed, and steam 6 hours. (If using small basins, 5 hours is sufficient.) Be sure to check water level every 45 minutes or so and replenish as needed. Remove pudding to cooling rack and let stand 15 minutes. Uncover; when pudding is completely cool, cover with fresh foil and refrigerate. (If you need to use the basin for another recipe, remove pudding and wrap in cheesecloth and then in foil. Before reheating, unwrap and return to basin.)

The pudding will need an additional 2 hours of steaming before serving. Proceed in the same manner as for the original steaming. Remove to a cooling rack and let stand 10 minutes. Uncover and invert onto a serving platter.

Serve warm with Yuletide Hard Sauce.

Mock Plum Pudding

The absence of suet in this Christmas plum pudding makes it a mock version. It may be made several weeks ahead as with the preceding traditional one; store in the same manner, dousing it with brandy if desired.

Bourbon Dessert Sauce or Foamy Rum Sauce is a nice change from the hard sauce usually served with this type of pudding.

SERVES 12 TO 16

1½ cups dark raisins	¾ cup butter, melted and cooled
1½ cups dried currants	
½ cup fruit cake mix	2½ cups sifted unbleached flour
¼ cup chopped candied cherries	
	1½ cups granulated sugar
½ cup coarsely chopped dates (use scissors)	1½ teaspoons baking soda
	1½ teaspoons ground cinnamon
1 cup finely chopped walnuts, pecans, or almonds	
	1½ teaspoons freshly grated nutmeg
¼ cup brandy	1 teaspoon salt
1½ cups grated carrot	Bourbon Sauce or Foamy Rum Sauce
1½ cups grated potato	
2 eggs, lightly beaten	

In a large mixing bowl combine raisins, currants, fruit cake mix, cherries, dates, nuts, and brandy. Let stand several hours, stirring occasionally.

Using a 2-quart basin, follow Basic Instructions for Steaming Puddings.

Place carrot and potato in a sieve and press out any moisture. Combine carrot and potato with eggs and butter. Stir into raisin mixture. Combine all dry ingredients in a sifter and sift into bowl with fruit mixture. Lifting and turning with 2 wooden spoons, mix well and spoon into prepared basin.

Cover as directed and steam 3 hours. Remove to rack and let cool 15 minutes. Uncover, cool completely, cover with fresh foil, and refrigerate. (If you need to use the basin for another recipe, remove pudding and wrap in cheesecloth and then in foil. Before reheating, unwrap and return to basin.)

To reheat, return covered basin to steamer and steam 1 hour. Remove to a cooling rack and let stand 10 minutes. Uncover and invert onto a serving platter.

Serve warm with Bourbon Sauce or Foamy Rum Sauce.

Amaretto Chocolate Pudding

This rich chocolate pudding and the brandied one that follows can be served with almost any of the dessert sauces. For a double-chocolate treat, use one of the chocolate sauces. For color, garnish each serving with a tiny sprig of mint.

SERVES 4 TO 6

½ cup butter, cut up and softened
½ cup granulated sugar
1 egg, separated
1 ounce square unsweetened chocolate, coarsely chopped or grated
¼ cup half-and-half cream
¼ cup amaretto

½ teaspoon pure vanilla extract
1 cup sifted unbleached flour
½ teaspoon baking powder
¼ teaspoon ground cardamom
   Pinch of cream of tartar
⅓ cup ground almonds, lightly toasted

Using a 6-cup mold, follow Basic Instructions for Steaming Puddings.

Beat butter in a mixing bowl with a wooden spoon. Blend in sugar until mixture is fluffy and smooth. Beat in egg yolk.

In a small heavy saucepan slowly melt chocolate in half-and-half, over medium heat, stirring often. Immediately remove from heat and stir in amaretto and vanilla. Gradually stir into butter mixture until well combined.

Combine flour, baking powder, and cardamom in a sifter and sift over chocolate mixture; stir just until dry ingredients are moistened. Beat egg white and cream of tartar until stiff peaks form. Gently fold in almonds. Stir about ½ cup of the egg white mixture into the batter to lighten it, then fold in remaining egg white mixture.

Spoon batter into prepared basin, cover basin as directed, and steam 40 to 45 minutes, or until cake tester inserted in center comes out clean and pudding has pulled slightly away from sides of basin.

Remove pudding from steamer, uncover, and let stand on cooling rack 5 to 10 minutes. Serve warm directly from the basin with a masking of sauce.

Chocolate Brandy Pudding

SERVES 8 TO 10

6 **tablespoons butter, cut up and softened**	2 **tablespoons double-strength coffee**
⅓ **cup sugar**	⅓ **cup brandy**
4 **eggs, separated**	1 **teaspoon pure vanilla extract**
1 **ounce square unsweetened chocolate, coarsely chopped or grated**	½ **cup fine dry breadcrumbs**
1 **ounce square semisweet chocolate, coarsely chopped or grated**	⅛ **teaspoon cream of tartar** **Dessert sauce of choice**

Using a 2-quart basin, follow Basic Instructions for Steaming Puddings.

In a large mixing bowl beat butter with a wooden spoon until creamy. Blend in sugar until fluffy and beat in egg yolks one at a time, mixing well after each addition.

In a heavy saucepan slowly melt chocolate in coffee over medium heat, stirring often. Immediately remove from heat. Beat in a little of the butter mixture, then return to remaining butter mixture. Stir in 2 tablespoons of the brandy, the vanilla, and the breadcrumbs.

Beat egg whites and cream of tartar until stiff peaks form. Stir about ½ cup of the whites into the batter to lighten it, then fold in remaining whites.

Spoon batter into prepared basin, cover as directed, and steam 1 hour, or until cake tester inserted in center comes out clean and pudding has pulled away slightly from sides of basin.

Remove pudding to cooling rack, uncover, and slowly pour remaining brandy over. Let stand 10 minutes before serving. Serve warm directly from the basin with sauce of choice.

Cocoa-topped Egg Custard

SERVES 4

2   eggs
2   tablespoons firmly packed
    brown sugar, sieved
2   tablespoons granulated
    sugar

¾   cup half-and-half cream or
    milk
    Unsweetened cocoa powder

Using 4 custard cups or soufflé dishes (about ¾-cup capacity), follow Basic Instructions for Steaming Puddings.

Beat eggs lightly in a mixing bowl, then beat in sugars until mixture is smooth and fluffy. Blend in half-and-half and pour into prepared custard cup. Sieve a light dusting of cocoa powder evenly over each filled cup.

Cover each cup as directed and steam gently 15 minutes, or until a thin-bladed knife inserted in center comes out clean. Remove custard to a cooling rack, uncover, and let stand 5 minutes. Serve warm, at room temperature, or chilled.

Variation: In a heavy saucepan, heat the cream with 1 tablespoon ground coffee 30 minutes. Strain through a sieve lined with a coffee filter and cool before proceeding with recipe.

Mexican Banana Flan

The step for preparing the caramel coating is easier to do than it sounds in the instructions, so don't be intimidated. To save time on the day of serving, caramelize the sugar as much as 48 hours ahead, cover with plastic wrap, and store at room temperature.

Unless you have a food processor with a 6-cup capacity (or if you are using a blender), you will need to mix this custard in two batches.

SERVES 10 TO 12

½ cup granulated sugar for the caramel	4 eggs
4 ripe bananas	⅓ cup granulated sugar
3 cups milk	⅓ cup brandy

Measure the ½ cup sugar into a cake pan 9 inches in diameter by 2 inches high. Place the pan over medium-high heat. As the sugar begins to melt, continually shake the pan to evenly distribute it; do not stir with a spoon or the sugar will lump. In about 5 minutes the sugar will have liquefied. Leave the pan on the heat, shaking and tilting it frequently, until the sugar is a deep hazelnut color.

Remove the pan from the stove and tip and turn it in a circular fashion to thoroughly coat the bottom. Once the bottom is evenly coated, position the pan perpendicular to the floor and carefully turn it clockwise a few turns; reverse the direction, turning the pan counterclockwise. The sides should now be evenly coated. The caramelized sugar thickens as it cools, making the coating process gradually easier. Set the pan aside while you prepare the custard mixture.

Peel the bananas, cut into pieces, and place in a blender or food processor fitted with metal blade. Blend to a smooth puree. Add the milk, eggs, ⅓ cup sugar, and brandy and blend well. Spoon the banana mixture into the prepared pan (the caramelized coating need not be completely cooled) and cover the pan tightly (see Improvised Lids).

Place the filled pan on a rack over boiling water, cover pot, and steam for 1 hour and 15 minutes, or until a knife inserted in the center comes out clean. Check the water level occasionally and add more as needed.

Remove the flan from the steamer and uncover. Let cool to room temperature. Invert a large serving platter on top of the pan, then invert the pan; the flan will unmold easily. Cut into wedges to serve. Serve warm or at room temperature.

Chinese Lemon Sponge Cake

Unlike most cake recipes, which don't rise properly when steamed, this cake steams extremely well. It has a wonderfully light texture and lemony flavor. The sauce is my nontraditional addition.

MAKES ONE 9-INCH CAKE

6 eggs, separated, at room temperature
1/4 teaspoon cream of tartar
1 cup granulated sugar
1 tablespoon freshly grated lemon peel
3 tablespoons fresh lemon juice

1/2 teaspoon pure vanilla extract
1 1/2 cups cake flour
1/2 teaspoon baking powder
1/4 teaspoon salt
Lemon Sauce

Butter a 9-inch round baking pan with lecithin butter and line with waxed paper. Set aside. Wrap lid of steamer in a towel and bring water in steamer almost to the boiling point.

Beat egg whites and cream of tartar in a large mixing bowl until soft peaks form. Beat in sugar, 2 tablespoons at a time until all is incorporated. Continue beating until whites are very stiff and glossy. Set aside.

Whisk egg yolks in a medium mixing bowl until slightly thickened and a rich yellow color. Whisk in lemon peel, lemon juice, and vanilla. Carefully fold yolk mixture into egg white mixture until just blended.

Combine flour, baking powder, and salt in a sifter. Sift about 2 table-spoons of flour mixture over egg mixture and gently fold in. Repeat with remaining flour mixture, about 2 tablespoons at a time; do not overmix.

Spoon batter into prepared pan, leveling gently with the back of a wooden spoon or with a spatula. Set pan on rack over gently boiling water, cover, and steam 30 minutes, or until cake tester inserted in center comes out clean.

Remove cake to cooling rack and let stand 10 minutes. Carefully invert cake on a serving plate and lift away the pan. Peel off and discard waxed paper. Turn cake right side up, slice, and serve warm with Lemon Sauce.

Sweet Couscous

In order to prepare this dessert you will need to refer to Couscous. Prepare Moroccan-style Chicken and steamed rice for the entrée and serve glasses of cold milk with the sweet couscous. Pass a bowl of sifted confectioner's sugar.

SERVES 6 TO 8

⅓ cup chopped blanched almonds	1 tablespoon olive oil
2 tablespoons granulated sugar	8 dried apricot halves, finely chopped (use scissors)
4 cups freshly steamed couscous	3 to 4 tablespoons coarsely chopped unsalted pistachios
4 tablespoons unsalted butter, cut up and softened	Mint sprigs Ground cinnamon

In a blender or food processor fitted with metal blade, grind almonds with sugar; set aside.

Transfer couscous to a large bowl and with fingers toss in butter and oil until grains are well coated. Toss in reserved almond mixture, apricots, and pistachios. Mound on a serving platter. Garnish platter with mint sprigs and sieve a light dusting of cinnamon over the couscous.

Chinese Buns with Sweet Bean Paste

The filling for this sweet ending to a *dim sum* spread is made with Chinese red beans, sometimes called azuki beans. They can be found in Chinese and Japanese markets, health-food stores, and many supermarkets. The sun-dried tangerine peel imparts a pleasant hint of citrus to the bean paste.

Refer to the recipe for Chinese Buns for directions on how to fill and steam the buns. Any bean paste that remains can be stored in a covered container in the refrigerator for up to 6 months.

FILLING FOR 16 BUNS

1   cup Chinese red beans
1   piece dried tangerine peel
*   (optional)*
½   cup granulated sugar, or to
*   taste*

¼   cup peanut oil, or as needed
1   recipe Chinese Buns (see
*   Appetizers and First Courses)*

Place beans and tangerine peel in a medium saucepan and add water to cover by about 2 inches. Cover, bring to a boil, reduce heat, and simmer, with lid slightly ajar, about 1½ hours, or until beans are very soft. Check occasionally and add water as needed to keep beans moist. When soft, uncover and let water boil almost away.

Place beans in a sieve and force the pulp through with the back of a spoon. The beans should form a thick puree and the hulls will remain in the sieve.

Transfer the puree to a saucepan and place over moderate heat. Add sugar and oil and cook, stirring constantly, until the paste is smooth and shiny. Taste for sweetness and add more sugar as needed. If the paste does not have a shiny appearance, gradually add more oil until it does. Remove the pan from the heat and let cool before filling buns.

Fill buns as directed, using about 2 teaspoons paste for each bun. Steam 20 minutes. Serve warm or at room temperature.

Thai Sticky Rice with Mangoes

Luscious ripe mangoes are mated with coconut-flavored sticky rice in this favorite Thai sweet. The addition of fresh ginger root slices is my own innovation. Time the preparation of the rice so that it is still warm when you add the sweetened coconut milk (see directions for Glutinous Rice). For richer dish, drizzle each serving with a little coconut cream (see instructions for preparing coconut milk, this recipe).

SERVES 4

¾   cup coconut milk (see Note)
2   slices ginger root
¼   cup granulated sugar
*   Pinch of salt*

3   cups warm steamed
*   glutinous rice*
4   ripe mangoes
4   mint sprigs

Place the coconut milk and ginger slices in a small saucepan over medium heat, bring to a boil, and boil gently to reduce to ½ cup. Remove from the heat, discard ginger root, and add the sugar and salt, stirring to dissolve. Pour this sweetened coconut milk into a large mixing bowl and add the warm rice. Mix gently so that all of the rice grains are lightly coated with the coconut milk. Let stand 1 hour.

Peel, halve, and pit the mangoes. Cut the flesh into long, thin slices and arrange them on individual serving plates. Spoon a mound of the coconut rice onto each plate. Garnish with a mint sprig.

Note: To make your own coconut milk, pierce one of the three black "eyes" on the pointed end of a fresh coconut and drain the liquid into a glass or pitcher. Chill this liquid and serve it as a beverage. With a hammer, crack the coconut in half and, with the point of a sharp knife, loosen the meat from the shell. (Warming the halved coconut in a low oven for 20 minutes makes the meat easier to remove.) Cut away the brown outer skin and shred the coconut meat.

Combine 1 part fresh coconut meat and 1½ parts hot water or milk in a large bowl and let steep 10 minutes. Alternatively, put the coconut meat and hot liquid in a blender or food processor and blend at high speed until coconut is completely pulverized. Pour the steeped or blended coconut mixture through a sieve, pressing out as much liquid as possible with the back of a spoon.

One cup of coconut meat and 1½ cups liquid will yield 1 cup of thick rich milk. The process can be repeated with the same coconut meat and new hot liquid for a thinner milk. Store the coconut milk in a covered jar in the refrigerator. It has essentially the same shelf life as cow's milk. The thick cream that rises to the top can be removed and used in recipes that call for coconut cream.

If fresh coconuts are unavailable, unsweetened dried (desiccated) coconut can be substituted for the fresh coconut meat. Coconut milk from Southeast Asia is available in cans in markets carrying Asian foodstuffs. Coconut cream may also be purchased in cans.

Fresh Fruit Desserts

Fresh pears, peaches, and apples that are normally poached can be steamed and they will better retain their fresh texture. These fruits make elegant desserts that are light enough to follow an elaborate meal and easy enough to put together in just a few minutes.

I have given a basic recipe for steaming pears. Peaches and apples can be prepared in the same way with different flavorings. Try peaches with Port, ground cinnamon, a tiny sprinkling of sugar, and grated lemon peel. Apples, cider, and grated orange peel are a natural combination. To add color, garnish each serving with fresh mint sprigs.

Pears with Gorgonzola

Select firm, ripe pears such as Bosc, Bartlett, or Anjou. Vary the liqueurs: Drambuie, orange Curaçao, crème de cacao, and anisette would also be good choices.

SERVES 4

4   *ripe firm pears*
    Fresh lemon juice
6   *tablespoons Grand Marnier*

¼   cup crumbled Gorgonzola
cheese

Peel and core the pears, rubbing each lightly with lemon juice as you work. Fill the center of each pear with 1 tablespoon of the Gorgonzola. Stand the pears upright in a shallow dish and pour 1½ tablespoons Grand Marnier over each pear. Set dish on rack over boiling water, cover pot, and steam 5 minutes.

Baste pears with liquid in dish, cover pot, and steam another 5 minutes. Test for doneness by inserting a cake tester or a thin-bladed knife into one of the pears; the tester should go in easily, but the flesh of the pear should still be slightly firm. Baste again and steam an additional 1 to 2 minutes if pears are not quite done.

Transfer pears to individual serving plates and pour steaming liquid evenly over each. Serve warm.

Variations:

Pears with Thin Chocolate Sauce: Prepare and steam pears as directed for Pears with Gorgonzola, but omit the cheese. Serve the pears warm with Thin Chocolate Sauce spooned over the top.

Gingered Pears with Custard Sauce: Prepare and steam pears as directed for Pears with Gorgonzola, but omit the cheese. Substitute sweet sherry for the Grand Marnier and sprinkle each pear with ⅛ teaspoon ground ginger. Serve the pears warm with Custard Sauce spooned over the top and garnish with semisweet chocolate curls.

Dessert Sauces

These delectable sauces will enhance the whole range of steamed desserts, from a complex English fruit pudding to a simple Chinese sponge cake. Some classics are here: a hard sauce, the Yuletide season favorite, updated with blanched almonds; and a silky smooth custard sauce, with a choice of flavorings.

For chocolate lovers, there are two liqueur-laced creations. For those who can eat rich dairy products without guilt, there is a pair of whipped cream sauces bolstered with rum or bourbon. And finally, there are the fruit-based toppings: a tart lemon version, a vibrantly colored persimmon puree, and a raspberry sauce that can be adapted to other fruits.

I have used unsalted butter in a number of these sauces because the flavor is more pleasing. Its use, however, is not essential; the consistency of the sauces is the same whether salted or unsalted butter is used.

Of course, sauces do add calories, but for the majority of people moderation in portioning is a realistic alternative to abstinence.

Yuletide Hard Sauce

MAKES APPROXIMATELY 1¼ CUPS

3 to 4 tablespoons slivered blanched almonds	1½ cups confectioner's sugar, sifted
4 tablespoons unsalted butter, cut into small bits, at room temperature	3 tablespoons brandy, or to taste
	¼ teaspoon freshly grated nutmeg, or to taste

Coarsely chop almonds in a blender or food processor fitted with metal blade. Add butter and blend well. Gradually add sugar and mix until smooth. Transfer mixture to a bowl. With a wooden spoon stir in brandy and nutmeg, then beat until light and fluffy.

If not serving immediately, let stand at room temperature for up to 2 hours, or cover and refrigerate for up to 1 week. Bring to room temperature before serving.

Thin Chocolate Sauce

MAKES APPROXIMATELY 1¼ CUPS

2 ounce squares unsweetened chocolate	⅓ cup brandy
1½ tablespoons unsalted butter	3 tablespoons water
	Pinch of salt

<table>
<tr><td>¾ cup granulated sugar</td><td>2 tablespoons crème de cacao</td></tr>
<tr><td>2 tablespoons light corn
   syrup</td><td>   or other liqueur</td></tr>
</table>

Coarsely chop chocolate and combine in a heavy saucepan with the butter, brandy, water, and salt. Place over medium-high heat and stir constantly with a wooden spoon until chocolate is melted and mixture is smooth. Thoroughly blend in sugar and corn syrup. Bring mixture to a boil, lower heat, and simmer without stirring for 5 minutes. Simmer, stirring occasionally, an additional 5 minutes, or until sauce is slightly thickened.

Remove saucepan from heat, cool slightly, and stir in crème de cacao. Serve warm or at room temperature.

If making ahead, transfer to jar, cool, cover, and refrigerate up to 3 days. To reheat, place jar, uncovered, in a saucepan with water reaching halfway up sides of jar. Slowly bring water to a simmer and, stirring sauce often, heat sauce to desired temperature.

Creamy Chocolate Sauce

MAKES APPROXIMATELY 1½ CUPS

2 ounce squares unsweetened
   chocolate
2 ounce squares semisweet
   chocolate
1 cup half-and-half cream

⅔ cup granulated sugar
3 tablespoons coffee liqueur
½ teaspoon pure vanilla
   extract

Coarsely chop chocolates and combine in a heavy saucepan with the half-and-half and sugar. Place over medium-high heat until chocolate is melted, beating until smooth. Bring to a boil, lower heat, and cook, stirring almost constantly, 5 minutes or until thick and creamy.

Remove saucepan from heat and let cool slightly. Blend in liqueur and vanilla. Serve warm or at room temperature.

If making ahead, transfer to jar, cool, cover, and refrigerate up to 3 days. To reheat, place jar, uncovered, in a saucepan with water reaching halfway up sides of jar. Slowly bring water to a simmer and, stirring sauce often, heat to desired temperature.

Bourbon Dessert Sauce

MAKES APPROXIMATELY 2 CUPS

4   tablespoons unsalted butter,
    cut into small bits, at room
    temperature
½   cup superfine sugar

1   egg, beaten
½   cup heavy cream, whipped
2   to 3 tablespoons bourbon,
    or to taste

In a mixing bowl cream butter with a wooden spoon until light and fluffy. Beat in sugar until mixture is very smooth. Thoroughly blend in egg. Stir a little of the whipped cream into the butter mixture to lighten it, then fold in remaining whipped cream. Carefully fold in bourbon.

If not using sauce immediately, cover and refrigerate. Sauce will keep 2 to 3 days.

Foamy Rum Sauce

MAKES APPROXIMATELY 1 CUP

1   egg yolk
½   cup confectioner's sugar,
    sifted

1½   tablespoons dark rum, or
     to taste
½   cup heavy cream, whipped

Beat egg yolk in a mixing bowl, then blend in ¼ cup of the sugar. Stir in rum, then beat in remaining sugar. Stir a little of the whipped cream into the sugar mixture to lighten it, then fold in remaining cream.

Cover and refrigerate several hours before serving. Sauce will keep 2 to 3 days.

Custard Sauce

MAKES APPROXIMATELY 1 CUP

4   egg yolks
¼   cup granulated sugar
    Pinch of salt

2   cups half-and-half cream or
    milk

2 teaspoons pure vanilla extract, rum, dry sherry, or Port	$\frac{1}{2}$ teaspoon freshly grated lemon peel (optional)

In a heavy saucepan or the top of a double boiler set over gently boiling water, beat together egg yolks, sugar, and salt. Blend in cream. Stirring almost constantly with a wooden spoon, cook until mixture thickens, 15 to 20 minutes. To test, lift spoon from the custard; if a coating of the custard remains on the spoon, then the sauce has cooked long enough.

Remove pan from heat and stir in vanilla and optional lemon peel. Serve immediately or let stand at room temperature several hours, stirring occasionally to prevent a skin from forming on the surface of the custard.

To store, jar, cover, and refrigerate for up to 1 day. Bring back to room temperature and stir well before serving. Do not attempt to reheat.

Lemon Sauce

MAKES APPROXIMATELY $\frac{3}{4}$ CUP

1 egg	2 to $2\frac{1}{2}$ tablespoons fresh lemon juice
4 tablespoons unsalted butter, cut into small bits	$\frac{1}{2}$ teaspoon distilled white vinegar
$\frac{3}{4}$ cup granulated sugar	Pinch of salt
$1\frac{1}{2}$ to 2 teaspoons freshly grated lemon peel	

Beat egg lightly in the top of a double boiler set over gently boiling water. With a wooden spoon, beat in all remaining ingredients and cook, stirring almost constantly, 10 to 15 minutes or until mixture thickens. To test, lift spoon from the lemon mixture; if a coating of the lemon mixture remains on the spoon, then the sauce has cooked long enough.

Serve immediately or let stand at room temperature for up to 2 hours, stirring occasionally to prevent a skin from forming on the surface of the sauce.

To store, jar, cover, and refrigerate for up to 3 days. Bring to room temperature and stir well before serving. Do not attempt to reheat.

Persimmon Sauce

MAKES APPROXIMATELY 2 CUPS

2   *cups persimmon pulp*
    (3 medium-size ripe
    persimmons)

1½   *tablespoons honey, or to*
     taste
     Fresh lemon or lime juice
     to taste

Combine all ingredients in a mixing bowl. Cover and chill until serving. Sauce will keep refrigerated for up to 2 days or frozen up to 2 weeks. Bring to room temperature and stir well before serving.

Raspberry Sauce

Fresh raspberries may be used for this recipe, but unless you live where there is an overabundance of these special berries, unsweetened frozen ones produce a very good and more economical sauce.

Other fruits can take the place of the raspberries. Try boysenberries or blackberries, or coarsely chopped peaches, or a combination of sliced strawberries and rhubarb. Substitute any liqueur for the amaretto.

MAKES APPROXIMATELY 2 CUPS

2   *10-ounce packages frozen*
    raspberries, defrosted and
    well drained, or 2 to 3 cups
    fresh raspberries
⅓   *to ½ cup sugar (optional)*
1   *teaspoon cornstarch,*
    dissolved in 1 tablespoon
    cold water

½   *teaspoon freshly grated*
    lemon or lime peel
1   *tablespoon fresh lemon or*
    lime juice, or to taste
1   *tablespoon amaretto, or to*
    taste (optional)

Combine raspberries and optional sugar in a saucepan. Bring to a gentle boil and cook, stirring often, 5 minutes. Stir in cornstarch mixture and cook, stirring, until sauce is slightly thickened.

Remove pan from heat and add lemon peel, lemon juice, and amaretto. Serve immediately or let stand at room temperature for up to 3 hours.

To store, jar, cover, and refrigerate for up to 2 days. If desired, reheat gently before serving.

Equipment Sources

All-Clad Metalcrafters, Inc. Canonsburg, PA 15317-9513 (412) 745-8300	Stainless steel steamer insert
Chantal by Lentrade, Inc. 10649 Haddington, #120 Houston, TX 77043 (713) 467-9949	Fish poacher with rack
General Housewares Corp. P.O. Box 4066 Terre Haute, IN 47804 (812) 232-1000	Magnalite: molded aluminum four-piece steamer, optional insert Leyse: stamped aluminum four-piece cooker/steamer (Priscillaware), steamer baskets (Bakeware), steamer plate (comes with wok set), stovetop rice steamer/cereal cooker, several types of steamers in the Leyson line Graniteware: blue-speckled porcelainware "5-piece Everything Pot" and a jumbo version

Hitachi Sales Corp. of America 401 West Artesia Blvd. Compton, CA 90220 (800) 262-1502 (CA) (800) 421-1040	Electric steamer: Chime-O-Matic Food Steamer/Rice Cooker
Gary Holt, Porcelain Stoneware Ceramics 1449 Fifth St. Berkeley, CA 94710 (415) 527-4183	Yunnan pot
Kaplan/Aronson 156 Fifth Ave. New York, NY 10010 (212) 242-0066	Universal Steamer Insert (graduated design, domed lid)
Kira Designs, Inc. 1 Faneuil Hall Marketplace Boston, MA 02109	Yunnan pot called The Steampot; available in 1-quart, 2-quart (the most practical), and 3-quart sizes
National Rice-O-Matic Nozawa Trading Co. 870 S. Western Ave. Los Angeles, CA 90005 (213) 385-7096	Electric rice cooker: Rice-O-Mat
Revere Copper & Brass Incorporated Revere Ware Division P.O. Box 250 Clinton, IL 61727 (217) 935-3111	1½-quart pot with insert, 3-quart pot with insert, and 6-quart pot with basket
Rival Manufacturing Company Kansas City, MO 64129 (816) 861-1000	Electric food steamer/rice cooker: Rival The Steamer
Waring Products New Hartford, CT 06057 (203) 379-0731	Food steamer/rice cooker: Waring Steam Chef
Williams Sonoma Mail Order Department P.O. Box 7456 San Francisco, CA 94120-7456 (415) 652-9007	Copper saucepot/steamer

Index